THE *BUSY* CLASSROOM

A Preschool Teacher's Monthly Book of Creative Activities

By Patty Claycomb

Illustrations by Linda Greigg

gryphon house

Beltsville, Maryland

Dedication

This book is dedicated to Patricia Dwight. Her special name is Teacher Pat! Teacher Pat knows the secret of being a great teacher. She radiates warmth and caring to each child in her classroom. She loves her children. Then she gives them a busy, happy classroom!

Library of Congress Catalog Number: 92-53891

Cover Design: Graves, Fowler & Associates Cover Photo: Photogroup, Inc.

Publisher's Cataloging in Publication
(Prepared by Quality Books, Inc.)

Claycomb, Patricia Lyle, 1950-
    The busy classroom : a preschool teacher's monthly book
 of creative activities / Patty Claycomb.

    P. cm.
    Includes index.
    ISBN 0-87659-159-4
1. Education, Preschool-Activity programs. 2. Creative
activities and seatwork. 3. Preschool teaching. 1. Title. 11. Title: A preschool teacher's monthly book of creative activities.
LB I 140.35.C75C5 1992   372.21
                    QBI92-805

Table of Contents

Chapter 4—December
Adventures in Arts and Crafts

Chapter 5—January
Our Beautiful Earth

Chapter 6—February
Fun and Giggles and Inside Games

Introduction

A busy classroom is a room full of children having fun. Along with fun, there are happy faces, busy hands and active minds. **The Busy Classroom** *was written and designed to provide children with experiences that are fun, creative and educational. The activities encourage the children's creative energy and develop their social skills. An understanding of social skills allows a child to learn and play successfully within a group setting. Feeling comfortable and confident is as important as the curriculum! Social skills, first explored in Chapter One, can be used throughout the year!*

With the active enjoyment of children in mind, I have written activities focusing on topics children find interesting and exciting. A monthly unit is offered for each topic. The teacher and children can fully explore an idea or topic. Throughout the month, the teacher and the children exchange ideas, share information and create spontaneous activities.

There's more! Within each month, the activities are presented in a special order. The first activity in each chapter introduces the children to the topic, and subsequent activities build skills and knowledge like building blocks, thought by thought, skill by skill, with fun from top to bottom! Review activities are at the end of the month.

The Busy Classroom *is a year of what to do every day! The activities are charged with creativity and imagination, and they have been child-tested in my classroom. This book holds endless possibilities for teachers and children. So start now! The children are waiting!*

Welcome to a New Classroom

At the start of every school year children experience many new situations and emotions. They may feel afraid or intimidated by all the other children and all the noise! They may lack confidence or social skills, or they may be spending time away from home for the first time. This chapter offers activities that help children adjust happily and successfully to a new classroom by encouraging confidence and a sense of trust. The activities offer fun and easy ways to learn and remember classroom rules. They help children feel that they are an important part of the group, and they teach children how to express themselves in a positive way. Above all, they provide a place where children can form and enjoy healthy friendships.

Welcome to a New Classroom

	Monday	Tuesday	Wednesday	Thursday	Friday
Week 1	**3+ Classroom Tour** *To learn about a new classroom*	**3+ Fun and Easy** *To learn to use classroom materials properly*	**3+ Sticker Hunt** *To become familiar with classroom rules*	**3+ Roll a Ball** *To learn about classmates*	**4+ I'm a VIP** *To highlight the special qualities of each child*
Week 2	**4+ Name Hunt** *To recognize first names*	**4+ Name-a-Saurus** *To recognize first names*	**3+ Wildflowers** *To learn that everyone is special*	**3+ Star Message** *To introduce positive classroom behavior*	**3+ Beanbag Hellos** *To learn to treat others kindly*
Week 3	**3+ Happy Hands** *To encourage positive classroom behavior*	**4+ Pet Store** *To encourage children to express themselves*	**4+ Copy Cats** *To learn what to do when someone copies you*	**4+ Secret Message** *To learn what to do about secrets*	**4+ Share a Bear** *To encourage children to share*
Week 4	**3+ Hide a Bug** *To learn to take turns*	**3+ Teddy Bear Talk** *To reinforce positive classroom behavior*	**4+ Caterpillar Crawl** *To work together*	**3+ Clubhouse** *To encourage group unity*	**3+ Happy Faces** *To review what was learned this month*

Classroom Tour

What to do

1. Point out and name the different areas of the classroom: the kitchen area, the library or the quiet area, the dress-up corner, the lunch tables, the art area, etc. Ask if anyone can remember the areas of the classroom just mentioned.

2. What can we do in our classroom? Make friends, play, listen to stories, take naps, learn about many interesting things and eat!

3. Briefly mention the basic classroom rules: walking instead of running, soft voices only, treating each other nicely, and listening to the teacher when he or she is speaking (add others appropriate for your classroom). You can brainstorm with the children on how to act nicely!

4. Now take a bus ride through the classroom! The teacher is the driver. Everyone stands, in pairs, behind you. When everyone is sitting in their pretend seats, start the motor and take off! Honk as you approach each classroom area. Have everyone repeat the name of each area. Mention parts of the classroom that you have not talked about, such as the cubbies, the trash can, the sink, the teacher's closet and the front door. Children feel more comfortable in their new surroundings with each additional piece of information. Take your time. As you leave each area, wave good-by.

More to do

Draw the different areas of the classroom on white posterboard. Color them different colors. Place the classroom drawing on the rug. Place an empty plastic bottle on the drawing. Spin the bottle and name the area the bottle is pointing to. Explain a special rule for that area. Toys are to stay outside of the library; when you are playing in the kitchen area, keep plastic food out of your mouth; lunch pails stay under your chair while you are eating. Can anyone think of any other rules that would be helpful to follow in the classroom?

Age level

3+

Objective

To learn about a new classroom

Materials

None

Preparation

None

Fun and Easy

Age level

3+

Objective

To learn to use classroom materials appropriately

Materials

Items from the classroom, such as felt pens, scissors, dolls or stuffed animals, blocks and puzzles
paper bag

Preparation

Place the chosen items in a paper bag.

What to do

1. Explain to the children that the items in the paper bag are from the classroom. They are fun and easy to use, but they must be taken care of and played with correctly.

2. As you talk about each item, remove it from the paper bag. Talk about the different ways to safely play with each item. Children do not always think of obvious reasons why or why not to do something. Helping them to understand these reasons will promote an awareness and confidence that will be reflected in positive, happy play.

For example:

Felt Pens—Place the top of a felt pen back on when you are finished with it. Demonstrate! Seeing will encourage remembering. Felt pens are not for chewing; food is for chewing! Press lightly when you are drawing. .

Scissors—Pretend you are holding scissors and demonstrate how to move your hand to cut with scissors. Have everyone hold scissors and practice moving them up and down. Demonstrate how to cut paper. Keep the scissor blades straight. If you turn your wrist and the sides of the blades touch the paper, it is hard to cut.

Dolls and Stuffed Animals—Treat them as if they were real! Hold them quietly and gently. Pass a stuffed animal around your circle. Each child can gently stroke it.

Blocks—Pass a block around your circle. Feel how heavy it is. A block dropped on someone's finger or toe can hurt! Slowly stack some blocks, one on top of the other. When is a good time to stop? A safe height is when they won't tumble over!

Puzzles—Display a puzzle. Talk about the picture on the puzzle. Notice the different colors and designs, such as the rippling of water or the color purple along the edges. Mention how helpful it is to study a puzzle before you try it. Take a puzzle piece away! Notice the shape that is left. All together, take the puzzle apart and put it back together.

More to do

Place the items you have discussed in a paper bag. One child closes her eyes and feels an item. Can she guess what the item is?

Sticker Hunt

What to do

1. Explain that everyone is going to learn about the classroom. A sticker hunt is a fun way!

2. Explain that there are different stickers hidden in each area of the classroom. Choose a child to hunt for a sticker. When a sticker is found, special information is given about that area. For example, if a caterpillar sticker is found in the library, have everyone stand in the library. Special information for the library: when we are through looking at a book, place it back on the bookshelf; we use whispering voices in the library.

3. Continue until each child has found a sticker in a special area.

4. Special information for different areas might be:
   In the Lunch Area—Demonstrate the proper way to sit in a chair. Feet on the floor and facing the table!
   At the Sink—Turn on the water. Turn off the water! Explain the importance of saving water.
   On the Rug or Block Area—Spill a container of toys on the rug. When you are through playing with toys, put them back! Everyone can help you place the toys in the container and back on the shelf.
   The Classroom Door—Talk to the children about keeping the classroom door closed. Explain that the teacher always needs to know where everyone is!

More to do

The teacher hides his or her eyes and slowly counts to ten. The children find a place to hide in their favorite area. When the teacher is through counting, he or she calls out the name of a child. He yells the name of his hiding place. Continue until everyone has been chosen. Next the children count to ten, and the teacher hides!

Age level

3+

Objective

To become familiar with classroom rules

Materials

Variety of stickers

Preparation

Place the stickers around the classroom in places where they are easily seen. Place one sticker in each area of the classroom.

Roll a Ball

Age level

3+

Objective

To learn about classmates

Materials

Large ball

Preparation

None

What to do

1. Ask the children to sit in a circle with their legs crossed.

2. The teacher rolls the ball to each child.

3. When a child receives the ball, she says her name and something she likes to do.

4. After her turn, she rolls the ball back to the teacher, and the teachers rolls the ball to another child.

5. Then play a memory game! Roll the ball to a child. See who remembers the name of the child and what he or she likes to do.

More to do

To start the game, the teacher rolls the ball to a child. This child answers a question and chooses another child to roll the ball to. Possible questions: Who is in your family? Do you have any pets? What is your favorite color? What did you eat for breakfast?

I'm a VIP

What to do

1. Pass out a circle paper to each child. The children draw their faces inside the circles. Encourage everyone to think about themselves. What color is your hair? How is it shaped? Is there anything in your hair? What color are your eyes? Now draw your body!

2. When everyone has finished their picture, sit together on the rug. What parts of our bodies do we all have? When a child responds, point to that part of the body. We all have the same body parts—eyes, ears, nose, mouth, eyebrows, hands, fingers and toes—but we all look different! Everyone shows their picture. Look how different we all look. That is what makes up special!

3. Tape the self-portraits on a wall. Title the wall, "I'm a VIP in My Classroom."

More to do

Everyone can draw a picture of something that they like! Brainstorm ideas before you pass out paper. Possible ideas: flowers, rainbows, your home, something to eat or even spiders! Tape these pictures on a wall near the self-portraits. Title the wall, "Special Things That I Like!"

Age level

4+

Objective

To highlight the special qualities of each child

Materials

Paper
crayons
tape

Preparation

Draw a 3" circle on a sheet of paper. Make one circle for each child. Spread a selection of crayons on the table.

Name Hunt

Age level

4+

Objective

To recognize the first names of the children in the class

Materials

Paper
scissors
black felt pen
matching stickers
tape

Preparation

Cut a 4" x 8" strip of paper for each child. Print a child's name on each one. Place a different sticker on each name strip. Tape the name strips around the room.

What to do

1. Explain to the children that their names are hidden around the room. Each name also has a sticker on it!

2. Give everyone a sticker that matches the sticker on their name strip.

3. Go on a Name Hunt! Everyone, at the same time, looks for their name with the matching sticker.

4. When each child finds his name, he places his sticker on his name strip and brings it to the teacher.

5. When all the name strips have been found, hold up each name strip and say the child's name.

More to do

Who can remember what his first name looks like? Play a game with the name strips! Hold up a name strip. See if the child can recognize his name. If not, then give clues! (It's someone who has blue shoes.) When the child is named, give an instruction such as jump up and down, or stand up and turn around!

Name-a-Saurus

What to do

1. Help everyone find their name by their special dinosaur. Now they are each a Name-a-Saurus!

2. Play the Name-a-Saurus Game! Place a plastic bottle on the floor. This is a dinosaur bone! Spin the bone. When the bottle stops, it will point to a child!

3. This child stands and places a heart sticker on her name. Everyone else pounds on the rug and says, "Dinosaur, dinosaur 1-2-3. Who is standing next to me?"

4. She is given ten seconds to study her Name-a-Saurus. The remaining children do the counting. On the count of ten, everyone spreads their arms wide and claps! Then the standing child says her name.

5. When she returns to the group ask her what color her Name-a-Saurus is? What is it doing? Does it have horns on its head?

More to do

Have everyone study the dinosaur pictures. Then have them close their eyes. Take one name away. See who can tell which name is no longer by its Name-a-Saurus! Take all the names off the wall. Who remembers what their Name-a-Saurus looks like? Who can place their name by their Name-a-Saurus?

Age level

4+

Objective

To recognize the first names of the children in the class

Materials

Paper
scissors
black felt pen
colorful dinosaur pictures
tape
an empty plastic bottle
heart stickers

Preparation

Cut a 4" x 8" paper strip for each child. Print a child's name on each one. Attach the dinosaur pictures on a wall and place a name strip by each dinosaur. Each dinosaur is now a Name-a-Saurus!

Wildflowers

Age level

3+

Objective

To reinforce the idea that everyone is special and different

Materials

Glue
paper cups
magazines
scissors
tape
pipe cleaners
white paper
different colored tissue paper
crepe paper
construction paper
optional—wildflowers

Preparation

Place glue in paper cups. Place all the materials on the table. Cut out picture of wildflowers from magazines. Tape the flower pictures on a wall near the work tables.

What to do

1. Look at the wildflowers or pictures of wildflowers. How can wildflowers be different? Their color? Their size? How they smell? Notice that all the flowers are different and special. Explain that in a field of wildflowers there are no two flowers alike!

2. Have the children stand and look at each other. We are wearing different colors. We are different sizes. We are all different and special like the wildflowers!

3. Make wildflowers! At the tables, glue a pipe cleaner on a sheet of white paper for a flower stem. Create beautiful petals and leaves from the colored papers. Tear off shapes and glue them on the flower. Crunch pieces of paper to add designs.

4. Tape the wildflower pictures on a wall. Notice how all the wildflowers look different and special!

More to do

Sit on the rug. Pass around a selection of live wildflowers. Notice their different colors. Do they have different shapes? Do they each have a different smell? Which one do you like the best? Why?

Star Message

What to do

1. Discuss what it means to be a star! A star is someone who is special. If you are a star, everyone wants to be your friend. People smile when they see you. You are liked for the wonderful things that you can do!

2. Have the children form a star with their hands. (Place both thumbs and first fingers together.) Look through your stars. Do you see everyone in the classroom? We are like stars! We are special and loved.

3. Display the star jar. The star jar will help us find out different ways to be stars in our classroom. One child chooses a star message. Read each message and give an example for each one.

More to do

Make Star Finders! Use paper towel rolls or roll different colored construction paper into tubes and tape closed. Place a sticky star on each roll. Place large star stickers around the room. Search through the Star Finders to find a star. When a child finds a star, give him a star sticker! When you are learning about the ocean, make Fish Finders and place fish stickers around the room. Make Ghost Finders at Halloween. Try Egg Finders at Easter!

Age level

$3+$

Objectives

To build self-esteem and to introduce positive classroom behavior

Materials

Paper
scissors
small sticky stars
pen
glass jar

Preparation

Cut 1" paper squares for each child. Place a sticky star on one side of each paper. Print a star message on the other side. Suggested star messages: be a friend to everyone; be kind; be polite; help others if they need it; and use nice words. Fold up the paper squares and place them in a glass jar.

Beanbag Hellos

Age level

3+

Objective

To learn to treat others kindly

Materials

Pretty rock
paper
crayons
toy cars
beanbag

Preparation

None

What to do

1. Talk about the word "friend." We have many friends in the classroom now. When we have a friend, we know something about that person.

2. Demonstrate different ways to treat a friend. For example:
   Sharing—Pass a pretty rock around. As the children pass the rock to the child next to them, mention how nice it is to share.
   Helping—A friend asks you to help color a picture. Give each child a crayon. Pass a sheet of paper around and each child colors it!
   Caring—If you see someone who looks sad, what would be a nice thing to do? Ask them to play with you! Have everyone roll a toy car to the person next to them.

3. Play the Beanbag Hello Game! It is nice to say hello to a friend. It shows them that you are thinking about them. The teacher throws a beanbag to a child. This child says hello to another child in the circle.

4. After the first child says hello, she thinks of something nice to say to the other child. For example, "Hello, Pat. I like your shirt!" The first child then throws the beanbag to another child. Continue until each child has caught the beanbag and said hello.

More to do

Talk about what it means to share ideas. When you share an idea, you tell someone something. Pass the beanbag around the circle. When a child receives the beanbag, she shares an idea. Help the children think of ideas! (What do you like to play? What do you like to draw?) Children find this concept interesting! They begin to think about communication. They find that speaking their thoughts is a safe and fun thing to do.

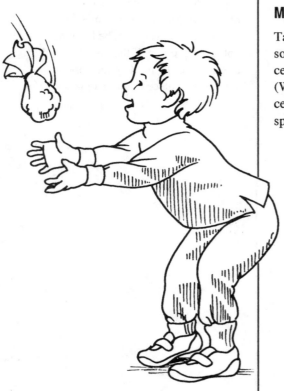

Happy Hands

What to do

1. We use our hands everyday in the classroom. How can we use them nicely? Brainstorm ideas! Clapping hands, touching someone gently, sharing our toys, waving hello to a friend, scratching someone's back.

2. Make hand tracings. Give everyone a sheet of paper. Spread a variety of felt pens on the table. Have everyone trace their hands on their paper. Color the hands, using many colors.

3. Sit on the rug with the hand tracings. Everyone tells the teacher a nice way to use their hands.

More to do

Have some fun with your hands! Think of a variety of hand signals. Act them out. Possible hand signals are palms up for standing up; palms down for sitting down; a finger circling in the air for turning around; a hand moving back and forth for a swaying motion; and hands together against a cheek for going to sleep. Use some of the hand signals in the classroom.

Age level

3+

Objective

To encourage positive behavior in a classroom

Materials

Paper
felt pens

Preparation

None

Pet Store

Age level

4+

Objective

To encourage children to express their feelings

Materials

Pictures of puppies (calendar pictures are great!)
tape

Preparation

Tape the puppy pictures on a wall or a bulletin board.

What to do

1. Pretend that you are puppies in a pet store, waiting for someone to take you home. Look at the puppy pictures on the wall. Choose a puppy that you would like to be!

2. Sit in a circle. Roll a small ball to a child. This child becomes the puppy he has chosen. The puppy sits in the middle of the circle. Have the puppy try to express how it is feeling without using words. Is he hungry, happy, scared, sleepy or lonely? Everyone else tries to guess what the puppy is feeling. When someone guesses correctly, the puppy rolls the ball to another child who becomes the puppy.

More to do

Look at the puppy pictures. Puppies can feel the same way that we do. They can feel tired, hungry, sleepy, happy, sad, lonely, bored, mad or ready to play. Draw puppy faces on paper. Add face parts, plus a tail and body. When everyone finishes their picture, they tell the teacher how their puppy is feeling. Print their responses on their papers!

Copy Cats

What to do

1. Discuss the feelings you have when someone copies you. It should be a good feeling! It's a compliment! It means that someone likes what you are doing.

2. Give everyone four blocks. Explain that everyone will copy the teacher! The teacher arranges the blocks in a certain way. The children place their blocks in the same pattern. Try a variety of patterns! Examples might be four blocks in a row; four blocks stacked; three blocks in a row with one on top of the middle block.

3. Play the Copy Cat Game! Choose a Copy Cat. Give this child a toy mouse. The Copy Cat chooses a block pattern or demonstrates an action such as wiggling fingers or pounding on the floor. The remaining children follow the action.

4. The Copy Cat gives the toy mouse to another child who becomes the new Copy Cat.

More to do

Sit at the table. Have the children follow the teacher's instructions with paper and crayon. The teacher might say, "Find a red crayon and color on your paper. Now find a yellow crayon and color on your paper. Find a blue crayon and make a big circle!" When the teacher has finished giving instructions, everyone shows their copy cat picture. It doesn't matter that everyone did the same thing. All the pictures are beautiful—and different!

Age level

4+

Objective

To understand feelings when someone copies you

Materials

blocks
toy mouse

Preparation

None

Secret Message

Age level

4+

Objective

To learn how to handle secrets

Materials

Pennies
wrapping paper
tape
paper
scissors
crayons

Preparation

Wrap a penny in wrapping paper. Tape it closed. Make one for each child. Draw a happy face for each child on a 3" square of paper. Draw a frowning face on the other side.

What to do

1. What is a secret? It is something that you are asked not to tell. What does a secret sound like? Sometimes it is a quiet sound and hard to understand. Have everyone whisper their name!

2. When is a secret good? When it is about something good! It will make you feel happy inside. Examples are a birthday present; a surprise party; or when you are planning to do something nice for someone.

3. Give each child a happy face. Place them, happy face up, on the rug. Ask for suggestions for happy secrets!

4. When is a secret not good? When it hurts a friend's feelings. When you get hurt and don't tell anyone! When you ask someone to do something that is not right.

5. Each child can turn over their happy face to show the sad face. Ask for suggestions for a sad secret.

6. Discuss how secrets in the classroom can hurt feelings. Everyone needs to feel part of the group!

More to do

Sing the secret songs, to the tune of "The Itsy Bitsy Spider." "Secret Song 1" is for keeping a good secret. "Secret Song 2" is for telling a secret!

Secret Song 1
I can feel a secret
Climbing up my throat.
I'll catch it in my mouth
And hide it in my coat.
If it tries to wiggle
So it can be heard,
I'll catch it in my fist and
Muffle every word!

Secret Song 2
I can feel a secret
Climbing up my throat.
I'll pull the secret out and
Wear it on my coat.
My secret is a button
That everyone can see
And that is how my secret
Wiggled out of me!

Share a Bear

What to do

1. What does it mean to share? Is it being a good friend? Can anyone remember a time when they have shared something?

2. Place the Share Bears and crayons on the rug. Each child chooses a Share Bear and colors it.

3. Play a share game. Choose two children. Have each child stand at opposite ends of the yarn.

4. Both children walk slowly towards each other. When they meet, they exchange Share Bears. Then they both return to their starting places.

5. The remaining children clap their hands. It feels great to share!

6. Choose two more children to share bears; continue until everyone has shared a bear!

More to do

Draw a large bear on a sheet of butcher paper. Tape it on a wall. Place crayons near the bear. The children share the crayons to help color the bear. Look at the giant Share Bear. It is a beautiful, shared picture!

Age level

3+

Objective

To encourage children to share

Materials

White construction paper
black felt pen
scissors
yarn
tape
crayons

Preparation

Draw a bear on a sheet of construction paper for each child. Cut them out. These are Share Bears! Cut a string of yarn 8' long. Tape it on the rug.

Hide-a-Bug

Age level

3+

Objective

To learn to take turns

Materials

Bug stickers
rocks

Preparation

Place a bug sticker on one of the rocks.

What to do

1. Talk about taking turns. Is it hard to wait your turn? Do you think everyone should get turns?

2. Place the rocks on the rug. Place the bug rock bug side down!

3. Explain that a bug is hiding under one of the rocks. Take turns turning over one of the rocks. If a child finds the bug, she can peel off the bug sticker.

4. The remaining children hide their eyes. Give the child who found the bug another bug sticker to place under another rock.

5. Continue until everyone has found the bug.

6. Place a bug sticker on all the rocks so each child can take a bug rock home. Hide the bug in a room in your house. Family members can take turns finding the bug!

More to do

At Halloween, hide a ghost sticker! At Hanukkah, hide star or candle stickers. Place the rocks in a container titled, "The Rock Box." The children can play the Hide-a-Bug Game by themselves or with each other.

Teddy Bear Talk

What to do

1. When you "Teddy Bear Talk," you speak nicely to your friends. You play nicely! You are a good listener, like a teddy bear. We should all be like teddy bears!

2. Pass out a handful of blocks to everyone.

3. Each child can build something from their blocks. Teddy bears only offer compliments to each other.

4. Have everyone bang two of their blocks together. A teddy bear says, "Please bang the blocks more softly."

5. Have everyone pile their blocks together. Clean-up time! All the Teddy Bears help clean up. We were all playing!

More to do

Have a special teddy bear in the classroom. When someone needs a reminder of how teddy bears play, point to the teddy bear! Playing, eating or napping with the teddy bear can be a special privilege!

Age level

3+

Objective

To reinforce positive behavior in the classroom

Materials

Blocks
teddy bear

Preparation

None

Caterpillar Crawl

Age level

3+

Objective

To foster the attitude that everyone works and plays together

Materials

None

Preparation

None

What to do

1. Explain how a caterpillar moves! It uses all its muscles together, slowly and smoothly. Everyone can move one finger on the rug like a caterpillar. Observe how carefully the caterpillars are moving. No one is bumping into each other!

2. Discuss how everyone should play like the caterpillars, working and playing together. Brainstorm ways to play nicely in the classroom.

3. Move together as a group. Do the Caterpillar Crawl! Have everyone kneel on the rug in a straight line. The teacher leads everyone in a swaying motion. Sway slow. Sway fast!

4. Move together in different positions! Give everyone a turn to think of ways to move together. Observe how nicely everyone is moving and playing together.

More to do

Place a variety of colored pipe cleaners on the rug. Make caterpillars! Choose a pipe cleaner and twist it around a finger. Now slide it off. Pull the caterpillar slightly apart. Have it crawl up your arm. Have it hide under a leaf (your hand). Take the caterpillars home. If the caterpillar loses its shape, twist it around your finger!

Clubhouse

What to do

1. Explain that everyone is an important part of the classroom. We are a group! We do many things together!

2. Call circle time a Club Meeting! Everyone can suggest a class cheer such as "hooray for us!" Think of a club greeting such as a handshake or slapping your knees. Do it! Think of a password to begin circle time. (Pizza!) Now the room is our clubhouse!

3. Play "Follow the Teacher." (Mention that everyone is doing it as a group!) The teacher can tiptoe around the room. Give each child a turn to think of something for everyone to do.

More to do

Sing the "I'm a Friend" song to the tune of "Put Your Finger In The Air."

With a hop and a skip and a jump. (On "hop" pound one fist on the other fist. On "skip" rotate two fists around each other. On "jump" clap your hands.)
With a hop and a skip and a jump. (Repeat directions above)
I can love a friend (Cross arms over chest)
To the very end, (Place one finger on the opposite shoulder. Run finger down arm to the end of hand.)

With a hop and a skip and a jump! (Repeat directions above)
With a hop and a skip and a jump. (Repeat directions above)
With a hop and a skip and a jump. (Repeat directions above)
I can help a friend (Clasp both hands together)
To the very end, (Repeat directions above)
With a hop and a skip and a jump! (Repeat directions above)

With a hop and a skip and a jump. (Repeat directions above)
With a hop and a skip and a jump. (Repeat directions above)
I can be a friend (Place thumb and first finger together. Move like a bee.)
To the very end, (Repeat directions above)
With a hop and a skip and a jump! (Repeat directions above)

Age level

3+

Objective

To encourage group unity

Materials

None

Preparation

None

Happy Faces

Age level

3+

Objective

To help children remember the many things that they have learned this past month

Materials

Yellow construction paper
scissors
butcher paper
black felt pen
tape

Preparation

Cut 3" circles from yellow construction paper. Make one for each child. Cut a large sheet of butcher paper. Draw a large square on the butcher paper. This is your classroom!

What to do

1. Place the yellow circles on the rug. Everyone will get a chance to turn one of the circles into a happy face!

2. Choose a child to be a Happy Face maker! Help this child remember something that he learned during the month. Mention the names of activities and what was talked about or done.

3. When the Happy Face maker remembers something, give him a black felt pen. Then he draws a happy face on a yellow circle and tapes the happy face in the paper classroom.

4. Continue until everyone has remembered something and made a happy face. Look at all the happy faces in the classroom! We have learned many things that can make us feel good and happy.

More to do

Make a giant happy face to take home! Draw two large eyes and a mouth on a large paper plate with a black felt pen. Cut yellow tissue into 6" strips. Place glue and the paper strips on the table. Crunch up the strips and glue them on the paper plate. Your giant happy face can remind you of all the special things that we have learned!

The Magical World of Our Senses

Children are a bundle of senses! They use their senses with enthusiasm and interest. The activities in this chapter offer a wide variety of learning experiences and teach an awareness of the body. Where is your finger tip? Do you have an earlobe? Observation and perception skills are enhanced. Who can see the tiny speck of color in this gray rock? Close your eyes! Raise your hand when you hear a very quiet sound. Sense activities also provide opportunities for mental stimulation and growth. What senses do you use in a rainstorm? If you were looking for a lost lion, what senses would help you? Our senses play an intricate part in our everyday actions. A child's natural sense of curiosity and wonder will be sparked at every activity time. So be prepared! With the following sense activities, it will be hard to end an activity. The combination of sense exploration, self-discovery and imagination makes this chapter a winner!

The Magical World of Our Senses

	Monday	Tuesday	Wednesday	Thursday	Friday
Week 1	3+ **Block Games** *To introduce the five senses*	3+ **Eye Spy** *To learn what eyes can do*	4+ **Sounds Around** *To understand sound*	3+ **The Nosey Bear Story** *To explore the sense of smell*	3+ **Mouth Munchies** *To learn about the sense of taste*
Week 2	4+ **The Touchy Pack Rat** *To introduce the sense of touch*	4+ **The Lost Puppy** *To use the sense of sight*	3+ **Find the Lion** *To increase listening skills*	3+ **Skunk Surprise** *To explore further the sense of smell*	4+ **Chef's Salad** *To learn more about the sense of taste*
Week 3	4+ **Trip to the Moon** *To explore the sense of touch*	4+ **Nature Hike** *To explore the five senses outdoors*	4+ **Camping Out** *To review the five senses*	3+ **Rain-storm** *To explore the five senses in a rainstorm*	4+ **Snow-storm** *To challenge the five senses in a snowstorm*
Week 4	4+ **The Five Sense Children** *To understand all five senses*	4+ **Haunted House** *To encourage imagination*	4+ **Cave Bats** *To improve cutting skills*	4+ **Closet Monster** *To encourage drawing skills*	3+ **1-2-3 Ghost!** *To seek and find the hidden ghosts*

Block Games

What to do

1. Talk about our five senses! Explain that there are five areas of the body that help us learn. Everyone can point to the areas as you mention them (eyes, ears, nose, mouth and fingers).

2. Give everyone two wooden blocks. Explain that the blocks will help us discover our senses! Suggestions to test our senses:

   Sense of Sight—Use your sight to play Follow the Leader! Balance a block on the back of your hand. Pick up a block using only two fingers. Put a block on your head! Each child can think of something to do with the blocks.

   Sense of Hearing—Bang the two blocks together. Bang them loudly. Bang them softly. Rub them together. Drop one of them on the rug. Who can hear it hit the rug?

   Sense of Smell—Smell the blocks! They have a wood smell. Place a block by your ear. Can you smell it now?

   Sense of Taste—If we ate wood, what part of our body would we use? Do you think it would taste good? What do you like to eat?

   Sense of Touch—Feel a block with your hands. Move your fingers all over the block. Now place the block on your cheek. Place it on your arm. We feel best with our fingers!

More to do

Give each child a sheet of paper. Place a variety of wooden blocks on the table. Give each child a handful of crayons and have them trace different shaped blocks on the paper. Color them in! (Notice how you are using two of your senses—your sight and touch!)

Age level

3+

Objective

To introduce the five senses

Materials

Wooden blocks

Preparation

None

Eye Spy

Age level

3+

Objective

To learn what eyes can do

Materials

Colored construction paper
scissors
tape

Preparation

Cut a sheet of construction paper 6" long. Roll it up into a tube. This is a color tunnel! Make them in a variety of colors. Make one for each child.

What to do

1. We see with our eyes. They can do many things! Close them. Open them! Move them up and down. Move them around and around. Move them side to side. Blink!

2. We see when our eyes are open. Everyone close their eyes. Is it dark? Open your eyes. Now you can see! Our eyes need the light in the room to see.

3. Display various colors of construction paper. Hold up one sheet at a time. What color do you see?

4. Play Eye Spy! Give everyone a color tunnel. Explain that each child will hunt for a special color in the room. What color is your color tunnel? That is the color you can look for!

5. Give everyone a few minutes to look for colors. Then each child finds her color and tells where it is.

6. Take the color tunnels home. Look for colors in your home. Look for colors outside!

More to do

Play Band Leader! Give a child a ruler to use as a baton. This child is the Band Leader. The Band Leader moves the ruler slowly in the air. Everyone follows the ruler with their eyes. Give each child a turn to be the Band Leader. (Play slow music for the Band Leader to conduct!)

Sounds Around

What to do

1. Find your ears! How many do you have? Feel the outside of your ear. Your ear is a special part of your body.

2. Your ear is like a baseball mitt. It catches sound! Make different sounds. Did your ears catch all the sounds?

3. You can hear many kinds of sounds! Place a variety of items on the rug. Examples are a bell, a ruler, a stuffed animal, two pencils, a jar, a penny. Make different sounds! Ring a bell loudly. Ring it softly. Hit a ruler on the rug. Hit it on a glass jar. Drop a stuffed animal on the rug. Shake a jar with a penny in it. Bang two pencils together. Ask for suggestions of ways to make sounds with classroom items!

4. Have all the children close their eyes. Make the same sounds with the classroom items. See who can identify how the sound is being made.

More to do

Have a sound party! Everyone finds two items in the classroom to make a sound. Each child sits with his items and gets a turn to make a special sound with them. Now place all the items on the rug. Everyone chooses two different items to make a sound. Experiment until you find your favorite sound!

Age level

4+

Objective

To understand sound

Materials

Variety of items from the classroom

Preparation

None

The Nosey Bear Story

Age level

3+

Objective

To explore the sense of smell and to introduce different scents

Materials

Lemon
cinnamon
cotton ball
perfume
soap
flower
paper bag

Preparation

Place the above items, except for the lemon, in a paper bag.

What to do

1. Where is your nose? Feel your nose with your hand.

2. Move the tip of your nose around. There are no bones at the tip! Feel the bone down the front of your nose. It feels hard.

3. What does your nose do? It can smell many things! Pass a lemon around. Take a deep breath! Now pass the lemon around again. Place it on your forehead. Does it smell as strong?

4. Tell the following story! As you tell the story, pull the selected items from the paper bag at the appropriate time.

The Nosey Bear Story

Once there was a baby bear who was very nosey. He liked to poke his nose into everything! He would always make such a mess that Mother Bear would say, "Don't poke your nose around the cave anymore!"

One day, Mother Bear went out to find some honey. She said to Baby Bear, "Watch your nose! And don't go sniffing at the flower bush!" After she left, Baby Bear got very excited. He loved to be alone in the bear cave. He could poke his nose into anything undisturbed. He found some cinnamon in the kitchen and sniff, sniff, sniffed it! (Pass around the cinnamon for everyone to smell.) Then he went into Mother Bear's bedroom and found some perfume, and he sniff, sniff, sniffed it! (Pass around a cotton ball dipped in perfume.) Then he climbed into the bathtub and found the soap, and guess what he did? He sniff, sniff, sniffed it! (Pass the soap around.) Then Baby Bear thought about the flower bush outside the bear cave. "Just one sniff," he thought. He poked his nose into a bright yellow flower. (Pass around a flower.) Then he took one big sniff. Bzzzzzzzzz—OUCH! A bee had stung Baby Bear on the nose!

"Ouch! Ouch! Ouch!" yelled Baby Bear, just as Mother Bear returned from the woods. "What's the matter?" said Mother Bear. Baby Bear told his mother all about the bright yellow flower and the bee.

Do you think Baby Bear still poked his nose into everything? Yes! But not in the flower bush!

More to do

Everyone can bring something from home to smell. Tell The Nosey Bear Story with the items from home!

Mouth Munchies

What to do

1. Pass out a small piece of bread to everyone. Place it on your finger. Can you taste it? Where can you taste it?

2. Chew the bread. Explain that your tongue is tasting the bread. What else is your tongue doing? It is moving the bread all around! It is pushing the food between your teeth to help chew it.

3. What does everyone like to eat? Everyone tastes things differently. What you like, someone else might not like!

4. Display the plate of food samples. Choose a food sample to taste. Ask each child how her food tasted. Give everyone a few turns to choose different food samples.

5. When the sampling is over, find out the children's favorites. Notice how the answers differ!

More to do

Talk about taste buds. They are the very small bumps on the tongue. Make a picture of taste buds. Give everyone pink construction paper cut in the shape of a tongue. Place small items on the table, such as beans or small marshmallows. These are taste buds! Glue the taste buds on the tongues.

Age level

3+

Objective

To introduce the connection between taste and tongue

Materials

Plate
knife
variety of foods, such as marshmallows, a pickle, an apple, cheese, nuts, crackers and bread

Preparation

Cut food items into small samples. Place them on a plate.

The Touchy Pack Rat

Age level

4+

Objective

To introduce the sense of touch

Materials

Small box
scissors
small stuffed mouse (look in pet stores)
variety of small objects, such as a ball, a block, a bow, a crayon, a truck, at least one object for each child
crayons

Preparation

Cut a small opening on one side of the box. This is an animal hole! Place the stuffed mouse and selected objects inside the box.

What to do

1. Talk about the sense of touch. Place a variety of crayons on the rug. Ask each child to pick up a color that they like. What part of your body touched the crayon first? Your fingers!

2. Explain that you feel best with your fingers. Ask where your fingertips are. Look at them! They are very sensitive. Now close your eyes and feel the crayon. Your fingers tell you about the shape of the crayon.

3. Display the box. A pack rat lives behind the hole. Pack rats collect anything! The pack rat will not care if you look at his stuff, but he wants you to put it all back!

4. Take out the pack rat! He is going to watch to make sure that none of his treasures are lost! Take turns sticking one hand in the hole and feeling an object. Before pulling the object out, guess what the object is!

5. When all the objects are on the rug, place them back in the hole. You do not want to upset the pack rat!

More to do

Bring a secret object from home in a small box. Pretend to be pack rats! Take turns feeling the object in someone's box and guessing what it is.

The Lost Puppy

What to do

1. There are lost puppies in the classroom! Each child chooses a puppy picture—that is his lost puppy.

2. Look at the pictures on the rug and talk about the differences in each puppy! Our eyes show us how each puppy is different.

3. Now it's time to find the lost puppies! Each child picks up his puppy picture from the rug and looks at it closely. Now find the picture in the classroom that matches his puppy.

4. When a child has found his matching picture, he has found his puppy!

5. Bring the puppies back to the rug. As the children return to the rug, give each child his puppy leash! Tape one end of the leash to the picture.

6. Send the matching pictures home with each child. They can play The Lost Puppy at home!

More to do

Play this game during the year, using different matching animals or objects. Use matching pumpkin faces at Halloween. Use matching fish when you learn about the ocean. When you study the weather, try matching snowflakes!

Age level

4+

Objective

To increase perception skills using the sense of sight

Materials

Yarn
scissors
paper
crayons
tape

Preparation

Cut a 2' piece of yarn (puppy leash) for each child. Draw a simple puppy face on a sheet of paper. Make two identical puppies for each child. Suggestions for different puppies are brown spots on the ears, black spots on the ears, blue eyes, yellow eyes, a pink nose, a black nose, a puppy with one red ear! Tape one set of the puppy pictures around the room and place the matching set on the rug.

Find the Lion

Age level

3+

Objective

To increase listening skills

Materials

Marbles
a jar
small plastic lion or a small picture of
a lion taped on a piece of posterboard
pictures of different animals including
a lion

Preparation

Place a few marbles in a jar. Hide the
lion in the classroom.

What to do

1. Explain that a lion has escaped from a nearby zoo. We are going to try to
   find the lion!

2. What does a lion look like? Possible answers are that it has a large mane,
   light brown hair, a long thin tail, large paws, whiskers and that it walks on
   four legs.

3. Show a few animal pictures, one at a time. After showing each picture,
   ask, "Is this a lion?" Show a picture of a lion last. Is this a lion? This is
   what we are looking for!

4. How can we find the lion? We know what he looks like, but we don't see
   him! We can't smell him! Can we hear him? Yes! Shake the jar of marbles. This is his growl!

5. The missing lion is somewhere in the room. The children can hunt for the
   lion. The teacher is the only one who knows where the lion is. When
   someone gets near the lion, listen for his growl!

6. Shake the jar of marbles to remind the children what the lion sounds like.
   When a child finds the lion, she shows everyone where the lion was hiding and then brings the lion back to the teacher. Everyone close their eyes.
   The child who found the lion can hide it! This child also shakes the jar of
   marbles to help the other children search.

More to do

Have different "hunt sounds" during the year. Hunt for a missing dinosaur!
Pound on a drum for the sound of dinosaur footsteps. Hunt for a runaway turkey at Thanksgiving. Gobble! Children who have found the turkey already
can help the teacher gobble!

Skunk Surprise

What to do

1. Place the cards face down on the rug. These cards represent a walk in the woods. Explain that there is a skunk in the woods, and we don't know where it is!

2. Tell the following story. The cards will be turned over when it is time to smell something in the story. Children take turns flipping a card over. Everyone identifies the picture on the card. When the skunk is turned over, everyone holds their noses, waves their hands in the air and yells "pew!"

3. After the skunk has been found, mix up the cards and start the story over. Give everyone a chance to find the skunk!

A Walk in The Woods

It was a beautiful day! The air was crisp. The sun streamed through the woods like long drips of honey. I went for a quiet walk in the woods. I smelled a (turn over a card and say what it is). Then I smelled a (turn over another card). Then I walked deeper into the woods and I smelled a (turn over another card). (Continue the story and turning over cards. When the skunk card is turned over say, "pew," hold your nose and wave your hand. Start over again!)

More to do

Make up different stories during the year. Draw related cards. Children often have ideas! Suggested ideas are *A Walk in the Grocery Store, A Walk in the Zoo*. Have a surprise smell in each story!

Age level

3+

Objective

To learn that the nose is used to smell and identify objects

Materials

White posterboard
scissors
felt pens

Preparation

Cut eight 3" x 5" shapes from the posterboard. These are playing cards for the story, *A Walk in The Woods*. Draw a picture on each card of something you might smell in the woods. Suggestions are pine trees, flowers, pond water, blackberries, a campfire, a licorice plant, a rain smell, a skunk!

Chef's Salad

Age level

4+

Objective

To learn about the sense of taste

Materials

Salad ingredients
knives
cutting boards
bowls
forks
optional—salad dressing

Preparation

Cut up the ingredients for salad. Place each item in a separate bowl.

What to do

1. Explain that everyone is going to make a Chef's Salad! Place the bowls of ingredients on the table.

2. Give everyone an empty bowl. Choose a child to start the salad. This child chooses ingredients for her salad.

3. After she makes her salad, the other children take turns.

4. Now the salads are ready to eat. Offer salad dressings, if desired. Talk about salads while you are eating. What food in your salad do you like the best? What would you like more of? What does not taste good? What tastes sweet? What tastes juicy? Is there anything else you would like in your salad?

More to do

Make submarine sandwiches. Make pizza! Watch imaginations make creative recipes!

Trip to the Moon

What to do

1. Take a trip to the moon! Pretend to put on spacesuits. Sit on the rug and fasten seat belts. Push an imaginary button to start the engine. Count down to ten. Blast off!

2. Tilt back as the spaceship takes off. When the spaceship changes direction, sit up straight!

3. Pretend to look out the spaceship windows. What can we see? (stars, planets, a creature!)

4. Now we are approaching the moon. Count down to ten. Land with a bump! Pass out paper bags. Leave the spaceship and look for a moon object to collect. Since there is no air on the moon, walk in slow motion!

5. Collect a moon object to take back to Earth (the hidden objects). Feel the various moon objects. Each child places one item in a paper bag. Return to the spaceship!

6. Count down to ten to blast off. Push a super speed button to fly fast! Count down to land on the Earth. Take off the spacesuits. Take turns showing the moon objects.

More to do

Place all the moon objects in a box. Take out one of the moon objects and place it in a paper bag. Choose a child to be a moon detective. This child feels the object in the paper bag and tries to guess which moon object it is. Play slow music to "moon" dance to. Encourage the children to move with slow movements to the music.

Age level

4+

Objective

To explore the sense of touch

Materials

Small paper bags
variety of interesting "moon" objects, such as a gourd, an eggplant, a wire whisk, an interesting rock, a funny looking stuffed animal, a rubber bug, a rubber glove, a candle, a small box with marbles in it!

Preparation

Hide the objects around the room.

Nature Hike

Age level

4+

Objective

To explore the five senses outdoors and to increase an awareness of nature

Materials

Marshmallows or tiny finger hot dogs
sticks

Preparation

None

What to do

1. Go on a nature hike! The five senses will help us learn and experience many things. Look for a stick. There will be a marshmallow roast at the end of the hike!

2. Stop many times to notice the different things in nature. Sit on grass. Feel it. Smell it! Lay on stomachs and look at it closely. Can you see anything else?

3. Smell flowers. What color are the stems, the petals? Feel how soft the petals are.

4. Find some leaves. Smell them. See if you can look through them. Can you see veins in the leaves? Do they feel smooth or rough?

5. Find a tree. Feel its bark. Smell the bark. Look up into the tree. Do you see any movement? What colors do you see on the tree?

6. Lie on backs. Take a deep breath. Relax. Feel the earth supporting you. Look at the sky! Do you see anything in the sky? Close your eyes. What sounds do you hear?

7. Find a grassy area. Have a marshmallow or hot dog roast! Pretend to build a fire. Collect small leaves and twigs. Make a pile of them. Sit around the pile with the collected sticks. Pretend to start a fire!

8. Pass out a marshmallow to each child. The children stick their marshmallows on one end of their sticks. Hold the marshmallows over the pile of leaves and twigs (the fire).

More to do

Go on other nature hikes and look for a special treasure each time. Look for a red leaf, an unusual rock or something brown! Go on a surprise hike! The children look for objects to surprise the class. Share the surprise objects when you return. Did anyone find a similar object? Who found the smallest object? Who found an object with the most color? Comment on each child's object!

Camping Out

What to do

1. Sit on the rug and pretend to drive to the campsite! Pass out paper plates. They are steering wheels! Start the engine. Push on the gas and go!

2. Weave back and forth to follow a winding mountain road. Wave at grazing cows. Honk at passing deer. Pull over at the campsite.

3. Pretend to pitch a tent. Walk around the tent in the classroom.

4. It's getting dark. Gather wood to build a fire! (Stack blocks together in the middle of the rug.)

5. Cook dinner! Give the children a sheet of tin foil and a block (a potato!). Wrap the potatoes in the tin foil and place them in the fire.

6. Sit around the fire to stay warm. What senses did the children use to camp out? Things to mention are seeing the animals with your eyes; the sound of your horn honking; feeling the warmth of the fire; smelling the potatoes cooking; and eating them!

7. Time for bed. Sit down under the sheet in the tent. Listen for nighttime sounds. Howl softly like a coyote. Hoot like an owl. Click like crickets.

8. Keep the tent in the classroom for the children to invent their own Camping Out.

More to do

At another time, build a "campfire" and sing songs! Read a story around the campfire. Then lay mats around the campfire to take naps! Take a drive to the mountains and look for bears! Hide a stuffed bear or a picture of a bear in the classroom. The children hunt for the bear. Hide it again!

Age level

4+

Objective

To review the five senses by going "camping"

Materials

Large sheet
tape
paper plates
tin foil
blocks

Preparation

Make a tent! Tape one side of a large bed sheet on a wall. Tape the opposite side on a table or solid structure in the classroom.

Rainstorm

Age level

3+

Objective

To discover the senses used in a rainstorm

Materials

String or yarn
tape
two cymbals or pot lids

Preparation

Tape circles of yarn or string on the rug a few feet apart. These are rain puddles.

What to do

1. There is a rainstorm in the classroom! Pretend to put on raincoats and boots. Take a walk in the rain. While the children are walking in the rain, the teacher can tap his or her fingers on a hard surface. This sounds like rain! Jump over any rain puddles.

2. When the teacher stops tapping, the rain has stopped and the children sit on the rug. Feel the raincoats. Are they wet? Take them off! Did anyone see any rain puddles? Did you hear the rain?

3. Listen for thunder! Close your eyes and listen. The teacher bangs two cymbals (or pot lids) together to make thunder. When the children hear thunder, they open their eyes and clap their hands to make a second boom. Take turns banging the cymbals together while the remaining children clap.

4. Make another rainstorm! The children pound the rug softly with their hands. A light rain is falling. Now pound a little louder, increasing the speed and force of the pounding. The rainstorm is getting louder! Now pound as hard as you can. It's pouring!

More to do

Sing "The Rain Song" to the tune of "Twinkle, Twinkle, Little Star."

I can hear a little rain (Pound softly on the rug)
Falling on my window pane. (Continue pounding)
Tap tap tapping at my door (Pound fist against open palm)
Growing to a monster roar. (Repeat above directions)
Should I cover up my eyes (Cover eyes)
Waiting for a big surprise! (Clap hands once)

Snowstorm

What to do

1. It's snowing! Who wants to go out in the cold? First, let's get warm. Do some exercises.

2. Now pretend to put on a thick jacket, earmuffs, mittens, thick socks and heavy shoes. Open the door of the house and walk out together!

3. Walk in the snow! Pick up your feet and walk slowly. The snow is deep! Walk quietly around the classroom. Walking in snow is a soft sound.

4. Build a snowman. Pretend to push snow together to form a ball. Make it bigger! Make two more balls and place them on top of each other. Are your hands feeling cold? Wiggle your fingers and shake your hands to increase circulation.

5. Stop and listen! Can you hear the snow falling? Hold a snowflake (a cotton ball). Now drop the snowflake. Did you hear it fall? Snow can fall without making a sound! Drop a few cotton balls on the rug. Throw them in the air! It's snowing!

More to do

When you walk in snow, you leave a footprint. Make one! Give everyone a sheet of white construction paper and a felt pen. The children trace their feet on their paper. Place the footprints around the room. Follow them! Take turns making a different path with the footprints.

Age level

4+

Objective

To challenge all five senses in a snowstorm

Materials

Bag of cotton balls

Preparation

None

The Five Sense Children

Age level

4+

Objective

To understand all five senses

Materials

Magazines
butcher paper
scissors
felt pen
tape

Preparation

Tear out magazine pictures that have parts of the body on them that relate to the senses, such as eyes, ears, noses, mouths and hands. Cut a sheet of butcher paper 5' long and draw five children 3' tall and standing in a row on the butcher paper. Tape it on a wall.

What to do

1. Place scissors and the magazine pictures on the table. The children cut out body parts relating to the five senses. Each child has her own pile of pictures.

2. When the children are finished cutting, sit on the rug with the pictures. The five figures on the butcher paper are the sense children! Each one likes to use a special sense. With a felt pen, draw an eye next to the first child, an ear next to the second child, a nose next to the third child, a mouth next to the fourth child and a hand next to the fifth child!

3. The first child likes to see, the second child likes to hear, the third child likes to smell, the fourth child likes to taste and the fifth child likes to touch! Look at the magazine pictures. There are parts of the body that each sense child likes to use!

4. Have one child choose a picture from her pile. This child tapes the picture on or near the appropriate sense child. For example, she would tape an eye on or near the sense child who likes to see!

5. Give each child a turn to choose a picture and tape it on or near the appropriate sense child. Tape all the pictures on the sense children.

More to do

Have a brainstorm session with the five sense children. Start with the first sense child. What do you think this sense child likes to see? Encourage everyone to think of something to see (a bird, a balloon, a rainbow). Brainstorm with each sense child. Be prepared for many imaginative answers!

Haunted House

What to do

1. Place paper, scissors and a variety of crayons on the table. The children draw a creature to live in the haunted house. Examples are monsters, bats, spiders and witches!

2. The children cut out the creatures and choose a window in the haunted house. Tape a creature behind each window. As an option, the teacher can hide special colorful Halloween cards behind some additional windows.

3. Sit in front of the haunted house. One child chooses a window and opens it! Look who's living in the haunted house!

4. Play a memory game. See who can remember what creature is hiding behind what window!

5. Leave the haunted house up until Halloween. Add something to the haunted house each day! Add spider webs (pulled apart cotton), Halloween stickers and any extra creepy crawlies drawn by the children.

More to do

Give the children a large sheet of paper to draw a creature. To help the children make an interesting creature, make available a variety of drawing tools. Drawing tools might be felt pens, crayons and colored chalk. Offer glue and cut up strings of yarn! When all the creatures are made, sit in a circle on the rug. Take turns showing the creatures. What kind of creature is it? What kind of noise does it make? Tape the creatures on a wall. Title the wall, "Waiting For A Room At The Haunted House!"

Age level

4+

Objective

To encourage imagination and memory skills

Materials

Butcher paper
scissors
tape
black felt pen
crayons
white paper
optional—Halloween cards from a card shop

Preparation

Cut two large sheets of butcher paper four feet long. Tape them on a wall, one above the other one. Draw a large haunted house on the paper. The children can color the haunted house! Cut windows on the haunted house. Cut only three sides of the windows so they can open and close. Make one window for each child.

Cave Bats

Age level

4+

Objective

To improve cutting skills

Materials

Black construction paper
white chalk
yarn
scissors
tape
hole puncher

Preparation

Using white chalk, draw a large bat on a sheet of black construction paper. Draw a bat for each child. Cut strings of yarn 1' long. Cut one for each child. Cut one string of yarn long enough to tape on a wall in the shape of an arch. This is a bat cave!

What to do

1. Sit at the table. Give everyone a cave bat and scissors. The cave bats need to rest in the bat cave! Show where the bat cave is on the wall. Have the children cut out their cave bats.

2. Then each child punches a hole on the feet of the bat and threads a string of yarn through the hole.

3. Fly the bats to the bat cave. At the bat cave, tape the free end of the string to the top and sides of the cave.

4. Look at all the cave bats resting upside down! Why are they resting? So they will feel strong to fly on Halloween night!

More to do

Say "The Scare-dy Cat Bat" chant! Make related sounds and body movements with the words that are capitalized.

Three friends out on Halloween night
To give the neighborhood a fright!
"OOOOOOO," said the ghost,
"SQUEEEEEAK," said the rat,
And a Scare-dy Cat BAT! (Clap hands once!)

Now the ghost would "OOOOOOO" and "SCREAM."
Pretending he was very mean!
The rat would JUMP and TWITCH his NOSE
Pretending he would bite your toes!
But the bat would WOOOOSH (Flap arms)
Around the air, pretending that he liked to scare!
When all he wanted was to EAT
And KNOCK on doors to trick or treat! (Bang fist against an open palm)

So, "OOOOOOO," said the ghost
and "SQUEEEEEAK," said the rat,
And trick or treat!
Said the Scare-dy Cat BAT! (Clap hands!)

Closet Monster

What to do

1. Make Closet Monsters! Closet Monsters are friendly monsters but very shy! They want to play, but they are too shy to come out of the closet. They never do! (Be sensitive to the fears of the children.)

2. Place black construction paper and a variety of colored chalk on the table. Have the children draw a closet monster that they would like to meet. Encourage the use of many colors!

3. When the Closet Monsters are finished, tape them on a wall. Title the wall, "The Monster In My Closet!"

More to do

Make different chalk pictures during the year. Use orange chalk to draw a pumpkin patch at night! Draw a large colorful Easter egg at Easter. Draw rainbows on white paper. Draw gray or black chalk lines around blue paper. Add a whale sticker. This is a whale migration path from cold to warmer waters!

Age level

4+

Objective

To encourage drawing skills and to help dissolve fear of the dark

Materials

Black construction paper
colored chalk
tape

Preparation

None

1-2-3 Ghost!

Age level

3+

Objective

To seek and find the hidden ghosts

Materials

Two ghosts, draw them or use two
ghost figures
white construction paper
tape
scissors

Preparation

Cut white construction paper into 4" x
5" pieces. Roll and tape to form tubes.
These are ghost callers! Make one for
each child.

What to do

1. Go on a ghost hunt! Show everyone the two ghosts. Have the children close their eyes. The teacher hides the two ghosts in the classroom.

2. When the ghosts are hidden, the children open their eyes and count, "1-2-3 Ghost!" On the count of "ghost," the hunt begins!

3. The children who find the two ghosts sit by the teacher on the rug. Give them each a ghost caller. When the remaining children hunt for the ghosts, the teacher and the two children can make ghost noises in their ghost callers. The noise will help call the ghosts from their hiding places!

4. As other children find the ghosts, they can join the children with the ghost callers.

5. Continue until all the children are sitting and making ghost noises!

More to do

Have different hunts during the year! Make turkey callers and hide turkeys! Make baby chick callers and hide Easter eggs. When you are learning about animals, make kitty callers and hide kittens.

I Am an Amazing Human Being

What a wonderful feeling to know who we are and what we can do! Learning about our human environment and our human bodies gives us a clear picture of ourselves. Learning about ourselves encourages a positive self-image. We are human! We can do many things!

The activities in this chapter begin with a view of children's immediate world. This includes their families, where they live and the kinds of things they do during the day. Fantasy play is an important part of these activities! Acting out the family environment is fun and enhances the learning experience. Large motor movement is also explored in this chapter. In what ways can our bodies move? Look what our bones and muscles allow us to do! Body awareness is also encouraged through experiments and discoveries. What allows us to sit straight without falling over? When we swallow food, where does it go? Is there a pump in our bodies? Being human is amazing!

The following activities offer interesting things to think about. What is the difference between the way we live and the way animals live? Would a wild animal be happy living in a human house? These activities will stretch a child's thinking! Children thrive on information about themselves. Activities that focus on who we are and what we can do provide many healthy and happy experiences. Learning about our world begins with learning about ourselves. So let the fun and learning begin. We are human! It's time to celebrate!

I Am an Amazing Human Being

	Monday	Tuesday	Wednesday	Thursday	Friday
Week 1	**3+ Living Shapes** *To discover that we are human*	**3+ My House** *To encourage an awareness of families*	**4+ Trick or Treat Review** *To sharpen memory skills*	**4+ The Brain Game** *To understand that brains make us special*	**3+ Magic Me** *To explore possible body movements*
Week 2	**3+ Skin Stretchers** *To learn about skin*	**4+ Body Bones** *To learn about bones*	**4+ Muscle Power** *To discover that muscles move bones*	**3+ Heart Beats** *To understand the importance of the heart*	**3+ Swamp Monster** *To move our bodies*
Week 3	**4+ Mouth House** *To understand the mouth*	**3+ Do the Stomach Mash** *To locate the stomach*	**3+ The Intestine Crunch** *To explore what the intestine does*	**3+ Hand Signals** *To learn about germs*	**3+ Call the Doctor** *To learn about doctors*
Week 4	**3+ The Human House** *To review what was learned this month*	**2+ Paper People** *To reinforce that we have human shapes*	**3+ Cut and Feather** *To improve cutting skills*	**3+ Pluck the Turkey** *To follow directions*	**3+ Thanks-giving Dinner** *To encourage imagination*

Living Shapes

What to do

1. What living things are on the Earth? Brainstorm answers! Possible answers are trees, grass, elephants, whales, worms.

2. What are we? Human! Have everyone repeat the word. Repeat it many ways. Say it softly. Say it loud. Whisper it!

3. Play a game to decide who is going to be your human helper. Everyone chooses a piece of paper from the bowl. Show the pictures. The child who chose the human shape is your helper!

4. The human helper stands by the teacher. The teacher talks about the human shape while the helper "shows" the appropriate part. Notice the round head, the two small ears, the short nose, the two long arms, the hands with five fingers, the waist, the two long legs, the two feet and the skin that covers your body.

5. Sing the "I Am Human" song to the tune of "If You're Happy and You Know It."

    I'm a human and I can turn around (Stand and turn around)
    I can sit very still on the ground, (Sit down)
    I can rock side to side (Rock from side to side)
    I can close my eyes and hide, (Put hands over eyes)
    I'm a human from my head to my toes! (Touch head and toes!)

    I'm a human and I can pound the floor, (With fists!)
    I can open and close a bedroom door, (Open arms wide and clap)
    I can throw a ball, (Throw a pretend ball)
    I can rock-a-bye a doll, (Fold arms and sway them)
    I'm human from my head to my toes! (Touch head and toes!)

More to do

Tear out pages from magazines that have human parts or shapes on them. Place the magazine pages on a table. Give everyone a sheet of paper, scissors and glue. Make collages of human shapes.

Age level

3+

Objective

To discover that we are human!

Materials

Paper
scissors
felt pen
a bowl

Preparation

Cut 3" x 3" squares of paper, one for each child. Draw a living shape on each piece of paper, such as a tree, a mouse, a butterfly and a flower. On one paper draw a human shape! Fold the papers in half and place them in a bowl.

My House

Age level

3+

Objective

To encourage an awareness of families

Materials

Posterboard
felt pen

Preparation

Draw the outline of a large house on the posterboard.

What to do

1. Humans like to live inside a nice warm house. When humans live together, they are called a family!

2. Act out many things that a house does for us! It keeps us warm. (Pretend to wrap up in a warm blanket.) It protects us from the weather. (Pretend to open up umbrellas.) It gives us a place to eat and sleep. (Pretend you are eating spaghetti! Then go to sleep.)

3. Display the posterboard of the house. Each child, in turn, chooses a felt pen and draws a person in the house. Ask each child who they are drawing—a mother, a grandfather, a baby? Print their answer by their picture. Title the posterboard, "We Live in Families"!

More to do

Play the Family Game! The teacher is the mother or father. Have everyone find a different place in the classroom to stand. Tell "your children" that they have all decided to live in a different house. Wave to each other! The teacher pretends to call each child on the phone. The children call each other! Now pretend to cook dinner. Everyone eats their dinner! Now stretch and yawn and go to sleep. Now the teacher says, "Who wants to come back and live with me! I'm lonely!" Is it more fun to live together? We need each other!

Trick or Treat Review

What to do

1. Explain that you are going to ask each child to tell you something that they remember about Halloween. This can be something they saw or heard! Possible things might be a pumpkin on someone's lawn or a child dressed as a bunny!

2. Say the "Trick or Treat" chant! At the end of the chant, roll the orange ball to someone. This child will tell something that he or she remembers. The number in the first line of the chant can be the number of children in the circle!

> *Ten little pumpkins (Place your fists in the air)*
> *Sitting on the rug, (Place one fist on the other open palm)*
> *Rolling all around, (Rotate both fists around each other)*
> *Upstairs, downstairs, (Clap hands above head and then in front of knees)*
> *What a sight, (Place both hands flat on cheeks, open mouth in surprise)*
> *What did (John) see (Point to one child)*
> *Halloween night!*

More to do

Everyone can draw a picture of something they saw on Halloween night. Tape them on a wall. Title the wall, "What Night Was This?"

Age level

4+

Objective

To encourage children to express themselves verbally and to sharpen memory skills

Materials

Orange ball

Preparation

None

The Brain Game

Age level

4+

Objective

To understand that brains make us special and unique

Materials

Marbles
paper cups

Preparation

None

What to do

1. We are human! How can we tell? Brainstorm ideas and act them out! Possible ideas are we brush our teeth; we bathe with soap; we cook our food.

2. There is a special part of our body that helps us to do these things. Can you guess what it is? Give clues! It is above your nose! It is under your hair! It is inside the top of your head! (Your brain!)

3. Our human brain is the best brain around. It helps us learn about everything! It helps us to think and remember. Play "The Brain Game." Place two paper cups on the rug. Place a marble under one of them. Mix them around! See who can remember which cup the marble is under.

4. Turn up your brain power! Use three paper cups and do it again! Now we really need to use our brains!

5. Send two paper cups and a marble home with each child. They can play "The Brain Game" at home!

More to do

Play many Brain Games during the year. Call a Brain Game circle time! Examples of Brain Games might be:

1. Display five items. Throw a scarf over the items. Take one of the items away. Reveal the items. Which one is missing?

2. Cut sponges into different shapes. Make two sets. Place one set on the rug. Place the other set in a paper bag. One child chooses a shape from the paper bag. Then find the matching shape on the rug!

3. Give each child the same amount of cards from a card deck. The teacher also receives the same amount of cards. Then the teacher makes a pattern on the rug with the cards. The children copy the pattern. Each child thinks of a new pattern for everyone to copy!

Magic Me

What to do

1. Where is your body? Is it your thumb? Is it your ear? It is all of you! Explain that each child will have a turn to find a special part of his or her body.

2. Show the magic wand! Give it to a child. This child can use the magic wand to point to a special part of his or her body. Then ask what this part of the body can do. If a leg is pointed to, jump up and down! If a knee is pointed to, march!

3. When the movement is finished, the child with the magic wand gives it to another child. Continue until everyone has had a turn.

More to do

Play the Magic Me Game! Choose a child to be the magician. Drape a large sheet or blanket over the magician. This child poses in a certain position under the covering. The remaining children say the words, "Magic, Magic Me"! Pull off the covering. Everyone copies the magician's body position.

Age level

3+

Objective

To become aware of the many wonderful things our bodies can do

Materials

Ruler
tin foil
glue
glitter

Preparation

Wrap tin foil around a ruler to cover it. Dab some glue on the ruler. Sprinkle the ruler with glitter. This is a magic wand!

Skin Stretchers

Age level

3+

Objective

To learn about skin

Materials

None

Preparation

None

What to do

1. Raise your hand if you have skin! Do you have skin on your hands? Where else do you have skin? Give everyone a turn to respond.

2. Do skin experiments! Allow time for comments and questions as you do each experiment. Suggestions for experiments are:
   Feel Your Skin—How does it feel? Feel the skin on your hand. Feel the skin on your cheek. Do they feel different or the same? Feel someone else's skin. Does it feel like yours?
   Look at Your Skin—Can you see the tiny thin lines on your hand? Do you see the lines around your knuckles? Look at your palm. Can you see the larger lines? Give everyone a turn to look at their skin through a magnifying glass!
   Skin Is Loose Fitting—Move your skin around on the back of your hand. Move your skin around on your neck. Move it around on your forehead! Where else can you move your skin?
   Skin Can Stretch—Pull the skin between your thumb and your first finger. It stretches! Tug on your earlobe. Puff your cheeks out! Your skin stretches with you as you grow.
   Skin Has Hair on It—Look at the hair on your arms. Look at the hair on your head! Is there hair on your face? Your eyebrows! The hair on your skin helps to keep your body warm!

3. Is there any place on your body that has no skin? Have everyone look at each other. Look at the teacher! Possible answers are eyes, gums, teeth and fingernails!

More to do

Make thumb print pictures. Give each child a sheet of white paper. The children place their thumbs on an ink pad and make thumb prints on their papers. Then they use felt pens to make the thumb prints into imaginative pictures! Add legs to the thumb print and it becomes a spider! Add a beak and two skinny legs to make a bird!

Body Bones

What to do

1. What is your skeleton made of? Bones! Look at your body. Can you see your bones? Where are they?

2. Feel your bones! Put your hands on your head. Feel your skull bone. It protects your brain! Gently feel around your eyes. There are two holes in your skull bone that protect your eyes. Feel the bones in your fingers. Bend your fingers! There are joints connecting your finger bones that allow your fingers to move. Place your hands above your waist. Do you feel your rib bones? Take a deep breath. Feel them move as you breathe! Feel your backbone. Your backbone helps you to move! Bend forward from the waist. Bend backwards! Bend from side to side.

3. Our bones give us our human shape! Get on your hands and knees. Do we look like puppy dogs? Bark! Do we look like seals? Sit on your knees. Sway back and forth! Do we look like frogs? Crouch down low. Croak! Do we look like humans? Stand straight and tall!

4. Your bones are alive. As you grow, they grow! Have everyone lay on the floor. You are tiny babies! Your bones are very small. Now you are growing. Slowly rise up and kneel. Your bones are growing too! Now they are growing again! Slowly stand. Your bones stop growing when you're an adult!

More to do

Cut white straws into one-inch pieces. These are bones! Place them on a table. Add cotton balls for the skull bone. Give everyone a sheet of black construction paper and glue. Glue the "bones" on the black paper to make human shapes. Make a family of bone people!

Age level

4+

Objective

To learn about bones—bones give us a human shape!

Materials

None

Preparation

None

Muscle Power

Age level

4+

Objective

To discover that muscles move bones!

Materials

Wooden blocks

Preparation

None

What to do

1. Where are your muscles? Hold your first finger out straight. Pretend this is a bone! Wrap your other hand around your first finger to cover it. Pretend this hand is a muscle. Muscles surround our bones!

2. Feel where your muscles are. Feel the lower back of your leg. Feel the muscle on the upper part of your arm. Feel your stomach muscles. Move them in and out!

3. Muscles help our bones to move!

- Spread your fingers apart. Close them! You are using muscles to move your fingers.
- Move your head from side to side. You are using your neck muscles!
- Squint your eyes. Open and close them. There are muscles around your eyes!
- Move your mouth around. Muscles help to move your mouth! Swallow! There are muscles in your throat!
- Stretch! This helps to warm up muscles so they can work properly.

4. Give everyone a wooden block. Hold the block in one hand. Move your arm up and down. You are exercising your arm muscles! They will develop into strong arm muscles.

More to do

Play The Mr. Muscle Game! Have everyone stand straight and still. Your muscles are holding you in this position! The teacher watches for anyone to move! When a child moves, the teacher says, "Please sit down Mr. (or Mrs.) Bones!" Continue until one child is left standing. This child is Mr. or Mrs. Muscle! Think of different positions for everyone to freeze in.

Heart Beats

What to do

1. We need to grow strong and healthy! What can help us do this? Eating healthy foods! Give everyone a turn to think of something that is healthy to eat.

2. Show the train picture. Explain that it is the Good Food Train. It only carries good food! Place the pictures of food on the floor, picture side down. Each child turns over a food picture and identifies it. If it is a healthy food to eat, the child tapes it on one of the cars of the Good Food Train. If it is not a healthy food to eat, remove it from the pile.

3. How does all this good food get to all the different parts of our body? Does a train carry the food through our body? Blood does! Show the picture of the human body. Each child, in turn, takes a red crayon and swirls a line through different parts of the body. This is our blood carrying food through our body to give us energy!

4. What pushes the blood through our body? A giant hand? The heart does! Place the red paper heart on the human body.

5. Have everyone clasp their hands together. Now squeeze and release. Do this many times! Our heart keeps pumping all day long and all through the night!

More to do

Give everyone a heart sticker to place on themselves. Now everyone is a member of the Healthy Heart Club! We eat good food and we exercise! Play music. Lead the children in easy warm-ups and exercise. Give everyone a turn to help think of an exercise to do. Call a meeting of the Healthy Heart Club many times during the year. Ask about what kinds of good food everyone has been eating, and do some exercising!

Age level

3+

Objective

To understand the importance of the heart

Materials

Magazines
scissors
butcher paper
felt pen
tape
red construction paper
red crayon

Preparation

Cut out pictures of food from magazines. Cut two sheets of butcher paper, 3' x 2', and tape them on a wall. Draw a large train on one sheet. Draw the outline of a human body on the other sheet. Draw and cut out a heart shape from red construction paper.

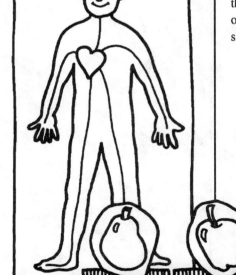

Swamp Monster

Age level

3+

Objective

To move our bodies in many different ways and to use our muscles

Materials

Yarn
scissors
tape

Preparation

Cut two strings of yarn 6' long. Lay them straight and tape them on the rug ten feet apart. This is a swamp!

What to do

1. Explain that the area between the yarn is a swamp. It is a wet soggy place. Maybe a swamp monster lives there!

2. Brainstorm different ways to cross the swamp. Possible ways might be jumping across, rolling across, walking backwards, walking on tiptoes and stomping across like a swamp monster! Remind everyone that we are moving our bones and muscles to move across.

3. Ask the rest of the class to be quiet while each child is crossing the swamp. The swamp monster is sleeping, and you don't want to wake him!

5. Continue until everyone has crossed the swamp to an opposite side. The teacher can cross the swamp too!

More to do

Choose a child to be the swamp monster! This child can sit in the middle of the swamp, pretending to be asleep. The remaining children sit around the swamp. Choose a child to think of a movement to wake up the swamp monster. Examples might be pounding on the rug, clapping, slapping your knees or swaying back and forth and making ghost noises! Decide on a movement, then everyone count to three and start the movement! When the swamp monster wakes up, he or she can growl back! The swamp monster now chooses a new swamp monster, and the teacher chooses another child to think of another swamp movement.

Mouth House

What to do

1. Point to the house picture. Whose house is it? Offer a clue. It is a Mouth House! Have everyone open their mouths. That is the door to your Mouth House. Close the door to your Mouth House. (Close your mouth!)

2. Now who do you think lives inside the Mouth House? Encourage answers, such as teeth, tongue, the inside of cheeks, gums, taste buds and the roof of the mouth! Point to these as they are mentioned.

3. What does your mouth do? Does it have a job? Let's find out! Give everyone a cracker to eat. Does it taste good? Your tongue is tasting it! Your mouth is moving up and down. Your teeth move up and down also. They are chewing the cracker into tiny pieces. What else is your tongue doing? It is moving the cracker all over your mouth! It helps your teeth to chew the cracker!

4. Swallow the cracker. Where is it going? Follow the cracker with your finger, down your throat and into your stomach.

More to do

Draw a large face on white posterboard. This is Ms. Hungry! Cut a large hole where her mouth is. Tape a small plastic bag behind the mouth. Have everyone cut out food pictures from magazines. Stick food pictures into Ms. Hungry's mouth (into the bag)!

Age level

4+

Objective

To understand the mouth

Materials

Posterboard
felt pen
scissors
tape
crackers

Preparation

Draw a large house shape on the posterboard. Tape it on a wall.

Do the Stomach Mash

Age level

3+

Objective

To find out where the stomach is and what it does!

Materials

Bananas
knife
bowls
forks

Preparation

None

What to do

1. Where is your stomach? Have everyone place their hand above their navel!

2. What does your stomach do? It mashes the food you swallow into tiny pieces. Have everyone press the palms of their hands together and twist them back and forth. This is what your stomach muscles do!

3. Cut bananas into 1" pieces. Give everyone a piece of banana in a bowl. Pass out forks. Mash the bananas with the forks! This is what your stomach does.

4. Eat mashed banana! In a few minutes, it will be in your stomach!

More to do

Do the stomach mash! Play music. Everyone stands and mashes their feet to the music. While you are mashing, say different kinds of foods to mash. Mash it!

The Intestine Crunch

What to do

1. Where does your food go after your stomach! To your ear? To your elbow? It goes to your intestines! Find them! Place one hand on your stomach (above your navel). Place your other hand below this one. You had found your intestines!

2. Your intestines mash food even smaller then your stomach! Give everyone a bowl with a tablespoon of sunflower seeds in it. Pass out a rock to everyone. Mash your sunflower seeds with your rock!

3. Eat your sunflower seeds! Before long, they will be in your intestines!

More to do

Do The Intestine Crawl! Explain that your intestines wind around inside of you. Have everyone get on their hands and knees. Follow the teacher in a crawl around the classroom. Wind around tables and furniture. End up where you started!

Age level

3+

Objective

To introduce the word "intestine" and to discover what it does

Materials

Sunflower seeds
bowls
tablespoon
rocks

Preparation

None

Hand Signals

Age level

3+

Objective

To learn about germs and to understand why you should cover your mouth when you sneeze or cough!

Materials

Glass jar

Preparation

None

What to do

1. Show the glass jar. Explain that there are invisible bugs inside the jar. They are germs! They are so small, you can't see them! Pass the jar around for everyone to take a look.

2. Empty the germs into your hand. Have everyone hold out their hand. Place an invisible germ on everyone's palm!

3. Look at your germ! Pick it up with your other hand. Now swallow it! You cannot taste or feel a germ inside you, but they can make you feel sick!

4. This is a cold germ! It often makes you cough. Have everyone cover their mouths and cough. Why is it important to cover your mouth when you cough? (You can cough the germs out of your mouth! They can make others sick, too!)

5. Pretend to sneeze! Cover your mouth. Who remembers why we should cover our mouths?

6. Have everyone yawn! Cover your mouth again. You are not spreading germs, but it is polite to cover a yawn.

7. Practice hand signals to cover your mouth! Say this chant and cover your mouth at the appropriate times.

> *Oh no, I feel a giant cough, (Cover mouth)*
> *Oh no, I have to sneeze, (Cover mouth)*
> *But now I feel a twitchy itch*
> *I'd better scratch my knee! (Scratch knee)*
> *I think I need a super stretch, (Stretch with arms)*
> *I know I have to yawn, (Cover mouth)*
> *Oh no, I feel. . I'm going. . to sneeze (Slowly bring hand up)*
> *It's gone! (Lower hand)*

More to do

Give everyone a sheet of paper and crayons. Everyone can draw what they think a cold germ looks like! Tape the germ pictures on a wall. Title the wall, "Cold Germs, Beware!"

Call the Doctor

What to do

1. Explain that a doctor is someone who has learned all about the human body. A doctor knows how to make you feel better when you are sick. Name different areas of the body that a doctor treats. Point to them!

2. Play Call The Doctor! Place the plastic bottle on the rug. Sit around the bottle. Choose a child to be the doctor. The doctor spins the bottle. When it points to a child, this child becomes the patient.

3. Now everyone says, "Call the doctor quick, quick! I am feeling sick, sick!" (Pretend to dial a phone for the first line, and hold your stomach for the second line.)

4. The patient now tells the doctor what part of his or her body hurts. Everyone says:

> *Check the heart, (Touch heart)*
> *Check the eyes, (Touch eyes)*
> *Check the ears, (Touch ears)*
> *No tears! (Move head back and forth)*
>
> *Wiggle fingers, (Wiggle fingers)*
> *Touch your toes, (Touch toes)*
> *All better, (Clap-clap)*
> *Doctor knows! (Move head up and down)*

5. The patient now becomes the doctor and spins the bottle. The bottle points to the new patient!

More to do

Play the game, Doctor Me! Cut white posterboard into card-size shapes. Draw a different part of the body on each card. On one of the cards, draw a happy face. This is the doctor! Make one card for each child. Place one card, face down on the rug, in front of each child. Say the following chant:

> *Who wears a white coat (Tap shoulders)*
> *And a stethoscope? (Place a fist on chest)*
> *Who taps you on the knee! (Tap knee)*
> *Who mends your bones (Grab a wrist)*
> *And hears your moans? (Hold stomach)*
> *It's Doctor Me! (Point to yourself)*

Everyone turns over their cards. Who has the doctor picture? This child collects the cards and passes them out again!

Age level

4+

Objective

To learn about doctors

Materials

Empty plastic bottle

Preparation

None

The Human House

Age level

3+

Objective

To review that we are human, we live in houses and we can do many things!

Materials

Blackboard
chalk

Preparation

Draw a large house on a blackboard. Include a door!

What to do

1. Explain that this is a human house! The teacher pretends that it is his or her house. Then the teacher asks if anyone would like to come over and play!

2. The teacher chooses a child to visit. This child stands in front of the house and knocks on the door.

3. The teacher says, "Hello! What's your name?" The child responds! The teacher then says, "What do you want to play?" The child thinks of something he would like to do!

4. The teacher then says, "Come on in!" This child then draws a small picture of himself in the house. Then choose someone else to come and visit! Continue until everyone has come over to play.

5. Look at all the people in the human house! We enjoy our friends. We live in safe, warm homes. We can do many wonderful things with our bodies. We are lucky to be human!

More to do

Give everyone a large sheet of paper. Draw a large house on the paper. Pass out crayons. The children draw the members of their families in their house. Include pets! Give out heart stickers to put on the pictures.

Paper People

What to do

1. The children lay flat on a sheet of butcher paper. Make an outline of their bodies with a felt pen. Add a face and a waistline!

2. When all the tracings are completed, lay the sheets of butcher paper on a hard surface such as the floor, tables and even taped on the wall.

3. Pass out a handful of crayons to each child. Color in the paper bodies! Try to match clothes, hair and eyes. (With the two year olds, make no mention of matching!)

4. Print the names on the paper bodies. Tape them all around the classroom walls. Look at all the paper people!

More to do

Draw the outline of a body on a sheet of paper. Give one to each child. Pass out crayons. Color in the tiny paper people! Tape the tiny paper people on a wall in the shape of a pyramid. Look what our bodies can do!

Age level

2+

Objective

To reinforce our special human shape

Materials

Butcher paper
scissors
felt pen
crayons
tape

Preparation

Cut a sheet of butcher paper for each child. Each sheet should be the length of the child.

Cut and Feather

Age level

3+

Objective

To improve cutting skills and to make feathers for the next activity!

Materials

Different colored construction paper
felt pen
scissors

Preparation

Draw a large feather, 3" x 8" long, on a sheet of colored construction paper. Make at least one for each child, using a variety of colors. These are turkey feathers!

What to do

1. Explain that a turkey is going to visit the classroom soon. But the poor turkey has lost his feathers! Help the turkey find his feathers!

2. Place the turkey feathers on the table. Pass out scissors, and cut out the turkey feathers!

3. Make a pile of cutout feathers. Print each child's name on the top feather of his or her pile.

4. Place the feather piles aside to use in the following activity, "Pluck The Turkey!"

More to do

Make hand turkeys! Trace a hand on a sheet of white paper. Color the hand in! Draw an eye on the thumb. The fingers are the feathers on the turkey. When the hand turkeys are colored in, place glue and feathers on the table. Glue feathers on the turkey pictures! Tape the turkey pictures on a wall. Title the wall, "Our Turkey Farm!"

Pluck the Turkey

What to do

1. Look at the turkey. He has found his feathers!

2. Choose a child to be a turkey "plucker"! This child chooses a feather on the tail and plucks it off! The teacher reads the turkey message on the back. Everyone does what the message says!

3. Continue until everyone has plucked the turkey. Look at the turkey now. He has lost his feathers again!

More to do

Act out different messages during the year. At Christmas, choose a tree message from Christmas balls on the tree. When learning about the weather, make cloud messages. When learning about the ocean, make fish messages!

Age level

3+

Objective

To follow directions and to explore large motor movement

Materials

White posterboard
felt pen
crayons
tape

Preparation

Draw a large turkey without feathers on the posterboard. The children can help color the turkey! Tape the turkey picture on the wall. Print a different turkey message on some of the feathers from the previous activity. Print one for each child. Suggested messages are clap your hands ten times, lay on your back with knees up and rock, shake hands with someone who has the same color on his or her clothes as you, and sing a favorite song. Tape the printed feathers around the tail of the turkey. The children can help tape the remaining feathers all over the turkey!

Thanksgiving Dinner

Age level

3+

Objective

To improve cutting skills and to encourage imagination!

Materials

Magazines
small paper cups
glue
scissors
paper plates
cotton swabs

Preparation

Tear out magazine pages with food pictures on them. Pour glue into paper cups. Make a glue cup for each child.

What to do

1. Place the food pictures on the table. Pass out scissors. The children make their own Thanksgiving dinner!

2. Cut out food pictures. Choose pictures that look delicious to eat!

3. Make a pile of food pictures. Pass out paper plates, glue cups and cotton swabs. Glue the pictures on the paper plates. Look at the Thanksgiving dinners. They look delicious!

More to do

Draw a turkey leg on a sheet of paper and cut it out. Place it on a paper plate. Sit on the rug around the paper plate. Say "The Turkey Leg" chant!

> *My Mother baked the turkey,*
> *Everybody cheered,*
> *But when the turkey plate was passed,*
> *The leg had disappeared!*
>
> *Who ate the turkey leg?*
> *All but a crumb,*
> *Uncle Henry softly said,*
> *Yum, yum, yum!*

Say the chant with the children as it is written. Then say it again! This time, after the word "disappeared," point to a child to grab the turkey leg and hide it in his or her lap. If the child's name is Daniel, say, "Uncle Daniel!" If the child's name is Katie, say, "Aunt Katie!" When you say the words "yum, yum, yum," say them softly and rub your stomach! Give everyone a chance to grab the turkey leg!

Adventures in Arts and Crafts

What is learned when coloring a picture?

   Listening Skills: *Choose one crayon at a time!*

   Decision Making: *What color should I choose next?*

   Color Awareness: *I need orange. Where is it?*

   Physical Development: *Strengthens small motor movement.*

   Social Development: *You're picture looks nice!*

The amount of fun and learning that can take place at an arts and crafts table is exciting! Children busy, children talking, children creating! Exploring many forms of art keeps interest and enthusiasm high.

Adventures in Arts and Crafts

	Monday	Tuesday	Wednesday	Thursday	Friday
Week 1	**3+ Felt Pen Artists** *To increase decision making skills*	**4+ Baby Bear's Quilt** *To encourage color aware-ness*	**3+ Shaping Up** *To become familiar with different shapes*	**4+ Elephants on Parade** *To recognize matching colors*	**4+ Color Cards** *To follow directions*
Week 2	**3+ Pretzels and Yarn** *To improve small motor skills*	**4+ Caterpillar Garden** *To improve small motor skills*	**3+ Seed Birds** *To control finger movements*	**3+ Popcorn Pops** *To introduce the concept of sequencing*	**4+ Bean Burritos** *To learn the names of colors*
Week 3	**3+ For the Birds** *To increase finger control*	**4+ Three Apple Trees** *To identify matching colors*	**3+ Cutting Roads** *To encourage creative thinking*	**4+ String of Hearts** *To improve cutting skills*	**4+ Snow Family** *To develop small motor control*
Week 4	**3+ Hanukkah Stars** *To learn about a Jewish holiday*	**4+ Menorah Lights** *To learn about menorahs*	**3+ Christmas Wish Whales** *To encourage creative thinking*	**4+ Christmas Hedgehogs** *To improve hand-eye coordination*	**3+ Christmas Cookies** *To recognize specific shapes*

Felt Pen Artists

What to do

1. Everyone can be an artist! Place a variety of felt pens nearby. Explain that artists use colors that they really enjoy. Have the children look at the felt pens and be thinking of colors that they really like.

2. Each child chooses a felt pen and makes a design on the butcher paper. Encourage designs that have no definite shape, such as large swirling lines and small wiggly shapes.

3. Let the children take a second or third turn! Encourage choosing different colors. When the picture is finished, admire the beautiful design!

4. What does the picture look like? What would be a good name for the picture? How does this picture make you feel when you look at it? Happy? Sad? Hungry? Do you like this picture?

More to do

Draw a half-inch border along the edges of a sheet of paper. This is a picture frame! Make one for each child! Place a variety of felt pens on a table. The children choose one felt pen at a time to draw designs on their papers. Think of a name for the pictures! Print the child's name inside the top border. Print the name of the picture inside the bottom border. Tape the pictures on a wall. Title the wall, "Art Show"!

Age level

3+

Objective

To increase decision making skills and to help children understand that each one of them draws and makes nice pictures

Materials

Butcher paper
scissors
tape
felt pens

Preparation

Cut a large sheet of butcher paper. Tape it on a wall, low enough for the children to touch.

Baby Bear's Quilt

Age level

4+

Objective

To encourage color awareness and to increase counting skills

Materials

White posterboard
black felt pen
paper
crayons
tape

Preparation

Using a black felt pen, draw four lines down the posterboard and six lines across, at least 4" apart. This is Baby Bear's Quilt! Draw a large teddy bear on a sheet of paper. Color it in. Tape it on the wall near the quilt.

What to do

1. Who has a quilt or blanket on their bed? What color is it? Point to the quilt on the wall. What color is Baby Bear's Quilt? (white) Let's help Baby Bear color his quilt!

2. Place a variety of crayons on the rug. The children choose a crayon and color in a square. Continue until all the squares are colored in.

3. Look at the quilt! Choose a child to show you a blue square. Choose a child to show you a green square. Who can find a corner square? Choose a child to show you his favorite color! Can anyone see two squares of the same color that are touching? Look at all the learning from a color quilt!

More to do

Draw three lines down and three lines across a sheet of paper. Make a color quilt for each child. Place a variety of crayons on the table. The children color in the squares on the color quilts. Draw small teddy bears for each child. Tape them on the finished quilts!

Shaping Up

What to do

1. Place a selection of crayons, felt pens and stencils on the table.

2. Point to the shapes on the wall. Identify them! Look closely at the shapes. Each child selects a shape, pulls it off the wall and brings it to the table.

3. Now add beautiful colors and designs to the shapes. Encourage drawing with the felt pens. Add many colors with the crayons. Make pictures on the shapes with the stencils.

4. When most of the children are close to finishing their shape pictures, pass out sticky stars! This can be a surprise that adds a final touch.

5. When the children have finished, sit in a circle. Then show the beautiful shapes and identify them!

More to do

Draw only square shapes! When the children have finished coloring their squares, sit in a circle. Then tape the squares on the wall to form a design! Try forming a special design with the squares, or a robot or a larger square! Try different shapes. Color triangles or rectangles. Form a special group shape with each of these!

Age level

3+

Objective

To become familiar with different shapes and to encourage imagination

Materials

White paper
felt pens
tape
scissors
crayons
stencils
sticky stars

Preparation

Draw a different shape on separate sheets of white paper. Draw them as large as the paper! Make a few extra. (Then the last few children can still have a choice.) Suggested shapes are a square, a rectangle, a circle, a triangle, a half moon, a star, a heart, an oval, a diamond and a cylinder. Tape these shapes on a wall low enough for a child to touch.

Elephants on Parade

Age level

4+

Objective

To recognize matching colors

Materials

White paper
crayons
scissors
yarn
tape

Preparation

Draw a large elephant on a sheet of paper for each child. These are circus elephants! Draw a 2" circle and cut it out. Tape a 6" string of yarn on the circle. This is a balloon! Make one for each child. Color the balloons different colors! Tape the balloons on a wall.

What to do

1. Place crayons on the table. Offer crayons that match the balloon colors.

2. Give everyone a circus elephant. They are white elephants! They need color to join the circus! The children choose one crayon to color their elephant.

3. Explain that the balloons on the wall match the crayon colors. As each child finishes coloring his elephant, he can take a matching balloon off the wall.

4. Then tape the finished elephant on the wall and tape the matching balloon on its tail!

5. Tape the elephants in a straight line. Look at the elephants on parade!

More to do

Make different matching pictures during the year. Color in mother birds and match them to their eggs! Color in tropical fish and match them to a tank with colored frames. Color in Easter eggs and match similar designs!

Color Cards

What to do

1. Place a variety of crayons on the table. Each child is going to make a card game!

2. Pass out the card bags. There are ten cards in each bag.

3. Pull two cards out of the bag. On one side only, color these two cards the same color! Continue pulling two cards out and coloring them matching colors.

4. When all the cards are colored, place them back in the bags.

5. Sit on the rug! Have the children place their cards on the rug, face down. One child turns over two of her cards, trying to make a match. Continue around the circle, until all cards have been turned over.

6. When a child makes a match, identify the color. Each child takes her color cards home so she can play at home!

More to do

Instead of matching colors, draw matching shapes on the cards. The children color in their ten shapes. Try matching ghosts at Halloween! Try matching dinosaur footprints when you are learning about dinosaurs. Play matching card games all during the year!

Age level

4+

Objective

To recognize matching colors and to follow directions

Materials

White posterboard
scissors
plastic bags
tape
felt pen
crayons

Preparation

Cut the posterboard into card-shaped sizes. Make ten cards for each child. Place ten cards in a plastic bag. Make a card bag for each child. Label each bag with a child's name.

Pretzels and Yarn

Age level

4+

Objective

To improve small motor skills and to learn about different shapes

Materials

Glue
small paper cups
yarn
scissors
stick pretzels
white construction paper

Preparation

Pour glue into small paper cups. Make a glue cup for each child. Cut yarn into 3" strings. Make at least ten strings for each child.

What to do

1. Place the pretzels and yarn on the table. Pass out the glue cups and white construction paper. Notice the shapes of the strings and yarn. They are thin shapes! You will be able to place many pretzels and pieces of yarn on your paper.

2. Brainstorm ideas on what you can make with the pretzels and yarn. Possible ideas are houses, people, trees, animals or a beautiful design!

3. Make pictures! Take your time! Use just enough glue to make the objects stick.

4. When the pictures have dried, share the pictures at a circle time. Let each child explain what he or she made with the pretzels and yarn!

More to do

Use different shapes of food to make pictures. Glue large heart-shaped pretzels on pink paper for Valentines! Glue square crackers and squares of construction paper together. Mention the various shapes of food pictures!

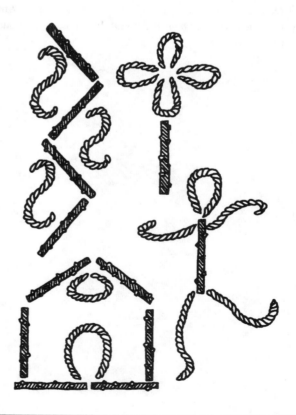

Caterpillar Garden

What to do

1. Give everyone a tomato garden! Pass out glue cups. How many tomatoes are in the garden? One! Who ate the other tomatoes? Caterpillars! Here they come!

2. Spread the paper caterpillars on the table. Show how to glue the caterpillars on the gardens. Place glue on both ends of the paper. Lay the caterpillar flat on the garden and push both ends towards each other. The paper will hump in the middle like a caterpillar!

3. Glue many caterpillars in the gardens. One of them will eat the last tomato!

4. Share the caterpillar gardens at a circle time. Have each child point out the caterpillar that is going to eat the last tomato!

More to do

Make a giant caterpillar garden! Color a large sheet of butcher paper green. Add circles of red to make tomatoes. Tape the tomato garden on the rug or low on a wall. Cut large strips of paper in different colors to make caterpillars. Glue or tape the caterpillars on the garden!

Age level

4+

Objective

To improve small motor skills

Materials

Different colored construction paper
scissors
green construction paper
red crayon
glue
small paper cups

Preparation

Cut 4" x 1" strips of different colored construction paper. Cut at least ten strips for each child. These are caterpillars! Color a small red circle on green construction paper. This is a tomato in a garden! Make a tomato garden for each child. Pour glue into paper cups. Make a glue cup for each child. Have the older children help with the preparation.

Seed Birds

Age level

3+

Objective

To control finger movements

Materials

Blue construction paper
felt pen
glue
paper cups
bird seed
brown yarn
scissors
paintbrushes

Preparation

Draw the outline of a large bird on blue construction paper for each child. The blue is the sky! Pour glue into paper cups. Make a glue cup for each child. Pour bird seed into paper cups. Make one for each child. Cut brown yarn into 3" strips. These are earthworms! Make one for each child.

What to do

1. Give everyone a bird picture. Pass out a glue cup, a seed cup and an earthworm to each child.

2. Make a Seed Bird! Dip the paintbrush into the glue and spread a layer of glue over the bird.

3. Pick up a pinch of bird seed and sprinkle it over the bird. It will become a Seed Bird when it is completely covered with seeds!

4. When each child finishes her Seed Bird, she glues her earthworm on her picture. Do you think your Seed Bird is going to eat the earthworm?

More to do

Make a variety of seed pictures! Draw fish and sprinkle with seeds. The seeds will feel like fish scales! Ask for suggestions for seed pictures. Draw each child's idea on their sheet of paper.

Popcorn Pops

What to do

1. Give each child a before and after sheet of paper, a popcorn cup, a glue cup and a toothpick.

2. Talk about the words "before" and "after!" Before is how something looks now. After is how it has changed! Look at the popcorn kernels. This is how they look before they are popped! The children dip toothpicks into glue and put a drop of glue on a popcorn kernel. Glue it on the "BEFORE" side. Glue many kernels on!

3. Now cook popcorn! Listen for the popping sound. The kernels are changing!

4. When the popcorn is done, glue the popped popcorn on the "AFTER" side of the sheet. How has the popcorn changed? Do you eat popcorn before or after is it popped?

More to do

Other activities to encourage the understanding of different concepts are:

BIG and LITTLE—The teacher traces his or her hand on the left-hand side of a sheet of paper, labeled "BIG." A child traces his or her hand on the right-hand side, labeled "SMALL." Color both hands.

ABOVE and BELOW—Print the word "ABOVE" on the left-hand side of a sheet of paper. Print the word "BELOW" on the right-hand side of the paper. Draw a table with long legs on both sides of the paper. Offer felt pens and stencils. The children trace stencil pictures above the table on the left-hand side and below the table on the right-hand side!

LIGHT and DARK—Cut a sheet of black construction paper and tape it on the right-hand side of a sheet of white paper. Label the left-hand side "LIGHT" and the right-hand side "DARK." Glue small white marshmallows on both sides. Notice how the white marshmallows show up more on the dark side. (Discuss how it is difficult to see the pale moon in the day sky but not the bright moon in the night sky.)

Age level

3+

Objective

To introduce the concept of sequencing and to understand the concept of before and after

Materials

Red construction paper
black felt pen
popcorn kernels
glue
small paper cups
toothpicks
popcorn machine

Preparation

Draw a black line down the middle of a sheet of red construction paper. Print "BEFORE" on the left-hand side and "AFTER" on the right-hand side. Make one for each child. Pour popcorn kernels into paper cups. Make a popcorn cup for each child. Pour glue into paper cups. Make a glue cup for each child.

Bean Burritos

Age level

4+

Objective

To learn the names of colors and to strengthen fingers by tearing paper

Materials

White, green, red and orange construction paper
scissors
yellow yarn
glue
paper cups
dried beans
small paper plates

Preparation

Cut a large circle from white construction paper. This is a tortilla! Make one for each child. Cut many 1" strips of yellow yarn. This is shredded cheese. Cut many 4" x 4" squares of green, red and orange construction paper. Pour glue into the paper cups. Make a glue cup for each child. The older children can help with the preparation.

What to do

1. Give everyone a paper tortilla. Pass out a glue cup and beans to each child. Let's make a delicious bean burrito!

2. Place the burrito ingredients on the table. Explain what they are! The yellow yarn is shredded cheese. The green construction paper is lettuce. The red is tomatoes. The orange is hot sauce! What's missing? The beans! Sprinkle the dried beans on the ingredients. Now they will be bean burritos!

3. Make bean burritos. Tear off small pieces of the colored construction paper. Dip these ingredients in the glue and place them on the paper tortilla. Don't forget cheese and beans! If you dare, try the hot sauce!

4. When the children finish, they place the bean burritos on a paper plate. Fold the sides of the tortilla over, so they are touching. Crease the folded edges so they will stay folded.

5. Take the burritos home. Open them at home and show the ingredients to your family!

More to do

Using different colored construction paper, try making a variety of food items. Make cheeseburgers, pizza or submarine sandwiches!

For the Birds

What to do

1. In the winter, birds have a harder time finding food. Let's help feed a winter bird!

2. Explain that the sheets of white paper are bread slices. Tear a bread slice (white paper) into tiny pieces. Place the bread pieces into a paper cup. Tear up another slice! Fill the cup with as much food as you want.

3. Give everyone a sheet of red construction paper. Tear a long strip off the red paper. This is a winter bird called a cardinal! Make many cardinals. Draw eyes on the cardinals with a felt pen.

4. Now fly the cardinals over to the rug. Place them on the rug. Look at all the birds looking for food!

5. The children take the food cups and slowly sprinkle the bread pieces on the rug. Sprinkle them near the birds. Feed them quietly. They are easily scared!

6. If you run out of bird food, you can make some more!

7. For a fun clean-up, pretend you are large crows. Swoop down on the rug and eat all the leftover food (pick up the pieces and place them in the trash can)!

More to do

Take a winter walk to feed the birds! Hold bird seed in paper cups. Remember to walk and speak quietly. The birds will learn that you are their friends.

Age level

3+

Objective

To increase finger control and to encourage fantasy play

Materials

White paper
paper cups
red construction paper
felt pens

Preparation

Place white paper on the table, at least one sheet for each child. They are slices of bread! Place paper cups on the table.

Three Apple Trees

Age level

4+

Objective

To encourage small motor movement and to identify matching colors

Materials

Small paper bags
black felt pen
three white posterboards
tape
red, yellow and green tissue paper
crayons
large paintbrush
glue

Preparation

Print a child's name on each paper bag. These are apple bags. Draw an outline of a large tree on each of the three posterboards. These are apple trees! Tape them on a wall in a straight line. Have the children help color them.

What to do

1. Give the children their apple bags. Explain that they will be collecting apples to put on the bare apple trees.

2. Place the sheets of red, yellow and green tissue paper on the table. The red is for red apples, the yellow is for yellow apples, and the green is for green apples!

3. Demonstrate how to collect the apples! Tear off a small piece from the red tissue paper. Crunch it up! Here is a red apple! Place it in the apple bag. Make yellow and green apples! Make many apples.

4. When all the children have finished, sit in front of the three apple trees with the apple bags.

5. The teacher draws a red apple on one tree, a yellow apple on one tree and a green apple on one tree. Each of the apples in the apple bags matches one of the trees!

6. The teacher now spreads a thin layer of glue over all three trees with a paintbrush.

7. Choose three children to stick their apples on the matching apple trees. (A red apple goes on the red apple tree!) Continue until all the apples are on the apple trees!

More to do

Make an apple pie! Mix the pie dough. Take turns with the rolling pin, flattening the dough. Cut apples into slices using red, yellow and green apples. Add sugar and spices; this makes a delicious apple pie!

Cutting Roads

What to do

1. Give each child a sheet of roads, scissors and a plastic bag.

2. Place a finger on one road. Follow the road with your finger! Do this with every road on the paper. Count how many roads are on the paper!

3. Now cut the roads out! Cut along the lines. The roads will appear! Mark each road with the child's name.

4. Then place the roads in a plastic bag.

5. Sit on the rug and have the children place their roads on the rug, end to end. Look how long your road is! Move the roads around to make different patterns. Make sure the end of each road is touching another road.

6. Everyone can take their roads home in their bag and build roads at home!

More to do

Make night roads! Cut roads from black construction paper. Make rain roads! Cut roads from grey construction paper. They have been wet by a rainstorm! Make a giant roadway! Tape a large sheet of butcher paper on the wall. Cut out paper roads and tape them on the butcher paper. Add car pictures cut from magazines!

Age level

3+

Objective

To improve cutting skills and to encourage creative thinking

Materials

White paper
black felt pen
scissors
plastic bags

Preparation

Using a black felt pen, draw lines 1" apart down a sheet of white paper. These are roads! Make at least one sheet of roads for each child. Older children can make their own roads.

String of Hearts

Age level

4+

Objective

To improve cutting skills

Materials

Different colored construction paper
black felt pen
scissors
yarn
hole puncher—more then one if
  possible
tape

Preparation

Cut 4" x 4" squares of different colored construction paper, at least ten
for each child. Draw a heart shape on
each square. Cut a 3' piece of yarn for
each child.

What to do

1. Place the paper hearts on the table. Pass out scissors. Let's make a string of hearts!

2. The children cut out the hearts. (If it is too difficult for some children to cut out the heart shapes, they can cut around the hearts.) Remember, the more hearts you cut out, the longer the string of hearts will be!

3. Make a pile of hearts. Use a hole punch to make a hole at the top of the hearts.

4. String the hearts on the yarn. When a string of hearts is finished, the teacher can tie or tape each heart in place on the string, about an inch or two apart.

5. Print the child's name on one of the hearts. Tape the string of hearts on the wall. They make a beautiful design!

More to do

Say "The Heart" chant! Start with the first String of Hearts on the wall. If there are two hearts on the string, count and clap to two. When you say the number two, say the line that rhymes with two! For example, clap and say, "1, 2, Hearts love you!" Say the chant with each String of Hearts, using the appropriate rhyming line.

Clapping 1—say, "Hearts have fun."
Clapping 2—say, "Hearts love you."
Clapping 3—say, "Hearts beat for you and me!"
Clapping 4—say, "Hearts marching out the door."
Clapping 5—say, "Hearts like to scuba dive."
Clapping 6—say, "Hearts can melt a candlestick!"
Clapping 7—say, "Hearts can fly to heaven."
Clapping 8—say, "Hearts can bake a birthday cake."
Clapping 9—say, "Hearts can wiggle in a line."
Clapping 10—say, "Hearts are to hug and mend!"

Repeat this activity in February for Valentine's Day.

Snow Family

What to do

1. Give everyone a large lump of dough. The lump of dough is a large snow-ball!

2. Demonstrate how to make smaller snowballs to make a snow family. Tear off a piece of dough from the large ball. Roll it between your palms. Show the round ball!

3. To make a snowman place three snowballs on top of each other. Then roll tiny pieces of dough for eyes. Roll a skinny string for a mouth!

4. When you have made a snowman, make a snow woman and a snow child. Make many snow people!

5. Each child places her snow family on a paper plate. Print the child's name on the plate.

More to do

Create a snow zoo! Make snow animals and place them in a shoe box from home. Label each box, "(Susan's) Snow Zoo!"

Age level

4+

Objective

To develop small motor control

Materials

Playdough
paper plates
felt pen

Preparation

None

Hanukkah Stars

Age level

3+

Objective

To learn about a Jewish holiday

Materials

White construction paper
black felt pen
crayons
sticky stars (make sure they are six-pointed stars)
glue
small paper cups
glitter
tape

Preparation

Draw a large Star of David on a sheet of white construction paper for each child. This is a six-pointed star. Pour glue into paper cups. Make a glue cup for each child.

What to do

1. Place crayons and sticky stars on the table. Give each child a Star of David. Explain that as the tree reminds many people of Christmas, the Star of David reminds Jewish people of their special beliefs!

2. The Star of David has six points. Together count the six points. It is a very beautiful star! Color the stars to help make them beautiful. Encourage everyone to choose colors that they feel would look pretty on the star. Use the sticky stars for an added glow.

3. Pass out the glue cups and glitter. Add sparkle to the stars! Dip a finger in the glue and make designs on the stars. Sprinkle with glitter.

4. When the stars are finished, tape them on a wall. The stars can help us to remember that we are all special.

More to do

Make different designs using the Star of David. Cut six-pointed stars from sponges. Dip the sponge stars in white paint and make star prints on dark blue construction paper. Cut Star of David shapes from white posterboard. Trace these on a sheet of white paper using a variety of felt pens. Color the stars!

Menorah Lights

What to do

1. Show one of the paper menorahs. Explain that it is a special candle holder. In a Jewish home, nine candles are placed in the menorah. Each one is lit on a different night. Count the nine candle holders!

2. Make a menorah. Pass out a candle sheet and scissors to each child. Who can see the candle that is shorter then the rest? It is called a Shamash. Have everyone repeat the word. It goes in the middle holder. It is lit first!

3. Cut out the nine candles. As the children finish, they choose a colored menorah from the teacher. Then they take a glue cup and glue their candles on their menorah.

4. As they finish, pass out nine gold sticker stars to place at the top of the candles. Remember to light the smaller candle first!

5. Tape the menorahs on a wall. Title the wall, "Festival of Lights"! Can someone guess why it is called this?

More to do

Draw a giant menorah with candles on a large sheet of butcher paper. Tape it on a wall. Color it! Color a flame above the middle candle. This candle is used to light the others! Color in one flame each day for the next eight days. This is how long Hanukkah lasts.

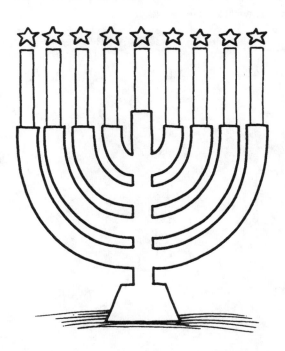

Age level

4+

Objective

To learn about menorahs and Hanukkah, The Festival of Lights

Materials

Different colored construction paper
white paper
scissors
black felt pen
glue
small paper cups
gold star stickers
tape

Preparation

Draw a large menorah on a sheet of construction paper. Draw one for each child using a variety of colored construction paper. Draw nine candles on a sheet of white paper. Draw one of the candles an inch shorter then the rest. Make a sheet of candles for each child.

Christmas Wish Whales

Age level

3+

Objective

To encouraging creative thinking

Materials

White construction paper
black felt pen
scissors
red and green crepe paper
glue
small paper cups
tape

Preparation

Draw the outline of a large whale on a sheet of white construction paper. Draw the mouth slightly open. Print the words, "Christmas Wish Whale," at the top of the paper. Make one for each child. Cut a 1" x 3" strip of white paper (wish paper) for each child. Cut red and green crepe paper into 1' long strips. Cut many!

What to do

1. Give each child a Christmas Wish Whale. Explain that a Wish Whale only eats wishes! Make a Wish Whale, and then tell it a Christmas wish.

2. Place the red and green strips on the table. Pass out the glue cups. Make Wish Whales! Crunch the red and green strips into small balls. Dip them in glue cups and glue them on the whales.

3. When a Wish Whale is finished, this child can tell the teacher his or her Christmas Wish. The teacher prints the wish on wish paper (white paper) and rolls it up. Now tape the rolled paper inside the Wish Whale's mouth. It will look like the Wish Whale is going to swallow the wish!

4. Take the Christmas Wish Whales home (with a note to parents about the Wish Whale). Have someone at home read the wish before the Wish Whale swallows it!

More to do

Tape a large sheet of butcher paper on a wall. Draw a large Wish Whale on the paper. Color the Wish Whale! Call a circle time. Have each child tell the teacher a Christmas wish. Print each child's wish on a separate strip of paper. Tape the wishes on the body of the whale. Encourage everyone to think of extra wishes during the week. When a child tells the teacher another wish, add this wish to his or her wish paper on the whale. At the end of a week, send the Christmas wishes home!

Christmas Hedgehogs

What to do

1. Give everyone a styrofoam ball and a handful of colored toothpicks. What is a hedgehog? It is an animal that has spines on its back. It can roll into a ball!

2. Have the children pick up a styrofoam ball. This is a hedgehog. What's missing? Spines! Make it into a Christmas Hedgehog!

3. Stick toothpicks into the hedgehogs until the hedgehog is completely covered.

4. When the hedgehogs are finished, help each child spray his or her hedgehog gold. NOTE: Be sure to spray them outside on newspaper.

5. When the hedgehogs have dried, tie yarn around them and hang them at home or at school.

More to do

Glue popsicle sticks together to form an interesting design. Spray paint it gold. Wrap red or green yarn around the design. Tie a string of yarn on one of the popsicle sticks. This makes a nice tree decoration!

Age level

4+

Objective

To improve hand-eye coordination and to introduce the word "hedgehog"

Materials

Medium styrofoam balls
colored toothpicks
gold spray paint
newspaper
yarn
scissors

Preparation

None

Christmas Cookies

Age level

3+

Objective

To recognize specific shapes and to encourage creative art and imagination

Materials

Butcher paper
scissors
tape
paper plate
red crayon
white paper
black felt pen
small paper cups
glue
crayons
glitter
small bottles of decorative candy sprinkles found in the cake section of your market

Preparation

Cut a 6' x 3' sheet of butcher paper. Tape it on a wall. This is an oven. Draw a large border along the inside edges to make an oven door. Tape a paper plate on the lower right corner and color it red. This is your oven ON button! Draw a large Christmas shape on a sheet of paper. Draw one for each child, using different shapes. Possible shapes are trees, Christmas balls, candy canes, bells, stars and wreaths. Pour glue into paper cups. Make a glue cup for each child.

What to do

1. Make and bake Christmas cookies! Place crayons, glue, glitter and decorative candy sprinkles on the table.

2. Place the cookie pictures on the rug. These are Christmas cookies to decorate and bake!

3. Each child chooses a "cookie" and brings it to the table. Now decorate the cookies! Use crayons to "frost" the cookies. Then glue on glitter and candy items to add decorations.

4. What else do the cookies need? To be baked! As each child finishes, he tapes the cookie on the oven. When all the cookies are in the oven, take turns pushing the ON button. When school is over, the cookies will be done and ready to take home!

More to do

Make a Christmas cookie tree! Draw a large tree on a sheet of butcher paper and tape it on a wall. Color the tree! Now draw and cut out cookie shapes from different colored construction paper. Tape the cookies on the Christmas cookie tree.

Our Beautiful Earth

The Earth is not only a planet, it is our home. The activities in this chapter are full of warmth and caring, along with observation and discovery. What is the Earth made of? Take a close look! What is a mountain made of? If you climbed to the top of the mountain, what would you see? Learning about the different environments on the Earth, such as deserts and rain forests, provides a backdrop for new information and high interest experiences. Discover the silence of the desert. Where are the hidden colors in the desert? Take a canoe ride to a rain forest. What lives in a rain forest?

Learning about your own backyard can also be exciting. Perception skills are challenged and enhanced. Look how the colors of flowers brighten up the grass! Is a tree alive? How can you tell? What kinds of things are growing in your neighborhood? Children will begin to notice and understand many things that surround them. While learning about the Earth, children think, explore and experiment. They learn that the Earth offers many exciting treasures to be discovered—and appreciated! This chapter will teach not only fact and observation but caring and respect.

Our Beautiful Earth

	Monday	Tuesday	Wednesday	Thursday	Friday
Week 1	**3+ Earth Play** *To learn about the Earth*	**3+ I Live on the Earth** *To understand land and water*	**3+ Dirt Digs** *To discover what the Earth is made of*	**4+ My Neighborhood** *To introduce the Earth as our home*	**4+ Get Down With Gravity** *To explore the concept of gravity*
Week 2	**3+ Our Beautiful Planet** *To appreciate the beauty of the Earth*	**3+ Make a Mountain** *To understand how a mountain is formed*	**4+ Mountain Climber** *To increase perception skills*	**3+ What's a Tree?** *To discover how trees and plants move*	**4+ Trees and Me** *To learn that trees are alive*
Week 3	**4+ Rain Forests** *To appreciate the beauty of a rain forest*	**3+ Flower Power** *To notice the beauty of a flower*	**4+ Follow the Stream** *To learn about streams*	**3+ Desert Snakes** *To learn about the desert*	**3+ The Cactus Story** *To learn about cactus*
Week 4	**4+ Cold Adventures** *To learn about icy, cold areas*	**5+ Island Home** *To understand what islands are*	**3+ My Home** *To reinforce that the Earth is our home*	**4+ Earth Memories** *To review what was learned this month*	**4+ Mother Earth** *To learn to take care of the Earth*

Earth Play

What to do

1. Display a globe or a blue ball. What is this? The Earth! Hold the globe high in the air. The Earth does not sit on anything. It is in space! The children can take turns holding the globe high in the air.

2. Have the children stand by the Earth on the wall. Look at the moon on the opposite wall. When we are standing on the Earth we can see the moon in the sky! Now stand by the moon. Look at the Earth! If we were standing on the moon, we would see the Earth in the sky!

3. Does the Earth move? It slowly turns around. Have the children slowly turn around! How else does the Earth move? It moves around the sun! Stand in a circle. Choose a child to be the sun. The remaining children make a circle around the sun and slowly move around the sun. The sun does not move! The sun tries to stand motionless. When the teacher sees the sun move, the sun chooses a new sun to stand still!

More to do

Cut large star shapes from white paper. Tape them around the classroom. Give each child a sturdy paper tube or construction paper rolled in a tube. These are telescopes! How do we know so much about the Earth and the sky? People study the sky through telescopes! Sit and look through the telescopes. Look for the paper Earth, moon and stars. Encourage questions and comments about the sky. An inquisitive and exciting brainstorm will follow!

Age level

3+

Objective

To learn about the Earth. What is it? Where is it?

Materials

White paper
felt pens
scissors
tape
globe or blue ball
crayons

Preparation

Draw a large circle on a sheet of paper and cut it out. This is the moon! Draw a large circle on a sheet of paper and color it blue. Cut it out. This is the Earth. Tape the moon and the Earth on opposite walls.

I Live on the Earth

Age level

3+

Objective

To understand the difference between land and water

Materials

Magazines
scissors
tape
butcher paper
crayons
pan of water
small rocks or stones

Preparation

Cut out magazine pictures of animals. Cut out pictures of people! Place a rolled piece of tape on the back of each picture. The older children in the class can help. Place the pictures on the rug, tape side up. Draw a large Earth on a sheet of butcher paper. Have the children help color the land brown and the ocean blue.

What to do

1. Place the paper Earth on the rug. Point out the land areas and the ocean areas.

2. Do most people live on the land? Yes! It is solid! Pound on the rug. Jump on the rug! We will not fall through it!

3. What is the ocean made of? Water! Place the pan of water on the rug. The ocean is not solid! Drop rocks into the water. Watch the rocks sink!

4. Place the taped pictures of people and animals near the paper Earth on the rug. Choose a child to turn over a picture. Identify the picture! Where does this person or animal live? The child places the picture on the land or the ocean. Continue until each child has had a turn.

More to do

Draw a large Earth on sheet of butcher paper. Have the children help color it in. Tape it on a wall. Give each child a sheet of paper. Place crayons on the table. Have the children draw pictures of themselves! Tape the pictures around the outside edge of the Earth. Save this Earth picture to use in the activity, "Earth Memories."

Dirt Digs

What to do

1. Give each child a paper bag and a spoon. Go on a Dirt Dig!

2. Look for some dirt and scoop some into their paper bags. Scoop at least a half an inch!

3. Take the dirt bags back to the classroom. Pass out bowls and have each child pour her dirt into a bowl. Lay on stomachs. Look closely at the dirt!

4. Dirt is the top layer of the Earth! Move your fingers in the dirt. How does it feel? Does it feel light? heavy? Does it fall easily between your fingers?

5. What colors do you see in the dirt?

6. Smell the dirt! How would you describe the smell?

7. Does anyone see anything interesting in their dirt? A small insect? A large rock? A leaf? Compare the children's observations.

More to do

When it rains or the dirt outside gets wet, how does the dirt change? Pour some water into the dirt bowls. Stir the dirt and water with spoons. Does the dirt look different? Does it feel different? Does it smell different? What have you made? Mud!

Age level

3+

Objective

To discover what the Earth is made of

Materials

Paper bags
spoons
bowls

Preparation

None

My Neighborhood

Age level

4+

Objective

To introduce the Earth as our home

Materials

Sand table or a large shallow pan
filled with dirt
pipe cleaners
scissors
small wooden blocks
straw
toothpicks

Preparation

Fill the sand table or pan with dirt.
Cut pipe cleaners into one-inch sticks.

What to do

1. Stand around the sand table (or rug if using a pan). Explain that the land on Earth gives us a place to live.

2. Make a neighborhood in the sand! Take out the wooden blocks. These are houses. Each child chooses a house and places it on the land.

3. Build roads! Take a straw and draw a road in the dirt.

4. Plant trees! Pass out toothpicks. These are young trees that do not have any leaves. Each child chooses a tree and plants it in the dirt.

5. Add people! Take out the cut pipe cleaners and stick a person in the neighborhood!

6. Look at the neighborhood. The Earth gives us a place to live!

More to do

Have each child bring a shoe box from home. Make a neighborhood! Put dirt in the shoe boxes. Offer a variety of items. Make neighborhood scenes in the boxes, using the items on the table.

Get Down With Gravity

What to do

1. Introduce the word gravity. Gravity is a special force that surrounds the Earth. It keeps you from falling off the Earth. It pulls you towards the Earth!

2. Experiment with gravity!

- Give each child a sheet of paper. Crunch up the paper into balls. Throw them in the air. What pulls them down? Gravity!
- Have each child take turns throwing a ball in the air. Count how many times it bounces before it stops. How many times did gravity pull it down?
- Take turns dropping a marble down a paper tube! A long paper tube is especially fun—use one from tin foil or a wrapping paper tube.
- Jump up and down! Can gravity pull you down ten times? Hold your arms out straight from your sides. Let them fall! How many times will gravity pull our arms down? Every time!

More to do

Play Beat the Gravity Game. Play music! Give each child a balloon. Have the children hit the balloons in the air. Try to hit the balloon back up before gravity pulls it down on the rug!

Age level

4+

Objective

To explore the concept of gravity

Materials

Pipe cleaners
scissors
paper
ball
marble
paper tube

Preparation

Cut pipe cleaners into 1/2" sticks. Make one for each child.

Our Beautiful Planet

Age level

3+

Objective

To learn that the Earth is a beautiful place to live

Materials

Butcher paper
scissors
tape
crayons
magazines
glue
paintbrush

Preparation

Cut a large sheet of butcher paper and tape it on a wall. Draw a large Earth on the paper. Have the children help color it. Tear out magazine pictures of beautiful things on the Earth. Possible ideas are flowers, trees, clouds, insects, mountains, rainbows, grassy fields and oceans.

What to do

1. The Earth is a very beautiful planet. Look outside. What do you see that looks beautiful? Each child says what he or she is looking at!

2. Sit at the table. Place the magazine pictures on the table. Pass out scissors. The children cut out pictures that they feel are beautiful.

3. When the children finish cutting, they bring their pictures to the paper Earth. With a paintbrush, spread glue on the Earth and stick the pictures on it.

4. When all the pictures are on the Earth, sit in a circle. Look at all the beautiful things on the Earth! Each child identifies a picture.

More to do

Draw a large Earth on a sheet of paper. Make one for each child. Place felt pens and crayons on the table for the children to draw beautiful things on their Earth. Brainstorm ideas!

Make a Mountain

What to do

1. Sit in a sand box. Feel the flat sand! Run your hands back and forth over the sand. Feel the flat sand with your eyes closed! There are no mountains on this land.

2. Who makes a mountain? A giant with large hands?! The Earth makes a mountain! Have the children place their hands under the sand, a foot apart. Now push your hands towards each other. When the Earth pushes together under the ground, a mountain is formed! Look at the mountain of sand that is forming. You have made a small mountain!

3. Now see how large a mountain you can make. Continue to push sand on the mountain. The ground is pushing up higher!

4. Roads are built on mountains. Make a road by swirling a finger around the mountain.

5. Tunnels are built through mountains. Poke a finger into the mountain to make a tunnel!

More to do

Build a mountain range in the sand. Make mountains in a line. Build roads by running your hands around the mountain range. Place sticks between the mountains for bridges. Find small rocks and place them in a row along a mountain. This is a train that follows a mountain track. Look what we can do with mountains!

Age level

3+

Objective

To understand how a mountain is formed

Materials

Sand box

Preparation

None

Mountain Climber

Age level

4+

Objective

To increase perception skills and to encourage creative thinking

Materials

White paper
tape
felt pen

Preparation

Tape a sheet of white paper on the rug. This is the top of a mountain that is covered with snow! Draw a simple map of the classroom on another sheet of paper and fold it up. A suggested map might be to draw an arrow around the lunch table, in and out of the kitchen area, stepping over three long blocks and then reaching the mountain peak a few feet away.

What to do

1. Climb a mountain! Pretend to put on hiking boots, wind a long rope around your arm and clip a canteen of water on your belt. Take a drink!

2. What do you think you will see at the top of the mountain? Brainstorm ideas! (Trees, a river, deer, snow, a cabin, animal tracks, a bear cave!)

3. Choose a mountain climber. Give this child the map. Explain that the map will show you how to get to the top of the mountain.

4. The mountain climber unfolds the map. The teacher explains the map to all the children. Point out the white paper on the rug. It is the top of the mountain that is covered with snow. Give the map back to the mountain climber. The mountain climber now follows the map to the top of the mountain.

5. When the mountain climber reaches the top of the mountain, ask him, "What do you see?" He tells the other children what he sees! Stand still or you might fall off!

6. Climb down the mountain the way you came. The mountain climber folds the map up and hands it to the next mountain climber.

More to do

For older children, a different map can be drawn for each mountain climber.

What's a Tree?

What to do

1. Explain that a tree is a giant plant! It is stronger and taller then all the other plants on the Earth. Act out different types of plants. Suggestions are:

- Roll up into a ball and pretend to be a bush!
- Stand straight with arms in different bent positions to be a cactus.
- Sit on your knees and make a circle shape with your arms. Sway back and forth. You are a garden of small flowers!
- Stand straight in a line with arms at your side. Sway. You are blades of grass.
- Hold hands and form a twisting pattern. You are clinging vines!
- Be a tree! Stand as tall as you can. Spread out your arms to form branches. Move your branches with the wind. You are beautiful strong trees!

More to do

Play a tree game! Cut cards shapes from white construction paper. Make thirty! Draw a tall tree on each card. Make matching tree cards! Color two trees red. Color two trees yellow. Color two apple trees and two banana trees! Place the tree cards face down on the rug. The children take turns turning over two cards to make a match.

Age level

3+

Objective

To discover how trees and plants move

Materials

None

Preparation

None

Trees and Me

Age level

4+

Objective

To learn that trees are alive and to treat them with respect

Materials

Butcher paper
scissors
felt pen
tape
leaves, real or paper ones
paper cups
straws

Preparation

Cut two 2' x 3' sheets of butcher paper. Draw a large tree with roots on one paper. Draw a large circle on the other paper. Draw nine concentric circles within the larger one, each circle smaller then the next. These are the rings on a tree stump! Tape the two pictures on a wall.

What to do

1. Trees are alive! They need to breathe! Give each child a leaf. What do we breathe through? Our noses! What does a tree breathe through? Its leaves! Have the children breathe in and breathe out on their leaf. You are like a tree breathing through your leaves!

2. How do we drink? With our mouths! A tree drinks through its roots! Show the roots of the tree that is on the wall. The tree sucks up water through its roots! Give each child a paper cup with an inch of water. Add a straw to each cup. Pretend the straw is a root! You are a thirsty tree. Suck the water up through your root!

3. Trees have birthdays just like we do! Show the tree stump with the rings. Each ring is one year. Count the rings. How old is the tree?

4. The tree is alive! How should we treat it? With care and respect!

More to do

Make a beautiful classroom tree! Draw a large tree on a sheet of butcher paper. Place the sheet on a table. Color it. The children can trace their hands on the tree for leaves. Or make hand prints with paint on the tree.

 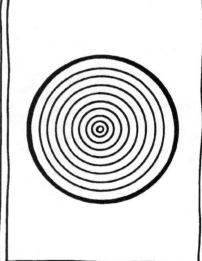

Rain Forests

What to do

1. Take a trip to a rain forest! Board your canoes! Sit in two straight rows, one behind each other. Paddle your canoes down the river towards the rain forest. Play jungle music or music with the sound of water!

2. Are you hungry! Pretend to throw fishing lines in the river. When you feel a tug, reel your fish in!

3. Paddle to land. Sit down at the edge of the rain forest. Listen! The forest is very still! Soon you will hear a storm coming. Pound lightly on the rug for a light rainfall. Now pound hard! The storm is over you! Rain falls often in a rain forest.

4. Now sit quietly. Place the animal pictures face down on the rug. By sitting quietly, the animals that live in the rain forest will not be frightened. Each child turns over a picture. If the child turns over a parrot, say, "Look! We see a parrot!" This child then tapes the parrot on the paper rain forest. Continue until all the animals have been placed in the rain forest.

5. Look at the beautiful rain forest! We are lucky to have such beautiful places on the Earth.

More to do

Some people who live in rain forests communicate by drum! Give two children a spoon and a pan each. These are their drums. One child beats out a message. The other child answers! Now switch and the child who answered sends the message! Give all the children a turn to send and answer a message.

Age level

4+

Objective

To appreciate the beauty of a rain forest

Materials

Butcher paper
scissors
felt pen
crayons
tape
calendars and magazines
optional—jungle or water music

Preparation

Cut at least three long sheets of butcher paper. Cut them as long as 6'! Draw a tall tree on each paper. Lay them on the floor or tables. Color them with the help of the children. Tape them near each other on a wall. This is the rain forest! Cut out pictures of animals that live in rain forests. Calendars and magazines are a great source of pictures! Common rain forest animals are frogs, sloths, anteaters, tigers, elephants, jaguars, ocelots, snakes, monkeys, parakeets, toucans, macaws, parrots, plus a variety of butterflies and flowers.

Flower Power

Age level

3+

Objective

To notice and appreciate the beauty of flowers

Materials

Flowers
white paper
crayons
paint
paintbrushes

Preparation

None

What to do

1. Pass around real flowers for the children to feel and smell. Where have you seen flowers? What colors do you remember seeing? Flowers make the Earth beautiful!

2. Place the paper, crayons, paint and paintbrushes on the table. The children draw or paint a flower picture, using the real flowers as models or creating flowers using their imaginations.

More to do

Make flowers to take home! Place pipe cleaners, scissors, glue and colored construction paper on the table. The children cut out flower shapes and leaves. Glue the flower shapes on a pipe cleaner. Be as creative as you can! Make as many flowers as you want! Send them home tied together with yarn.

Follow the Stream

What to do

1. Stand at the beginning of the stream (opposite the ocean). Pretend that the stream is near a mountain. It starts to snow! The snow melts and forms a stream. Act out this part! Wiggle your fingers slowly and move your hands downward for snow. Then slowly melt to the floor for melting snow! Now move a hand up and down in a wavy motion for a stream.

2. Now follow the stream! Walk slowly. Comment on each animal as you come to it. Suggested comments might be:
   Salamanders need to keep their skin moist.
   Frogs lay their eggs in water.
   Some **turtles** need to keep their shells wet.
   Ducks live in and out of the water. They teach their babies how to swim!
   Raccoons wash their food in streams!
   Beavers build their homes in water.
   Water spiders catch their food on the water.
   Mother **birds** feed baby birds worms that live near streams.
   Bears catch fish in streams.

3. When you reach the end of the stream, look at the larger body of water. It has grown into a river. Then look at the large circle of ribbon. The river has flowed into an ocean.

More to do

Look at the stream. What's missing? Fish! Have the children draw fish on a sheet of colored construction paper and cut them out. Offer a variety of colors! Make as many fish as you want. When a fish is finished, place it on the stream.

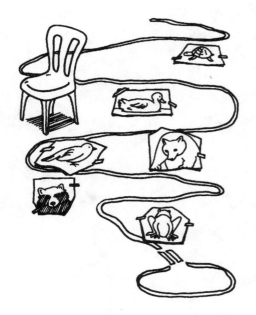

Age level

4+

Objective

To learn about streams and wildlife living nearby

Materials

Blue ribbon or yarn
scissors
magazines

Preparation

Cut a piece of blue ribbon or yarn longer than the classroom. Place the ribbon on the floor in a winding path around the classroom. This is a stream! Cut out pictures of animals that live near streams from magazines. Tape them along the stream. Animals you might use are salamanders, frogs, turtles, ducks, raccoons, beavers, water spiders, birds and bears! Cut two 6" pieces of ribbon. Place these parallel to each other at the end of the stream. Cut a piece of ribbon to form a 10" circle. Place this piece on the floor in a circle at the end of the river. This is the ocean!

Desert Snakes

Age level

3+

Objective

To learn about the desert and discover its beauty

Materials

Butcher paper
scissors
yellow crayons
tape
yellow crepe paper
felt pens
green crayons

Preparation

Cut out a 3' wide circle from butcher paper. Have the children help color it yellow. This is the sun. Tape it high on a wall. Cut long streams of yellow crepe paper. Tape them sticking out from the sun. They are sun rays. Draw a small cactus on butcher paper and color it green. Tape it low on a wall in the classroom.

What to do

1. The desert is a very quiet place. Sit very still! What sounds do you hear outside? Let each child say what he hears. You will not hear these sounds in a desert!

2. It is very hot in the desert. Look at the bright sun. Animals need to find shade! Pretend to be desert snakes. Crawl quietly to a place in the classroom to cool off. The teacher walks around the room and says to each child, "You look like a cool snake!" After the teacher has talked to each child, call the snakes back to the rug. The evening air is cooling the desert.

3. Explain that a special plant grows in the desert. A cactus! Go on a cactus hunt! Look for the cactus in the classroom.

More to do

Make a cactus to take home! Give each child a mound of dough. Shape the dough into a cactus shape. Spread out the base of the cactus so it will stand. Cut colored toothpicks and plain toothpicks into 1/2" pieces. Give each child a handful! Stick the toothpicks in the cactus to make the needles. The colorful toothpicks are the cactus blossoms!

The Cactus Story

What to do

1. Place the pictures on the rug, picture side down. Tell *The Cactus Story*. During the story, choose different children to turn over the appropriate picture. Number 1 picture will be turned over first!

The Cactus Story

Once there was a giant cactus. He lived in the desert. Today it was very hot, but he didn't mind. It was his birthday! He knew that his desert friends would visit him and wish him a happy day. First, *(turn over number 1)* a lizard came and sat on a warm rock near the cactus. Then *(turn over number 2)* a mouse stopped by and twitched his nose. He was hoping to smell a birthday cake! Then *(turn over number 3)* a spider crawled up the cactus. She made the cactus a beautiful silver web. Then *(turn over number 4)* a beetle ran past the cactus. Was he looking for the birthday party? Then *(turn over number 5)* a snake slid across the sand. She was an old friend and had shed her skin many times by the cactus. Then *(turn over number 6)* a butterfly flew around the cactus. He wanted the cactus to notice his beautiful wings! Then *(turn over number 7)* an owl flew into a small hole in the cactus. The owl lived in the cactus and was planning to sing a special birthday song. What do you think it would sound like? Then *(turn over number 8)* a coyote sat in front of the cactus. She would sing a birthday song with the owl. What do you think the coyote would sound like? The animals singing made the cactus so happy that *(turn over number 9)* a flower blossomed at the very top of the cactus. The cactus felt proud to be a cactus. He felt absolutely beautiful!

More to do

Now ask a question about each animal in the order presented in the story. For example, "What sat on a warm rock near the cactus?" The child who guesses the lizard tapes the lizard near the cactus. Continue until all the animal pictures are taped on or around the cactus.

Age level

3+

Objective

To learn about cactus and the variety of life in a desert

Materials

Butcher paper
scissors
tape
felt pen
various shades of green crayons
magazines
white paper

Preparation

Cut a large sheet of butcher paper and tape it on a wall. Draw a large cactus on the paper. Have the children help color the cactus many shades of green. Draw or cut out magazine pictures of the following animals: a lizard, a mouse, a spider, a beetle, a snake, a butterfly, an owl, a coyote and a flower. Print a large number on the back of each picture. Number them in the order listed. For example, the lizard would be number 1, the mouse number 2.

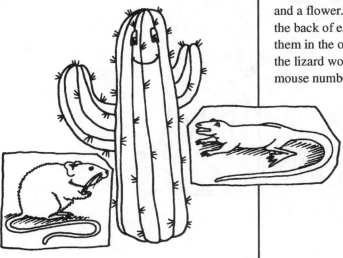

Cold Adventures

Age level

4+

Objective

To learn about cold, icy areas on the Earth—the North and South Poles

Materials

Globe
tape
felt pens
scissors

Preparation

None

What to do

1. Pretend the rug is covered with ice. Walk carefully on the ice. It's slippery! Now sit down. Display a globe. Who can see the white areas on the Earth? They are layers of ice! Give each child a chance to point out the North and South Poles.

2. It's very cold at the Poles! Animals who live there stay warm with a thick layer of fat and fur. Pretend to be penguins! Stand with arms straight down and hands out like flippers. Waddle around the ice! Sit together on the ice and huddle close. Now pretend to be huge walruses. Move slowly together as a group. Weave back and forth! Now stand up. Your hands are large furry paws.

3. How would you stay warm if you lived in such a cold place? Pretend to put on thick clothing. Now exercise! Give each child a chance to think of an exercise to do.

4. Look around the ice. Do you see many fruits and plants growing? It is hard for things to grow in the cold! What would you eat? You can fish for your food! Pretend to chop a hole in the ice (rug). Now drop a fishing line into your hole. Wait patiently for thirty seconds! Who feels a tug? Reel up your line and see if you have caught a fish.

More to do

Sit at the table. Explain that igloos are homes that are built in the cold, icy areas of the Earth. They are made from blocks of ice. Make igloos! Give the children a paper plate, glue and a handful of sugar cubes. These are blocks of ice. Glue the sugar cubes together to make igloos!

Island Home

What to do

1. Act out the birth of an island! Sit on the rug, around the island. Pretend there is an earthquake! Rock back and forth while you are sitting. Shake and tremble! A mountain is growing from the bottom of the ocean. The island is the top of the mountain!

2. Notice the island. There is nothing on it! Move to the other side of the classroom. The children are plant seeds, blown to the island by the wind. They can walk slowly, rocking back and forth, until they reach the island. The seeds can lay where they want! They will turn into green fruits and plants!

3. Return again to the other side of the classroom. Give each child a wooden block to hold. Now the children are lizards! They are carried across the ocean to the island on pieces of wood. Make swishing sounds. Weave back and forth to the island, carried by huge waves.

4. Snails come to the island attached to leaves, floating in the ocean. Give each child a leaf. Slowly float to the island!

5. Now birds come to the island because there are things for the birds to eat! Fly to the island!

6. People are the last to come to the island. They arrive in boats. Sit together on the rug and rock back and forth. You are heading towards the island in your boat! Now the island is ready for you to build your homes. It is a beautiful place to live!

7. Build island homes! The children move chairs and furniture to make forts. Provide sheets and blankets! Play in the island homes all day!

More to do

Make island pictures. Give each child a large sheet of blue construction paper. This is an ocean. Give each child a sheet of brown construction paper to cut out an island shape. Place glue on the table. Glue the islands on the ocean. Now place items on the table to glue on the islands. Possible items are bird seed, flower seeds, twigs, leaves, pebbles and small pictures of animals and insects. Have each child think of a name for his or her island. Print the island names on the papers!

Age level

5+

Objective

To understand islands and to follow a sequence of events

Materials

Butcher paper
scissors
brown, gold and yellow crayons
tape
wooden blocks
leaves, real or paper ones
sheets and blankets

Preparation

Cut two large sheets of butcher paper. Place them on the floor or on tables. Have the children help color the sheets with brown, gold and yellow crayons. Tape the sheets of butcher paper together on the rug. They form an island!

My Home

Age level

3+

Objective

To reinforce the idea that our home is on the Earth

Materials

None

Preparation

None

What to do

1. Stand to say "The Earth" chant!

> *I live on the Earth, (Make a circle with your arms)*
> *In my very own house, (Put fingers together to form a roof)*
> *That sits on my very own street. (Place a fist on an opened palm)*
>
> *I live on the Earth, (Make a circle with your arms)*
> *I dance and I play, (Twirl around then, pound two fists together)*
> *I walk with my own two feet! (Stomp both feet on the rug)*
>
> *The Earth is my home (Make a circle with your arms)*
> *High in the sky, (Point to the sky)*
> *Circling round and round, (Turn around and around)*
>
> *I live on the Earth, (Make a circle with you arms)*
> *In my very own house, (Put fingers together to form a roof)*
> *That sits upon the ground. (Sit down)*

More to do

Make an Earth home to take home. Have the children bring in an empty box. The teacher cuts a small opening on one side of each box. This is the front door. Give each child a sheet of paper and felt pens. They draw the members of their family. Draw them to fit inside the box. Now cut them out. Glue them inside the box, on the side opposite the front door. Look through the front door. You will see your family! This is your home on the Earth.

Earth Memories

What to do

1. A memory helps us to remember things! Ask the children if they remember what they ate for breakfast.

2. Show the picture of the Earth. Place a variety of felt pens on the rug. Ask the children to be thinking of something they remember about the Earth.

3. Help them remember by offering clues. We talked about a green plant in the desert! What is an animal that lives in a rain forest? What did we see in the dirt we dug up? Each child takes a turn to say something that she remembers about the Earth.

4. When a child remembers something, she chooses a felt pen and draws it on the Earth. When all the pictures have been drawn, look at all the wonderful things on the Earth!

More to do

Play The Vacation Game! The teacher says, "I took a vacation and I saw a mountain!" The child sitting next to the teacher repeats the sentence but instead of "mountain" adds a different word. Each child, in turn, thinks of something she saw on her vacation on the Earth! Play it again. This time the children say what the teacher said, plus their own answer! Keep adding more and more words.

Age level

4+

Objective

To remember what was learned about the Earth

Materials

Felt pens
tape

Preparation

Tape the picture from the activity, "I Live on the Earth" on the wall.

Mother Earth

Age level

4+

Objective

To learn how to take care of the Earth

Materials

Large paper bag

Preparation

None

What to do

1. The Earth is our home. We need to help take care of her! Talk about the different ways you can do this!

2. Talk about water! Water is a part of the earth and should not be wasted! Pretend to brush your teeth. Squeeze toothpaste on your toothbrush. Turn on the tap and wet the toothbrush. Now turn off the tap and brush your teeth! This saves water!

3. Show a large paper bag. You see these at the market. Beautiful trees are cut down to make paper bags. Re-use them as many times as you can! If you only buy one or two things at the market, carry your items out in your arms! Pretend you are at the market. The children find something in the classroom that they want to buy. Bring the item to the teacher. Give the teacher some money and carry the item in your arms to the rug. Sit down in your car (on the rug)! When all the children are sitting on the rug, drive home. That was easy! You might have saved a tree from being cut down!

3. Go outside! Look around. Can you see anything that needs your help? Possible things might be to sweep sand back into the sand area, to water a plant, to plant grass seeds where they are needed, to straighten up an outside area that is messy.

More to do

Go on a litter hunt! Give each child a small paper bag. Walk outside and look for litter. When the children find litter, they can put it in their paper bags. When you return to the classroom, throw the litter bags in the trash can. You have helped to make the Earth beautiful! Start a glass and can recycling collection in your classroom. The money you collect can buy something to help the Earth. Buy flower seeds or plant a small tree!

Fun and Giggles and Inside Games

The question, "Who wants to play a game?," always receives an enthusiastic response! Games attract children like ducks to water. You can't keep them away! In the classroom, games provide valuable learning through fun, movement, concentration, following directions, learning new skills and imagination! The fun comes naturally. Movement provides great opportunities for strengthening muscles and small motor movement. The ability to concentrate on rules increases the children's perception and awareness skills. Following directions develops good listening skills and the ability to remember. Learning new skills is just part of the magic of inside games. Many of the games involve matching colors, counting, letter recognition, spatial awareness and positive social interaction. Imagination is perhaps one of the most important learning experiences. With an imagination, anything can happen! With an imagination, you can do anything!

Fun and Giggles and Inside Games

	Monday	Tuesday	Wednesday	Thursday	Friday
Week 1	**3+ Yancy Yarn** *To follow directions*	**4+ Roll the Gopher** *To increase hand-eye coordination*	**4+ Late one Stormy Night** *To stimulate imagination*	**4+ Cat's Eye** *To improve small motor skills*	**3+ Mother's Silly Soup** *To follow directions*
Week 2	**3+ Pass the Python** *To improve dexterity*	**3+ Walk the Plank** *To learn how to balance*	**4+ The Deep Blue Sea** *To develop cutting skills*	**3+ Birdie Ate the Worm** *To learn to take turns*	**3+ Hungry Birds** *To improve cutting skills*
Week 3	**4+ Secret Mission** *To identify matching colors*	**4+ The 20 Second Cat Nap** *To improve counting skills*	**3+ Flying Saucer Sightings** *To encourage decision making skills*	**3+ The Big Bad Wolf** *To develop large motor skills*	**3+ The Golden Egg** *To increase perception skills*
Week 4	**4+ Stop That Penny** *To learn to count*	**3+ Cotton Tails** *To develop memory skills*	**4+ Pig In, Pig Out** *To increase hand-eye coordination*	**4+ Jump Fish** *To improve color matching skills*	**3+ Bug Collector** *To recognize colors*

Yancy Yarn

What to do

1. Give each child a string of yarn. Stand in a circle. Each child places his yarn in his own circle on the rug and stands by his circle.

2. Explain that the yarn's name is Yancy. Say, "hi," to Yancy! Explain that the class is going to play a game together called Yancy Yarn!

3. Yancy Yarn is similar to Simple Simon. All the children sit down inside their circle. Make sure your entire body is inside! Now give a direction, such as, "Yancy Yarn says, 'stand in your circle!'" All stand! Now say, "turn around." No one should turn around! Yancy Yarn did not tell you to!

4. Suggested directions might be (use Yancy Yarn when you want):

- Step outside of your circle.
- Step inside of your circle.
- Walk around the outside of your circle.
- Jump up and down inside your circle.
- Sit in your circle and stick only one foot outside your circle!
- Walk around your circle with one foot inside your circle and one foot outside your circle.
- Jump across your circle to the other side!

5. When a child follows a direction given without the Yancy Yarn phrase, this child sits in his circle for the remainder of the game. Continue until there is only one child standing.

More to do

Each child stands in front of the group and gives a direction. With this variation do not use the Yancy Yarn phrase. Use cotton balls! The cotton ball says, "Hide me in your fist!" "Place me on the rug." Use scarfs! The scarf says, "Roll me in a ball and throw me in the air!" "Lay me over a shoulder." "Swirl me in the air!"

Age level

3+

Objective

To follow directions, to control large motor skills and to increase spatial awareness

Materials

Yarn
scissors

Preparation

Cut 5' pieces of yarn for each child.

Roll the Gopher

Age level

4+

Objective

To increase hand-eye coordination

Materials

Brown construction paper
tape
small ball

Preparation

Push the shorter ends of a sheet of brown construction paper slightly together. This forms a tunnel shape! Tape the short ends on the floor or rug. Now you have a tunnel! Make many tunnels. Tape them a few feet apart facing in different directions.

What to do

1. Show the small ball. This is a gopher! Show the many tunnels that the gopher has built. Now he is very tired. He wants to go back to his tunnels! Who wants to help him?

2. Choose a child to roll the gopher! This child holds the gopher (ball) and sits on the rug. She tries to roll the gopher through one of the tunnels. It is best to roll slowly!

3. Give each child three turns. The second roll starts at the place where the gopher stopped rolling. The same rule applies to the third roll. If a gopher stops inside a tunnel, the gopher has fallen asleep. It is then another child's turn.

4. Continue until all the children have rolled the gopher!

More to do

Tape the tunnels in a straight line. Try to roll the gopher through the long tunnel! Play in groups of two. Have two children sit on either side of a tunnel. They can roll the gopher to each other through the tunnel!

Late One Stormy Night

What to do

1. Sit down on the rug and turn off the lights.

2. Tell the children that when there is a blank in the poem, they can try to guess what was really seen or heard. Remember that it is dark in the house and hard to see. Is the child in the poem imagining everything?

3. After the children guess at the first blank, choose a child to turn over the imagination card number 1. It will show what was really seen or heard! After the second blank, turn over card number 2. Continue until the seventh blank is guessed, and card number 7 is revealed.

4. Read the following poem slowly and with an air of suspense!

Late one night as I lay in bed,
My feather quilt pulled over my head,
I heard a noise outside my door,
It sounded like a dinosaur!
But it was only _____ (thunder)

I sneaked downstairs to turn on the
*   light,*
My wristwatch mouse watch said mid-
*   night!*
I heard a crack and then a creek,
It was a pair of giant feet!
But it was only _____ (the sound of
*   rain)*

Then I sat down upon the floor,
I needed time to think some more,
Was I awake or still asleep?
Then every floorboard seemed to
*   squeak!*
But it was only _____ (my pet
*   mouse)*

I stood back up and rubbed my eyes,
I smelled my mother's apple pie,
I headed towards the kitchen door;

And saw a gorilla on the floor!
But it was only _____ (an old blan-
*   ket)*

I ate my pie and drank some juice,
I wished I had my cuddle-moose,
But I had left him waaaay upstairs,
I think I see a grizzly bear!
But it was only _____ (a couch)

I'm getting cold, right to my feet,
My knees are just a little weak,
I think I'll hide behind a chair,
I see a monster on the stair!
But it was only _____ (my dog)

This cannot be, I'm going to bed,
I'm just a tired sleepyhead,
But as I reached my bedroom door,
I heard a hungry lion roar!
But it was only _____ (the wind)

I covered up and hid my head,
I loved my safe and cozy bed,
Oh no, I thought, I cannot bother,
Now I want a drink of water!
(See who can guess the word water!)

More to do

Tell the story again so other children have a chance to turn over the imagination cards! Make up different answers to the blanks!

Age level

4+

Objective

To stimulate imagination and creative thinking skills and to learn to use visual imagery during a story

Materials

White posterboard
scissors
felt pens

Preparation

Cut white posterboard into seven card-size shapes. These are imagination cards! Print a large number 1 on a card. Print a number 2 on the next card. Continue printing a number on each card up to number 7. On the other side of each card, draw a picture relating to the story. On card 1, draw thunder (swirling black lines with the word Boom!); on card 2, draw rain; on card 3, draw a mouse; on card 4, an old blanket; on card 5, draw a couch; on card 6, draw a dog; on card 7, draw the wind! Place the cards on the rug, number side up.

Cat's Eye

Age level

4+

Objective

To improve small motor skills and to encourage letter recognition

Materials

Paper cup and marble for each child. The marbles should be crystal or clear with only one cat's eye marble. A cat's eye marble has a thin ribbon of color in it and looks like a cat's eye! small box
felt pen

Preparation

Place all the marbles in a box. Print the letter G or M or C on the bottom of the paper cups. The M is for moose, the G is for goose and the C is for cow!

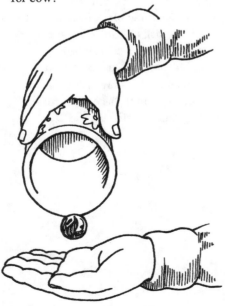

What to do

1. Give each child a paper cup. Tell the following story!

The Cat's Eye Story

Once there was a rabbit who lived in the woods. His best friends were a goose, a moose and a cow. One day, Rabbit went to play in his marble box. His favorite marble was missing! Where was his beautiful cat's eye? Rabbit said what he always said when he was sad, "Oh, Jellybeans!" But Rabbit had a plan. He went to see Goose, Moose and Cow. "I promise," said Rabbit, "that the one who finds my cat's eye can eat a piece of my carrot pie!" When Goose, Moose and Cow heard this, they all claimed to have found the cat's eye. But who really found the cat's eye? Find out!

2. Have the children close their eyes. Bring the box of marbles to each child. They choose a marble from the box and drop it in their paper cup. Have them cover their cup with their other hand.

3. Say the following chant. While saying the chant, the children shake their marble cup, keeping their hands over the top!

> *Who has the cat's eye?*
> *"I," said the goose!*
> *Who has the cat's eye?*
> *"I," said the moose!*
> *Who has the cat's eye?*
> *"I," said the cow!*
> *Now, shake and rattle*
> *And roll it out!*

4. After the last line, the children roll their marbles into their hands. The child who has the cat's eye looks on the bottom of her paper cup. If the G is there, Goose found the cat's eye. If the M is there, Moose found the cat's eye. If the C is there, Cow found the cat's eye! Now play again!

More to do

Cut out pie shapes from orange construction paper. Place the pie shapes on a paper plate. The child who has the cat's eye takes a piece of carrot pie!

Mother's Silly Soup

What to do

1. Sit in a circle. Place the pot and wooden spoon in the middle of the circle. Who would like to have a taste of Mother's Silly Soup? The class can help make it!

2. Say the Silly Soup fingerplay.

   > *Turn on the fire, (Hold thumb and first finger together, twist)*
   > *Pour in the water, (Pretend to pour water)*
   > *Grind in the pepper, (Make two fists, turn the one on top)*
   > *Shake in the salt. (Shake fist up and down)*
   > *Stirring round and round the pot (Move hand in a circle)*
   > *To make the Silly's hot! (Blow over fist)*

3. Now it's time to put in the ingredients. Tell the children to find something in the classroom that has red on it. Bring the object back to the circle.

5. Each child places his object in the pot and stirs it with the wooden spoon.

6. Now Mother's Silly Soup is ready to eat. Pretend to give the children a taste with the wooden spoon. How does the soup make you feel? Silly? Act silly! Wiggle! Make funny faces. Make silly sounds. If the soup begins to wear off, taste it again!

7. Make soup with another kind of classroom item—something yellow, blue, soft, heavy, round, small, etc. How does this soup make you feel? Happy, bouncy, small, sleepy, etc.

More to do

At Halloween, be a witch and make a scary soup! After tasting the soup, make scary sounds! Make a wish soup. It can turn you into anything you want to be. Make a quiet soup. Taste the soup and take slow, deep breaths. Slowly fall to the rug. Relax! Ask for suggestions on what kind of soup to make.

Age level

3+

Objective

To follow directions and to learn the meaning of descriptive words, such as red, blue, soft or heavy

Materials

Large pot
wooden spoon
various classroom items

Preparation

None

Pass the Python

Age level

3+

Objective

To improve dexterity

Materials

Thick stick at least 10" long
newspaper or wrapping paper
tape
recorded music

Preparation

Wrap a sheet of newspaper or wrapping paper around the stick so it is completely covered. This is the skin of the python! Continue to wrap sheets of paper around the stick so there is at least one sheet for each child.

What to do

1. Sit in a circle. Show the wrapped paper stick. Explain that the stick underneath the paper is the python. The layers of paper are the skin that he sheds!

2. The teacher hands the python to a child and starts the music. The python is passed around the circle. When the music is stopped, the child holding the python unwraps a layer of skin. The snake has shed a layer!

3. Start the music. The python is passed around the circle. When the music stops, another child peels off a layer of skin.

4. Continue until the python has shed all his skin! The child who is left holding the skinless python throws him in the middle of the circle. The children say, "He looks hungry!" The teacher says, "Everyone hide!" Then the children quickly find a place to hide.

5. When the teacher puts the python away, the children come out from their hiding places.

More to do

The children can make individual pythons. Go on a python hunt! Hunt for sticks. Place many sheets of newspaper, wrapping paper and even foil on the table. Wrap many layers of skin around the pythons. Take the pythons home. Play Pass The Python at home!

Walk the Plank

What to do

1. Explain the game. We are on a boat that is sinking! The quickest way off is to walk the plank. Jump off the plank, but do not swim into an alligator, or you will be eaten! Show the children where the island and the alligator's stomach are located in the classroom.

2. Before a child walks the plank, say the following chant with the children:

   I'm going to walk (Walk fingers along hand)
   A creak-ity plank (Walk fingers along hand)
   Off into the sea, (Jump fingers off hand)
   And swim to shore (Make a wavy motion with a hand)
   Before an alligator (Place palms flat against each other)
   Swallows me! (Open hands slowly and then clap together)

3. Now choose a child to walk the plank. When she jumps off, she tries to reach the island without swimming into an alligator. If she touches an alligator, it eats her! Then she will sit in the alligator's stomach for the rest of the game. If she does not get eaten by an alligator, she sits on the island.

4. After she walks the plank, repeat the chant and choose another child. Play ocean music while a child walks the plank!

More to do

Think of different ways to walk the plank. Try them! Possible ideas might be walking sideways, walking on tiptoe, walking backwards, and crawling across!

Age level

3+

Objective

To learn how to balance and to develop spatial awareness by walking between defined spaces

Materials

Board at least 3' long
two large wooden blocks
green construction paper
scissors
black felt pen
optional—ocean music

Preparation

Place a wooden block under each end of the board. This is a plank. Cut green construction paper into 3" x 6" oval shapes. Draw two large eyes on each one. Make at least ten. These are alligators! Place them around one end of the plank at least 1' apart. Choose a place in the classroom to be the island. Choose a place in the classroom to be the alligator's stomach!

The Deep Blue Sea

Age level

4+

Objective

To develop cutting skills

Materials

Different colored construction paper
black felt pen
yarn
scissors
tape
pencils

Preparation

Draw large fish on a sheet of construction paper. Make at least two for each child. Use a variety of colors! Cut a string of yarn 3' long. Tape one end to a pencil to make a fishing pole. Make a fishing pole for each child.

What to do

1. Place the paper fish on the table. Pass out scissors. Each child cuts out two paper fish.

2. When they are finished, they place their fish in the deep blue sea (the rug)!

3. When all the fish have been cut out, give the children their fishing poles. Show how to turn the pencil so the fishing line is brought up and let down. Now it's time to catch a fish!

4. Stand around the deep blue sea. Unroll the fishing lines. Place a wad of tape on the end of the yarn. Sing, "The Fishing Song!" Sing it to the tune of, "The Wheels on the Bus."

   I'm going fishing in the deep blue sea
   The deep blue sea, the deep blue sea,
   I'm going fishing in the deep blue sea,
   For mommy and me!

5. Now the children lower the end of their fishing line on a fish. When it sticks, reel it up.

6. Throw it back and catch another fish! Sing "The Fishing Song" again. This time, instead of mommy, say daddy! Catch more fish and substitute the words daddy, grandma, grandpa, sister and brother for mommy.

More to do

Instead of standing around the deep blue sea, try sitting and laying down to catch fish. Play a jumping game! Jump over the fish. Before each child jumps, say this verse substituting a child's name for the word Jack.

   Jack be nimble,
   Jack be quick,
   Jack jump over the paper fish!

Birdie Ate the Worm

What to do

1. Sit in a circle. Pass out brown socks to the children. They place the sock on their hand like a puppet. These are earthworms!

2. Hold the earthworms high in the air. They are playing above the ground.

3. Choose a child to be the birdie. The birdie walks around the outside of the circle. The rest of the children sway their earthworm back and forth while saying "The Earthworm" chant.

    Worm, Worm
    Slippery slide,
    I smell a bird,
    And I better hide!
    Down, down
    Under the ground,
    Squirmy, wormy
    Round and round.

4. At the end of the chant, the teacher calls out, "Freeze Birdie!" The birdie stops and taps the child in front of him on the head.

5. The birdie pulls off his worm and throws it into the nest (center of the circle).

6. The birdie now sits in the circle with his earthworm. The child whose worm was eaten now becomes the birdie.

More to do

Play Freeze Bird! The children are birds and each one holds a 12" piece of string. These are earthworms! Play music. The birds dance around with their earthworms. When the music stops, the birds freeze. Any bird who moves sits in a special area labeled the nest. Continue until only one bird remains out of the nest.

Age level

3+

Objective

To learn to follow directions and take turns

Materials

Brown socks—these are earthworms

Preparation

None

Hungry Birds

Age level

3+

Objective

To improve counting skills and to increase color recognition

Materials

Green construction paper
crayons
scissors
white paper
tape
musical instrument, such as a cymbal, drum or bells
optional—contact paper

Preparation

Have the older children in the class draw large leaves on green construction paper. Cut them out. (Cover the leaves with contact paper and use them throughout the year.) Draw caterpillars on white paper and color each of them a different color. Cut out the caterpillars and tape each one on a leaf. Make one set for each child. Place the leaves at least 1' apart on the rug.

What to do

1. Have the children take off their shoes. They start to walk slowly around the leaves. They are the hungry birds looking for caterpillars to eat.

2. While they are walking, the teacher plays an instrument such as a cymbal, drum or bells. When a beat is established, the teacher says "The Hungry Bird" chant!

   Before I go to sleep, sleep, sleep,
   I will have to eat, eat, eat.
   Fat and juicy, jolly good
   Caterpillars on a leaf!

3. When the chant is over, the teacher slowly counts to a number between one and ten and then claps at the end! After the clap, the children jump on a caterpillar leaf. They found their caterpillar to eat! What color is the caterpillar that you found to eat?

4. Now play the game again but with one less caterpillar leaf on the rug. The child who is left without a leaf after the clap did not find a caterpillar to eat. This hungry bird sits down in a chosen spot, the bird nest!

5. Continue until there is only one hungry bird on a caterpillar leaf. This bird ate the most caterpillars! What color is the last caterpillar on the leaf?

More to do

Twirl pipe cleaners around a finger and pull them off. Now they look like caterpillars!

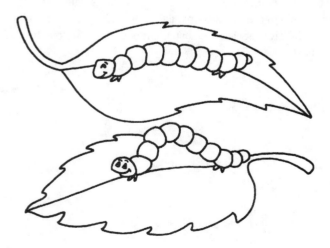

Secret Mission

What to do

1. Sit in a circle. We are on a Secret Mission! Pass out an envelope to each child. Explain that there are clues inside the envelopes.

2. Count slowly to ten. On the count of ten, the children open the envelopes! Look at the color on the clue card. This is a secret mission! Keep your color a secret.

3. Now it is time to go on the Secret Mission. Each child hunts for an object in the classroom that matches the color on her clue card. If the color is yellow, she hunts for an object that is all yellow or part yellow!

4. When each child finds an object, she returns to the rug. When all the children have returned, share clue cards and objects.

More to do

Take the clue cards home in the envelopes. Encourage the children to bring in an object from home that matches the color on their clue card. Have a special sharing time with the objects from home.

Age level

4+

Objective

To identify matching colors

Materials

White posterboard
scissors
crayons
envelopes

Preparation

Cut posterboard into card-size shapes. Draw a 1" diameter circle on each card. Color each circle. Use many different colors! These are clue cards! Make one for each child. Place each clue card in an envelope.

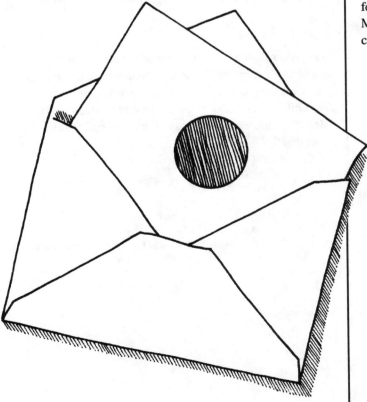

The 20 Second Cat Nap

Age level

4+

Objective

To improve counting skills

Materials

Bag of large white cotton balls
shoe box

Preparation

Hide 40-50 white cotton balls around
the classroom. A few can be hidden in
the same spot! Place the shoe box on
the rug.

What to do

1. Explain that there are white mice (cotton balls) hiding all around the class-room. The teacher is the hungry cat!

2. The cat pretends to take a 20 second cat nap. During the cat nap, the cat **slowly** counts to 20.

3. While the cat is napping, the children look for the white mice. As they find the mice, they place them in the mouse house (shoe box). These mice are safe from the cat!

4. When the cat reaches the count of 20, the cat meows loudly. The children stop looking for the mice and sit on the rug. The cat says, "I'm hungry!" Now the cat goes hunting for the remaining mice. These mice are placed on the rug outside the mouse house (shoe box). They have been caught by the cat!

5. Count how many mice are safe in the mouse house. Count how many mice have been caught by the cat!

6. Now choose a child to be the cat. The remaining children hide their eyes. The teacher hides the mice again and then the cat counts with the teacher.

More to do

Use yellow cotton balls and hide baby chicks around the room. The teacher can be the hungry wolf! Use blue cotton balls and hide tropical fish. The teacher is the shark! Give each child a white cotton ball. This is a mouse! The children place the mouse in front of them on the rug. Say "The Little Mouse" chant. The teacher says each line, and the children repeat it. Say the lines quietly!

> *I see a little mouse*
> *As quiet as can be,*
> *He wants to be my friend*
> *He's not afraid of me!*
> *But when he sees a pointed ear*
> *And spots a furry tail,*
> *He runs into his little house (Push the mouse under one hand)*
> *And waits....right....there!*

Flying Saucer Sightings

What to do

1. The children sit in a circle holding their flying saucers. Explain that many people claim they have seen a flying saucer. When someone sees a ship from outer space, it is called a sighting!

2. Play recorded music. The children fly their flying saucers slowly around the room.

3. Stop the music! Each child finds a place to land his or her flying saucer. Each flying saucer must land on a different spot in the classroom.

4. Now the teacher turns over the top card on the rug. If it is the sink card, the teacher says, "I see a flying saucer! It is a sighting on..... the sink!"

5. If a child landed his flying saucer on the sink, this child flies his saucer to the teacher. Start the music again. Now this child stops the music, chooses a sighting card and says where the saucer has been seen. (If no one landed on the sink, the teacher chooses another sighting card.)

More to do

The children can be flying saucers! Play music. The children fly around the room. When the music stops, find a place to land. The teacher chooses a card and says the location of the sighting. If a child landed on that spot, then he chooses the next sighting card.

Age level

3+

Objective

To encourage decision making skills and to increase listening skills

Materials

Paper plates
crayons
stapler
felt pens
white paper
scissors
recorded music

Preparation

Give each child two paper plates to color. Have them color the bottom of each plate. Staple the two plates together along the rim. These are flying saucers! Print the children's names on the saucers. Cut white paper into card-size shapes. Draw or print the name of an object in the classroom on each card. Ideas are the sink, a chair, a table, cubbies, a stuffed animal, the play oven, the block shelf. These are sighting cards! Place them face down in a pile on the rug.

The Big Bad Wolf

Age level

3+

Objective

To develop large motor skills and to learn to follow verbal directions

Materials

None

Preparation

None

What to do

1. Sit on the rug. The room is now the woods! Choose a child to be the Big Bad Wolf.

2. The wolf sits apart from the group. The remaining children need to reach grandma's house before the wolf does. Say "The Wolf" chant with the children! Say the first verse slowly. As you say it, slap the rug with your hands. Slap slowly. Say the second verse faster. Slap the rug faster.

   I'm walking in the woods to grandma's house
   Grandma's house, grandma's house,
   I'm walking in the woods to grandma's house
   To beat the Big Bad Wolf!

   I'm running in the woods to grandma's house
   Grandma's house, grandma's house,
   I'm running in the woods to grandma's house,
   To beat the Big Bad Wolf!

3. When you finish the chant, the wolf slowly creeps towards the group. The teacher says, "Go hide!" The wolf stops and closes her eyes! The rest of the children find a hiding place in the woods (the classroom).

4. When they have found a hiding place, The teacher says, "Go wolf!" The wolf slowly walks around the woods. The wolf taps children on the shoulder while walking around. When the wolf taps a child **and growls**, this child has been caught while on the way to grandma's house. The wolf then walks her back to the rug and she becomes the wolf.

5. Repeat "The Wolf" chant and continue the game.

More to do

Play a variation of the game. To begin the game choose half the children to be wolves. The remaining children say "The Wolf" chant and hide! Each wolf taps a child on the shoulder and returns to the rug area. When all the wolves have returned, the children who were tapped try to guess which wolf tapped them. Only one guess allowed! Children who guess correctly become wolves for the next game.

The Golden Egg

What to do

1. Choose a giant! The giant sits in his "castle," facing a wall.

2. The remaining children sit on the rug, each holding a golden egg (a yellow cotton ball).

3. The children say, "Fee Fi Fo Fum!" Then the giant turns around and hunts for the magic goose.

4. After he finds the goose, he needs a golden egg to go with his magic goose. The giant takes one child's golden egg! This child becomes the giant! The child who was the giant hides the magic goose and sits on the rug with the other children, holding a golden egg.

More to do

Make golden eggs to take home. Go on a rock hunt! The children paint the rocks yellow. Play the game with the yellow rocks. Take the yellow rocks home to play the golden egg game at home.

Age level

3+

Objective

To increase perception skills

Materials

Picture of a white goose
yellow cotton balls (golden eggs!)

Preparation

Hide a picture of a goose somewhere in the classroom. This is a magic goose!

Stop That Penny

Age level

4+

Objective

To increase perception skills and to learn to count

Materials

Pennies
box
marker

Preparation

Print the word "BANK" on the box.

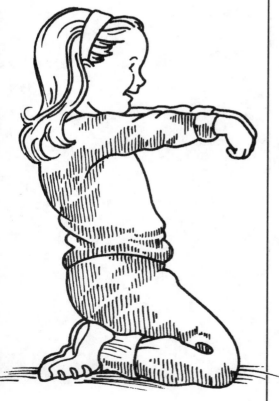

What to do

1. Sit in a circle. Choose a Penny Picker! This child sits in the middle of the circle. Give the remaining children a penny.

2. Have the children hold their penny in their fists. Say "The Penny" chant! Each child passes her penny back and forth from one fist to another while saying the chant.

   Penny, penny,
   To and fro,
   Pennies dancing in a row,
   Stop that penny on the go!

3. When the children say the last word, they stop passing the pennies from one fist to another! The Penny Picker tries to pick a fist that has a penny in it.

4. If the Penny Picker finds a penny, she takes a penny from the penny bag and places it in the bank (box).

5. Then the Penny Picker chooses another child to be the Penny Picker. Continue until all the children have had a turn.

6. When the game is over, count all the pennies in the bank. How many pennies were found?

7. Play again! See if you can put more pennies in the bank the second time.

More to do

Pass only one penny around the circle. The children pass the penny from one child to another until the end of the chant. The Penny Picker tries to guess who has the penny!

Cotton Tails

What to do

1. Point to the basket (or box) on the rug. This is filled with nice fresh grass that bunnies like to eat! But where are the bunnies? Who would like to help find them?

2. Explain that the bunnies are hiding under the cups. One child turns over two of the cups. If he finds a bunny under both cups, he takes the bunnies and puts them in the basket.

3. The teacher replaces the bunnies (cotton balls) under the two cups with two more cotton balls. Now mix up the cups again.

4. If he does not find two bunnies, he quickly hides the bunny under the cup. A hungry fox might be looking for dinner. Then the next child takes a turn.

5. Continue until all the children have found two bunnies, then count how many bunnies are in the basket!

More to do

Use different colored cotton balls! Use white, blue, yellow and pink. Have the children try to find two bunnies that match in color. For older children, use fewer bunnies or more cups.

Age level

3+

Objective

To develop memory skills

Materials

10 paper cups
basket or box
small white cotton balls

Preparation

Place the paper cups upside down on the rug. Hide a cotton ball under eight of them. Mix them up!

Pig In, Pig Out

Age level

4+

Objective

To increase hand-eye coordination

Materials

White posterboard
black felt pen
pink crayon
pennies

Preparation

Draw horizontal and vertical lines across the posterboard. The squares that you make are pig pens! Draw a large pig face in half of the squares. Color the pigs pink!

What to do

1. Place the posterboard on the rug and sit around it. Give each child a penny. The white squares are pig pens, but the pigs are hiding. We can't see them! The pink squares are pigs that are out of their pig pens!

2. The children take turns trying to throw their penny on a square.

3. If a penny lands on a pink square, all yell,"Pig out!" Duck down, we don't want to get run over by a pig! Leave the penny in this square.

4. If the penny lands on a white square, pick up the penny and wait for another turn.

5. When all the pink squares have been covered (all the pigs have escaped from their pens), the game is over!

More to do

Play this game using different animals. Try dinosaurs! When a penny lands on a dinosaur space, all yell, "Dinosaur out!" Pound the rug to make a noise like a dinosaur running.

Jump Fish

What to do

1. Sit by the fish tank. Look at all the colorful fish! Identify the colors. Explain that fish can jump out of their tank! They jump when no one is looking!

2. Have the children hide their eyes. The teacher takes off one fish from each matching pair and hides them around the room.

3. The teacher now says, "Jumping fish!" The children open their eyes and hunt for the fish that have jumped out of the tank.

4. When each child finds a fish, she sits on the rug. When all the fish have been found, take turns taping them in the fish tank. Tape each fish near one that it matches!

5. Play again! Choose a child to hide the jumping fish!

More to do

Give each child a sheet of white paper. They draw their own fish, color it and cut it out. Encourage many designs! When a child finishes, she tapes her fish on the fish tank. Now play a memory game. Have the children close their eyes. Take one of the fish away. Open your eyes! Who can tell which fish has jumped out of the fish tank?

Age level

4+

Objective

To improve color matching skills

Materials

White posterboard
felt pen
crayons
different colored construction paper
scissors
tape

Preparation

Draw a 2" border along the inside edge of the posterboard. This makes a fish tank. Have the children help color the inside of the tank blue. Draw 3" fish using a variety of colored construction paper. Draw two identical fish for each child. Cut them out and tape them in the tank. Tape the fish tank on the wall.

Bug Collector

Age level

3+

Objective

To learn to recognize colors

Materials

White posterboard
black felt pen
crayons
scissors

Preparation

Draw 2" circles on white posterboard. Draw two circles for each child. Draw another, smaller circle inside each of the circles (these are bugs). Draw eyes and feelers and legs! Color the bugs. Make matching sets. For example, make two blue bugs, two yellow bugs, two striped bugs, two spotted bugs. Cut the bugs out, cutting around the larger, outside circle.

What to do

1. Place the bug circles bug side down on the rug. Sit around the bugs. Sit down carefully. You are bug collectors. You are going to catch them, not squish them!

2. Sing "The Bug Song," to the tune of "The Farmer in The Dell."

   > Don't squish a bug, (Mash palms together)
   > Don't squish a bug, (Mash palms together)
   > I going to look so carefully, (Peer through circles made with thumb and forefinger)
   > To catch a little bug! (Gently clasp hands together)

3. Now the teacher chooses a bug collector. This child turns over two bug cards and identifies the bug colors. If the bugs match, he catches them (carefully picks them up and keeps them). If the bugs don't match, keep turning over cards until a match is made.

4. Then he chooses another child to be the bug collector. Continue until all the children have had a chance to be the bug collector.

More to do

For younger children use solid colors for the bugs. More complex designs can be used with older children. Have the children make their own bug on a sheet of paper and color it. Make many bugs! Cut them out and place them on the rug a few inches apart. Play music. The children take turns starting at one spot and walking carefully through the bugs. Don't step on one!

Hold on to Your Umbrellas—
An Exciting Look at the Weather

The weather is exciting! Snow is almost magical! Rain sparks a special energy in the classroom—an air of mystery and different sounds. The wind stirs a wonderful free feeling that makes you want to run with it! The warmth of the sun makes you feel relaxed and good inside. The weather affects us daily, and learning about the weather encourages an awareness of the world around us. Look outside! Are the branches of trees swaying? What is moving them? Does it look dark or light outside? Why? Does the pavement feel warm or cold?

Hold on to Your Umbrellas–
An Exciting Look at the Weather

	Monday	Tuesday	Wednesday	Thursday	Friday
Week 1	**4+ Weather Report** *To learn about the weather*	**3+ Weather Window** *To use imagination*	**4+ Weather Forecaster** *To learn what a weather forecaster does*	**3+ Sky Map** *To learn about weather conditions*	**3+ Thunder Claps** *To review different kinds of weather*
Week 2	**4+ Air Tricks** *To learn about air*	**3+ Windy Days** *To understand what wind is*	**4+ Cloudy Sky** *To find out what clouds are made of*	**4+ Stormy Weather** *To learn about weather changes*	**4+ Wind Dancing** *To learn how weather changes the Earth*
Week 3	**3+ It's Raining** *To learn about rain*	**3+ Shiver and Shake** *To learn how the body reacts to cold weather*	**3+ Snowy Ideas** *To find out how snow is formed*	**4+ It's Snowing** *To improve cutting skills*	**3+ Detective Snow** *To increase memory skills*
Week 4	**4+ Weather Proverbs** *To predict the weather with proverbs*	**4+ A Hot Riddle** *To understand why weather becomes warmer*	**4+ Warm Wishes** *To learn about warm days and cool nights*	**3+ Weather Blankets** *To review what was learned this month*	**3+ The Weather House** *To review different weather conditions*

Weather Report

What to do

1. Where is the weather? Have the children look outside. The weather is out-side! Does it look cold, hot, wet or windy? Now step outside. How does it feel? Look at the sky. Look at the ground, the trees and the grass. We can see and feel the weather!

2. Show the Weather Report chart on the wall. Explain that each square is a different day. The chart will show us how often the weather changes! Choose a child to be the weather reporter. This child looks out the win-dow or steps outside. Then she draws a picture of the weather on the chart with crayons. Choose a different weather reporter each day.

3. On subsequent days when the weather reporter has finished the picture, notice the picture drawn the day before. Is the weather the same? Is it dif-ferent?

4. At the end of the month count how many days were sunny! How many days were cloudy or rainy? Ask each child to tell the class about her favor-ite kind of weather.

More to do

Act out different weather conditions. Possible ideas are raining —pretend to open up umbrellas and walk around the classroom stepping over large pud-dles! A thunderstorm—clap your hands loudly and say boom! Then cover your ears! Try growling like the sound of thunder. Snowing—stand up, slowly wiggle your fingers and softly fall to the ground. You are quiet snow-flakes falling! Windy—sway gently back and forth. A hurricane—find some-thing to hold on to. Make wind noises and sway forcefully. A foggy day—try to look through the fog! Walk carefully around the room with your hands feeling for objects in front of you.

Age level

4+

Objective

To learn about the weather—it changes daily

Materials

Butcher paper
scissors
black felt pen
tape
crayons

Preparation

Cut a 5' x 4' sheet of butcher paper. Tape it on a wall. Draw eight vertical and six horizontal lines to form a chart. Draw thirty squares! Each square is a day of the month. Print the days of the week across the top of the chart. Tape the chart on the wall and title it, "A Daily Weather Report!"

Weather Window

Age level

3+

Objective

To encourage an awareness of the weather and to use imagination

Materials

Posterboard
scissors
wax paper
tape
empty spray bottle

Preparation

Make a large picture frame shape from posterboard by drawing an inch border along the edge. Cut out the inside and leave the frame! Cut wax paper to fit the frame. Tape it to cover the open area. This is a Weather Window!

What to do

1. Play the Weather Window Game! Sit in a circle and sing "The Window" song to the tune of "Pop Goes The Weasel."

   Wash the window (Rotate flat hand around and around)
   Round and round, (Rotate flat hand around and around)
   Spray the window cleaner, (Move first finger up and down)
   Brrrrr, it's getting cold outside, (Hug yourself, then shiver)
   Slam the window shut! (Clap hands on the word "slam")

2. Spin an empty spray bottle. When the spray bottle stops and points to a child, give this child the Weather Window.

3. He looks through the window and pretends to see outside. He describes the weather he sees!

4. Encourage imagination! If he sees snow, the teacher can ask him, "Do you see any snow on the roofs of houses?" If he sees rain, the teacher can ask him, "Are there large puddles on the ground?"

More to do

Make Weather Windows to take home. Cut out the window shapes for each child. Leave a large border. Pass out crayons so the children can color the borders. Have the children cut out a wax paper window. Some children may need help taping their wax paper window on their Weather Window.

Weather Forecaster

What to do

1. There are different kinds of weather all over the Earth. We only see the weather over our house!

2. There is a person who tells us what the weather is going to be. Who is this person? A weather forecaster! This person studies the weather and talks to different weather forecasters all around the Earth! Then they report the weather to you! Choose a child to be the weather forecaster in your town (class)!

3. Place the weather condition cards face down on the rug. Explain that there is a different weather picture on each card.

4. The weather forecaster chooses a weather card and studies it! No one else sees the card but the teacher. The weather is often a surprise!

5. The weather forecaster gives the weather report! She tells the rest of the class what she thinks the weather will be tomorrow (the weather condition on the card)!

6. Continue this activity over a few days.

7. Keep the weather cards to use in the activity, "Thunder Claps," later on this week.

More to do

Cut out one side from a large cardboard box. This is a television. Place the television on a chair. The cut side is facing the audience. The Weather Forecaster kneels behind the box. Her face is showing through the cutout side. The Weather Forecaster gives a weather report! She tells us what she thinks the weather will be tomorrow

Age level

4+

Objective

To learn what a weather forecaster does and that different weather conditions exist all over the Earth

Materials

White posterboard
scissors
felt pens
crayons
white construction paper

Preparation

Cut white posterboard into 3" x 4" cards. Cut out 11 cards. Draw a different weather picture on each one. Suggested pictures are the sun—draw a large yellow sun; light rain—draw five large raindrops; heavy rain—draw many raindrops; snow—draw snowflakes; hail—draw round circles; the wind—draw gray lines circling around and around; a tornado—draw funnel-shaped lines; fog—color the card gray; a rainbow—draw a large rainbow; lightning—draw an orange streak; and thunder—draw a large black cloud!

Sky Map

Age level

3+

Objective

To learn that the sky is a good clue about weather conditions

Materials

White paper
crayons
glue or tape
black yarn
scissors

Preparation

None

What to do

1. The sky is like a giant weather map! You can see what the weather is like or what is coming! You can see a rain storm approaching! Have the children draw rain storm pictures. After they draw clouds on their pictures, they glue or tape black strings of yarn on their clouds. Glue them close to each other. The distant rain storm is approaching!

2. Now have the children draw pictures of different weather conditions. Try to remember the different weather pictures in the previous activity, "Weather Forecaster."

3. Notice all the different sky pictures!

More to do

Place a sheet of white butcher paper on a table. Place crayons on the paper. Have the children draw a special weather picture together. If it is a sunny day, draw suns and color them. If it is a thunderstorm, draw the rain or the thunder or the lightning. Rainbows would make a beautiful picture! Draw different group pictures during the month and tape them on a wall.

Thunder Claps

What to do

1. Place the weather cards face up on the rug. Point to each one and say what they are. Then explain movements that are associated with each picture. The movements are important to the game of Thunder Claps! Suggested movements are the sun—make a large circle with both arms; light rain—pound lightly on the rug; heavy rain—pound hard on the rug; snow—make a circle by placing your thumbs and first fingers together. Slowly make the snowball fall from the sky; hail—pound your two fists together; the wind—weave gently back and forth; a tornado—move your bodies around and around; fog—push the air away from you with both hands; a rainbow—make a large arch shape in the air with one hand; lightning—make a long streak downward with one hand; and thunder—clap!

2. Turn the weather cards face down. Each child, in turn, chooses a weather card and turns it over. He looks at the card and does the suggested movement with the rest of the children. The cards with the sun, snow, wind, tornado, fog, rainbow and lightning are silent cards. The movements are made without any noise!

3. When a child turns over the black cloud, clap as quickly as you can! Then cover your ears. The child who turned over the thunder card mixes them up. This child begins the game again by choosing another weather card.

More to do

Have the children think of different movements to the weather cards, either silent or with noise. Play again with these movements! (The children will want to play this game many times!)

Age level

3+

Objective

To review of the many kinds of weather and to increase memory skills

Materials

Weather cards from the "Weather Forecaster" activity

Preparation

None

Air Tricks

Age level

4+

Objective

To learn about air

Materials

Straws
paper cups
water
balloon

Preparation

None

What to do

1. Why are there different kinds of weather? Air is one reason! Can you see air? Look between your fingers. Look under your foot! Clasp your hands together and peek inside. Air is everywhere, but you can't see it!

2. Have the children find a place in the room where there is air. They stand in their chosen place. The teacher walks around and agrees that there is air there!

3. Return to the circle. You can feel air! Blow on your palm. Move your hand back and forth in front of you. Have someone blow on the back of your head!

4. Give each child a straw. Blow through the straw on your hand. Air is traveling through the straw! Now give each child a paper cup. Pour an inch of water in each cup. Blow through your straw into the water. The bubbles that you see have air in them!

5. Blow up a balloon. Watch the air making the balloon bigger. Now release the balloon. The air is pouring out! It has made the balloon smaller.

More to do

Visit a place that has no air. Visit the moon! Have the children jump as high as they can. Pretend you have landed on the moon. Stand very still. Place your hand in front of you. You will not feel any wind! There is not any rain or snow on the moon either. In fact, it is impossible to breathe! Jump off the moon and land back on Earth. Take a deep breath. The air makes our Earth very special!

Windy Days

What to do

1. Give each child a sheet of construction paper. Have them fold it to make a fan. Then move the air in front of you to make breeze! Move your fan back and forth gently. Can you feel the air moving? You have made a gentle breeze.

2. Make a breeze on different parts of your body. Try your face, your ear, the top of your head, your elbow and your leg. Now fan the air quickly. You have made your breeze into a wind! Winds are stronger. The air is moving faster!

3. Now place a ball on the rug. Pretend it is the Earth. Give each child a crepe paper streamer. The streamers are the wind! Winds travel around the Earth. Play music. Have the children walk slowly around the Earth, waving their streamers. Stop the music! The winds have stopped. A wind can blow through your town and then travel on to blow somewhere else. Start the music! The winds have come back!

4. What does the wind do?

- It can make you feel cold! Shake and shiver!
- It can make it hard to ride a bicycle. Place your hands on pretend handlebars. Move your body forward and backward with great effort!
- It can push sailboats. Place the tips of your fingers together. Sway your sail back and forth on a wavy ocean.
- It can fly your kite! Pretend to hold onto the string of a kite.
- The wind can also carry flower seeds in the air. Pretend to be flower seeds blown by the wind. Fly slowly around the room. Now drop down. Grow into a beautiful flower where you have landed.

More to do

Act out different stages of wind. Pretend you are trees while you are acting them out.
- Calm air—nothing is moving. Stand very still.
- A gentle breeze—leaves are slightly moving. Slowly wiggle your fingers.
- A strong breeze—branches are moving. Sway your arms around.
- A strong wind—keep your feet on the ground. Sway your entire body back and forth with gusto!
- A storm—trees can fall over! Bend at the waist. Fall to the ground!

Age level

3+

Objective

To understand what wind is and what it can do

Materials

Crepe paper
construction paper
large ball
recorded music

Preparation

Tear a 3' crepe paper strip for each child.

Week 2
March

Cloudy Sky

Age level

4+

Objective

To find out what clouds are made of

Materials

Paper towels

Preparation

None

What to do

1. Where are clouds? In the sky! What are they made of? Find out! Give each child a paper towel. They find a place in the classroom to dust.

2. Show each other the dust. Clouds are made of dust! What else? Feel the warm air from a radiator or a sunny window on your hands. As warm air rises, it cools and it forms tiny drops of water. Divide the children into three groups. One group is the warm air. They sit on the rug. The second group is cool air rising. They sit on the rug and then slowly stand up! The third group are water drops. They slowly stand and turn around and around. A cloud is made of dust and drops of water crowded together!

3. Become a large cloud. Stand close together and form a shape! The wind pushes clouds and changes their shape. Move around together. Stay close while you move! Stop moving. Look at the different shape! Change shapes many times.

More to do

Go outside and lay down on your backs. Observe clouds! What color are they? Can you see them moving? Do you see any special shapes? Make clouds! Cut cloud shapes from white paper. Tape the clouds on a blue poster-board. Look at all the different shapes! What do some of them look like?

Stormy Weather

What to do

1. Show the blue posterboard. Does this look like a clear sky or a storm sky? If a storm was approaching, what would appear in the sky? (clouds)

2. Give each child a sheet of white paper and scissors to cut out one cloud and tape it on the clear sky. Now look at the clear sky—it's cloudy! If these were storm clouds, what color would they be?.

3. Distribute the gray and black crayons. The children choose a crayon and color in part of a cloud. Now there are a few dark clouds. It could rain!

4. What else is part of stormy weather? Offer a clue! It blows the rain clouds over town (wind). Make wind sounds. Before it gets too stormy, what do you think would be fun to fly in the wind (a kite)? Choose a child to be the wind. This child make wind sounds. The remaining children are kites. When they hear the wind, they gently fly around the classroom. Give other children a chance to be the wind.

More to do

Make kites. Have the children cut large kites shapes from white paper and color the kites. Tape a crepe paper streamer on the end of each kite. Punch a hole in the top of each kite. Thread a string of yarn through the hole. Run outside, waving the kites in the air.

Age level

4+

Objective

To learn about weather changes during a storm

Materials

Blue posterboard
tape
white paper
scissors
black and gray crayons

Preparation

Tape the blue posterboard on a wall.

Wind Dancing

Age level

4+

Objective

To learn how the weather changes the appearance of the Earth

Materials

Green crepe paper
scissors
white, pink and green balloons
scarf
red ball
white or silver yarn
recorded music

Preparation

Cut the green crepe paper into 3' streamers. Blow up the white, pink and green balloons. Have at least one balloon or object (see the activity instructions) for each child.

What to do

1. Explain that when the wind blows, there is movement outside! Brainstorm ideas on what outside objects move when the wind blows. Possible ideas are trees, flowers, grass, clouds, insects, spider webs, and even people!

2. Display the following objects and explain what each object represents. The green crepe paper is grass; the scarf is the wind; the white balloons are clouds; the green balloons are trees; the pink balloons are flowers; the red ball is a ladybug; and the white or silver yarn pieces are spider webs!

3. Each child chooses an object. Have the children sit on the rug with their objects. Play a slow tune. The music is a slow and gentle wind.

4. As the teacher calls each child's name, he stands up and dances with his object. If Jerome has the red ball, say, "Ladybug Jerome, dance with the wind!" Call each child to dance.

5. When the music stops, the wind has blown away. Sit down on the rug. Exchange objects! Start the music again and continue to wind dance.

More to do

Make a dancing spider to take home. Give each child a sheet of paper, scissors and felt pens. They draw and cut out their spiders. When each child finishes his spider, he cuts a string of yarn for a spider web. Tape the spider at one end of the yarn. Now swish the yarn through the air. You have a dancing spider!

It's Raining

What to do

1. Place the pan of water on the rug. Pretend the water is a large puddle of rain water. Give each child a turn to stir the rain water with the stick. It's fun to play in a puddle!

2. Where did the rain water come from? Demonstrate! Pretend a sponge is a large rain cloud. Carefully dip the sponge in the water. Now squeeze! The rain pours out of the cloud. Why? When the cloud becomes too heavy with water, it rains!

3. Now the children become the cloud! Give each child a balloon. They are large rain drops. Stand in a circle. The teacher sits in the middle of the circle and says the following chant:

   Rain cloud, rain cloud
   One-two-three,
   Drop your rain all over me!

   As the teacher says the chant, the children slowly raise their balloons over their heads. At the end of the chant, they drop their rain on the teacher!

4. Now choose a child to sit in the middle of the circle. This time all the children say the chant! After the child is rained on, he chooses the next child to sit in the middle.

More to do

Say "The Rain" chant. Use a different child's name each time.

_____, _____, knocking at my door, (Knock with fist)
Come inside and tell me more! (Open pretend door)
Teacher, teacher, it looks like rain (Wiggle fingers in air)
Close your open window pane! (Clap on "Close")
The coooooooooold wind blows (Sway arms back and forth)
Before it pours, (Wiggle fingers in air)
Who's that knocking at my door! (Knock with fist)

Age level

3+

Objective

To learn about rain

Materials

Large shallow pan
water
balloons
stick
sponge

Preparation

Fill the pan half full with water. Blow up the balloons.

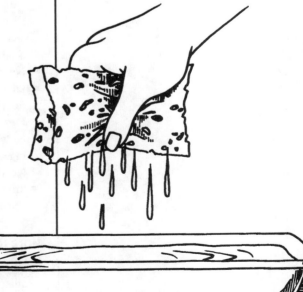

Shiver and Shake

Age level

3+

Objective

To learn how the body reacts to cold weather

Materials

ice cube
bowl
large sheet

Preparation

None

What to do

1. What do our bodies do in cold weather? They shiver and shake! Have the children shiver and shake! Shiver and shake from head to toe. All this movement makes our bodies feel warmer!

2. When you shiver and shake, your muscles tighten. Have the children squeeze their fists. Now place your hands on your shoulders. Squeeze your arm muscles. Sit with your legs straight. Squeeze your leg muscles. Squeeze your toes!

3. What part of the body feels the cold? Our skin! Pass an ice cube around in a bowl. Feel the cold ice on your skin.

4. We can put on extra clothes when the air is cold, or we can wrap up in a warm blanket! Sit close together. Place a large sheet over everyone. Cuddle up! You are trapping the air under the blanket. The air will become warm. Hold the blanket close. Don't let any of the warm air out!

5. How else can we stay warm in cold weather? Exercise! Lead the children in a five minute routine. The more you move your body, the warmer you will feel! Begin by standing. The following is a suggested routine.

- Rotate your neck. Rotate to the left and then to the right.
- Rotate your shoulders. Rotate them forward and backwards. Move them up and down.
- Wiggle your fingers. Shake your hands. Now place your arms straight out from your side. Rotate your arms forwards and backward.
- Place your hands on your hips. Bend from your waist. Bend from side to side and forward and backward.
- Shake your legs one at a time.
- Now sit down. Place your legs straight in front of you. Bend one leg at the knee. Straighten the leg and bend the other knee. Do this in a smooth motion, alternating knees.
- Flex your feet. Keep your heel on the rug and point your feet down and up.
- Now stand. Place your arms up in the air and stretch! Try to touch the ceiling.
- Now slowly march in place. March around the room! When you are through marching, sit on the rug. Take a deep breath. Your body is feeling warmer. If you went outside in cold air, you would feel more comfortable.

More to do

Form an exercise club! Think of a name for the club. Meet whenever the weather is cold! Choose an exercise leader each time. The exercise leader chooses a form of exercise. Suggestions are jogging around the play yard, dancing to music or running in place!

Snowy Ideas

What to do

1. Where does snow come from? It falls from clouds! Act out the formation of snow. Divide the children into two groups. The children in one group are rain drops. The children in the second group are ice crystals!

2. Have the children take off their shoes. Give each rain drop a blue balloon. Give each ice crystal a silver or white balloon.

3. Play music. The children dance around the classroom with their balloons.

4. Stop the music! Have each rain drop find an ice crystal. The teacher says, "It's snowing!" Now the pairs of children slowly fall to the ground. Each pair has turned into a snowflake! (When a water drop attaches to an ice crystal and falls from a cloud, it turns to snow!)

5. Play music again. Exchange the balloons. The water drops are now ice crystals. Ice crystals are now water drops! Continue to become snow-flakes.

More to do

Make snow pictures! Place white paper and crayons on the table. Have the children draw a picture of something outside, such as a street with houses, fields of flowers or a forest of trees. When the pictures are finished, place cut up sponges and white paint on the table. The children dip a sponge in the white paper and dab the paint over their pictures. The pictures will look like a recent snowfall has covered them. Look how white the world looks when it snows!

Age level

3+

Objective

To find out how snow is formed

Materials

Blue and white or silver balloons recorded music

Preparation

Inflate the balloons.

It's Snowing

Age level

4+

Objective

To learn about snowflakes and icicles and to improve cutting skills

Materials

Different sizes of white paper
markers
scissors

Preparation

Draw long skinny triangles on a sheet of white paper. These are icicles! Make an icicle sheet for each child. Fold small sheets of white paper in half and in half again. Make at least two folded sheets for each child.

What to do

1. Demonstrate how to make snowflakes! Cut out designs on the folded edge of a folded sheet of paper. Round off the corners and also make cuts on this side. Open the paper and you have a snowflake! (The older children can make more folds to make more intricate designs.) A snowflake is a tiny drop of snow. Each snowflake has a beautiful design!

2. Show an icicle sheet. Explain that icicles form in cold weather. Water drips from an object such as a tree branch. The water drop freezes and forms an icicle!

3. Place the folded papers and icicle sheets on the table. The children cut out snowflake designs and a sheet of icicles!

4. Print the children's names on the backs of their snowflakes and icicles. They can be used for the activity in the "More to do" section that follows.

More to do

Explain to the children that a surprise is coming! The children will have to go to sleep! Lay on the rug and close your eyes! While the children are sleeping, tape the paper snowflakes and icicles around the classroom. Tape some of the snowflakes on windows. Place cotton batting (snow) over objects in the classroom. Now say, "Wake up! It's snowing!" The children sit up and look around. Did anyone hear the snow falling? What color is the snow? If you touched the snow would it feel cold or hot? Pretend to take a walk in the snow. Walk quietly around the room. Notice how snow changes the shape of objects.

Detective Snow

What to do

1. Explain that each child will become Detective Snow! Walk slowly around the classroom. Notice the many things in the classroom, where the objects are located and their size. Talk about what you are seeing.

2. Now have the children close their eyes. The teacher places cotton batting (snow) over objects in the classroom that are pictured on the folded papers.

3. The children open their eyes. Objects have changed shape! Do they look different?

4. Choose a child to be Detective Snow. This child chooses a paper square from the box and identifies the picture.

5. Detective Snow tries to remember where she saw the object. She searches the classroom and uncovers the object. The teacher replaces the snow (cotton batting) over the object.

6. Now choose another child to be Detective Snow!

More to do

Play a memory game. Choose five small objects in the classroom. Place them a few inches apart on the rug. Study the objects. What are they? What colors are they? Now place a sheet or cloth over the objects. Remove one of the objects. Now say the magic words, "Abracadabra, Snowball!" Who can tell what object is missing?

Age level

3+

Objective

To increase perception and memory skills

Materials

White paper
scissors
felt pen
small classroom items
small box
cotton batting

Preparation

Cut white paper in half. Make a half sheet for each child. On each sheet draw a picture of a small object in the classroom, such as a block, a small toy, a box of crayons, a pot in the kitchen area, a small stuffed animal. Fold each sheet in half twice. Place them in a small box.

Weather Proverbs

Age level

4+

Objective

To predict the weather with weather proverbs

Materials

None

Preparation

None

What to do

1. By observing nature, we become more aware of our surroundings. The sky, plants and animals help us guess what the weather might be. Weather proverbs can help us guess!

2. Choose one or two proverbs a day to read to the children. Have the children repeat them line by line! Children enjoy repeating words and hearing their different sounds. Many of the proverbs are funny! See if you can guess what the proverb means. Afterwards, reveal their meaning!

Sky Proverbs

A ring around the sun or moon,
Means that rain will come real soon.
(The light from the sun or moon is surrounded by ice crystals. This means that stormy air is coming!)

Pale moon rains,
Red moon blows,
White moon neither
Rains nor blows!
(The moon can show us changes in the weather.)

When clouds appear like rocks and towers
The Earth is wet with frequent showers.
(Clouds can be pushed upward to great heights by cool moist air that surrounds them. Large rain drops form!)

Mackerel skies and mares' tails
Make tall ships carry low sails.
(A mackerel is a fish. When the clouds look like fish scales and thin mares tails this means a storm is coming.)

Rainbow in the morning,
Sailor's warning.
Rainbow at night,
Sailor's delight.
(A rainbow is surrounded by raindrops! In the morning, it means that rain is coming. A rainbow at night means the rain is moving away!)

Animal Proverbs

When frogs jump across the road,
They are looking for rain!

The first thunder of the year
Awakens all the frogs and snakes.
(Frogs can feel rain coming and become active!)

The goose and the gander
Begin to meander;
The matter is plain,
They are dancing for rain.
(Geese get nervous when they feel rain!)

Everything is lovely
When the goose honks high.
(If geese fly high, the weather is nice.)

Pigs carry sticks and straw before rain!
(Pigs feel nervous before it rains.)

If dogs and horses sniff the air,
A summer shower will soon be there.
(Animals feel a change in the weather!)

A fly on your nose, you slap and it goes.
If it comes back again,
It will bring a good rain!
(Flies become more active before it rains.)

Plant Proverbs

Open crocus
Warm weather;
Closed crocus
Cold weather.
(When the air is warm, many flowers
*   open. When the weather is cold, they*
*   close.)*

The daisy shuts its eye before it rains.
(It closes its petals.)

Onion skins very thin
Mild winter coming in;
Onion skins thick and tough
Coming winter cold and rough.
(The onion's thicker skin will protect it.)

Sap from the maple tree
Flows faster and faster,
Before the wet and rainy showers.
(Rainy weather can cause a rise of
*   water under the ground. This can*
*   push the sap out of trees!)*

Silver maple leaves
Turning over before it rains.
(Cold weather can bring a wind. The
*   wind can flip the leaves over!)*

Trees are light green
When the weather is fair;
They turn quite dark
When a storm's in the air!
(The leaves are turned over by wind.
*   The trees appear dark.)*

The ash before the oak
Choke, choke, choke,
The oak before the ash,
Splash, splash, splash.
(If ash trees bud before the oak trees,
*   there will be little rain. The trees will*
*   need a drink! If oak trees bud before*
*   the ash, there will be plenty of rain!)*

More to do

Draw a picture of some of the proverbs! Attach a copy of the proverb to each picture. Make up some proverbs of your own with the children! Draw a picture of these proverbs. The teacher can print the proverb on the papers.

A Hot Riddle

Age level

4+

Objective

To understand why weather becomes warmer

Materials

White paper
felt pen
tape
a yellow crayon

Preparation

Print clues about the sun on separate sheets of paper. Make a paper clue for each child. Tape the papers clue side down on a wall. Tape them in a row. Draw a large yellow sun on a sheet of paper. Tape it sun side down next to the last clue. Possible sun clues are it is round; it is bright yellow; sometimes it can look orange; it is in the sky; it can hurt your eyes if you look at it; it is very hot; it can make you feel warm; it is larger than the Earth; it does not move!

What to do

1. Sit near the paper clues on the wall. Explain that there is a clue behind each paper. The clues will tell us about something that affects the weather. The last paper has the answer!

2. Choose a child to pick a clue. It can be any of the papers except the last one. The teacher reads the clue. The child guesses! Accept all guesses. If the right answer is guessed, do not reveal the answer! Reveal the answer only after all the children have had a turn to pick a clue and make a guess.

3. When all the children have had a turn, show the sun picture! Explain that the sun gives us warm weather. Sit close to the sun picture. When the weather is warmer, the Earth has moved closer to the sun.

4. Now have everyone sit away from the sun. If you move away from the sun will you feel warmer or colder? Do you like warm weather or cold weather the best?

More to do

Explain that the sun is so hot that you cannot touch it. Play Hot Potato with the sun! Sit in a circle. Play music. Pass a yellow balloon around quickly. When the music stops, the child holding the sun is out. Continue until one child is left holding the sun. Play music. Tap a yellow balloon in the air with your hands. The sun is hot! Don't catch the balloon! Tap it quickly back up in the air.

Warm Wishes

What to do

1. It's daytime! Look outside. Does it look light or dark? What is everyone wearing? Do you see any animals? Do you hear many noises, such as cars or people talking? We do more things during the day. The sun keeps the air warm. The weather is more comfortable!

2. Sit on the rug. Now pretend it's nighttime. At night, it looks darker! How are you dressed at night? Are people inside or outside more? It's colder at night. The sun is not shining on us!

3. Say the "Warm Wish" chant. Slap your knees while you say the chant!

   I'm hot, I'm hot,
   The sun is very bright,
   I'm wishing for the sun to set,
   To cool the night!

4. Now say the chant again. This time leave out the word night! Choose a child to replace the word with something he would like the night to cool. It could be a puppy, an elephant, a tree or a friend!

More to do

Have the children draw two pictures. Draw one on yellow construction paper. Use felt pens. Draw anything you like! This is a warm daytime picture. Use black construction paper for the second picture. Draw with colored chalk. This is a nighttime picture!

Age level

4+

Objective

To learn about warm days and cool nights

Materials

None

Preparation

None

Weather Blankets

Age level

3+

Objective

To help children remember the many things they learned about the weather

Materials

Butcher paper
crayons
scissors
tape

Preparation

Cut butcher paper into 2' x 3' rectangles. These are weather blankets. Make one for each child.

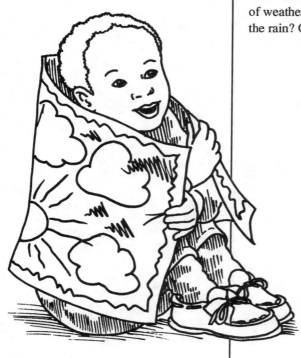

What to do

1. Place the weather blankets on the tables and the floor. Place crayons by each weather blanket. Each child chooses a blanket to color.

2. Encourage the children to make beautiful blankets! Use many colors. Add designs. Draw a weather picture on the blanket.

3. As each child finishes her blanket, tape it on a wall. When all the blankets are on the wall, sit on the rug. Ask each child to remember something she learned about the weather.

4. As each child remembers something about the weather, she takes her blanket off the wall and covers herself!

5. After all the children are wrapped in their weather blankets, take them off and fold them up so the children can take them home! The weather blanket can remind them of the many things they have learned about the weather.

More to do

Have the children bring a blanket from home. The teacher also brings in a blanket! Cuddle up with your blanket on the rug. Encourage a nice quiet brainstorm about the weather by asking questions. What is your favorite kind of weather? Why? Has anyone seen lightning? Has anyone taken a walk in the rain? Children will enjoy this cozy time to talk and share ideas.

The Weather House

What to do

1. Place the box on the rug. This is the Weather House! Sit around the Weather House. Explain that everyone can help the weather come outside where it belongs!

2. First, we have to get the weather's attention. Pound on the rug! Now we need to trick the weather into coming outside. Say "The Weather" chant!

   Come out, come out, come out today,
   Come out or I shall run away!

3. Give the jar of marbles to a child. The teacher now says, "I think I hear the weather!" The child shakes the jar of marbles. The weather is ready to come out! The child with the marbles opens the paper door and lets the weather out. She tells everyone the kind of weather that has come out of the Weather House!

More to do

Have the children make a Weather House to take home. They draw a house shape on a sheet of paper (younger children may need help). Add designs on the houses. Color the houses! Cut a scrap of material to cover the door. Tape or glue the left side of the material over the door. Let the weather out when you get home!

Age level

3+

Objective

To review different weather conditions

Materials

Cardboard box
scissors
paper
tape
jar
marbles

Preparation

Cut two windows and a door on one side of the box. Cut a piece of paper to fit over the box door. Tape the left side of the paper over the door. It should open like a door! Place a few marbles in a jar.

Can You Recognize an Orangutan— Exploring the Animal World

What is more appealing to children than a playful puppy? To children, the animal world is a never-ending source of wonder. Finding a caterpillar under a leaf is like finding gold! Trying to catch a bird in the grass is always a temptation! Children are naturally drawn toward animals, so teaching children about animals is a natural! Animals are very much like ourselves. The Earth is their home too. They breathe, eat and sleep. Many live in families. Some animals share our homes! Our pets especially need our care and attention. Children who are taught these concepts will respect animals and treat them with kindness., since children are naturally inclined to nurture and protect their world. The animal world is a large and important part of this Earth. Animals touch all of our lives. The first day you visit the animal world you will hear rumblings that precede explosions of fun. Animals and children have connected!

Orangutan?
Exploring the Animal World

	Monday	Tuesday	Wednesday	Thursday	Friday
Week 1	**3+ Bright Ideas** *To introduce animals*	**3+ Animal Groupies** *To learn about different kinds of animals*	**3+ House Pets** *To learn about tame animals*	**3+ Baby Gorilla** *To learn that animals have babies*	**4+ Quiet Camouflage** *To understand the word "camouflage"*
Week 2	**4+ Happy Habitats** *To learn about habitats*	**4+ The Wild Grass** *To understand the grassland habitat*	**3+ The Great Big Elephant** *To learn about the elephant*	**4+ The Heavy Hippo** *To learn about the habits of the hippopotamus*	**3+ Bounding Kangaroos** *To learn about the kangaroo*
Week 3	**4+ Mountain Homes** *To explore the mountain habitat*	**4+ Baby Bears** *To learn about mother and baby bears*	**3+ Nice Wolf** *To understand the wolf*	**3+ The Wobbly Fawn** *To learn about fawns*	**4+ Eagle Eyes** *To appreciate the beautiful bald eagle*
Week 4	**4+ Love Me, I'm En-dangered** *To understand what "endan-gered" means*	**5+ The Jungle House** *To learn about the jungle habitat*	**3+ The Creep-ing Tiger** *To learn about the tiger*	**3+ Pretty Parrots** *To discover how parrots communicate*	**4+ Orange Orangutan** *To learn about the orangutan*

Bright Ideas

What to do

1. Place the yellow squares sun side down on the rug. Ask the children questions. Who can tell me something about animals? When a child gives you an answer, she can turn over a bright idea!

2. Accept all answers! Encourage "brainstorming" as long as you can by listening to the answers and asking more questions. Are animals alive? Where do animals live? What do animals eat? Do animals sleep when they feel tired? Do they live in families? Do animals take care of their babies? Can animals swim? Can some animals be our pets? What is a wild animal? What animals live in trees? What animals can swim? What animals live in the jungle? Can an animal feel cold at night? Can an animal feel hungry or lonely? How does an animal show it is happy? Do we share the Earth with animals?

3. If there are more ideas than yellow squares, clap at the additional Bright Ideas!

More to do

Send a yellow square home with each child. Encourage the children to remember a bright idea about animals and tell someone at home. Make bright ideas for different topics of study! When learning about the ocean, use blue posterboard. When learning about the weather, use white for a snowstorm! When learning about the Earth, use brown or green. Always send a Bright Idea home!

Age level

3+

Objective

To introduce animals

Materials

Yellow posterboard
scissors
black felt pen

Preparation

Cut the posterboard into 3" squares. Draw a sun on each square. These are Bright Ideas!

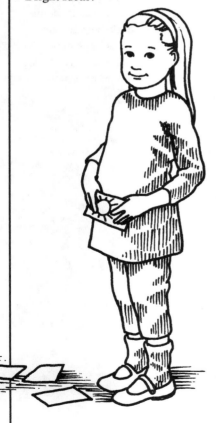

Animal Groupies

Age level

3+

Objective

To learn about different kinds of animals

Materials

Magazines
scissors
posterboard
tape

Preparation

Cut out pictures of animals from different animal groups, such as land animals, sea animals, birds, insects and reptiles. Cut out squares of posterboard. Mount one picture from each animal group on a square of posterboard.

What to do

1. Place the mounted pictures on the rug a few inches apart. Talk about these animals. They are all a part of the animal world! Say the name of each mounted animal. Say something special about each animal. For example, a rabbit is a land animal. The starfish lives in water. The parrot is a bird. Parrots can fly! The snake is a reptile. It does not have any legs. The ladybug is an insect. Insects have six legs.

2. Give each child an equal amount of animal pictures. The child to the right of the teacher begins. He shows one of his animal pictures. First, he identifies the animal. Second, he places the animal on one of the posterboard squares of animal groups (land animal, sea animal, bird, insect or reptile).

3. The next child takes a turn. If her picture is a crocodile, she places it on the reptile posterboard. Continue until all the children have shown and grouped all their pictures.

4. Look at all the animals with which we share the Earth! Each belongs to the animal world. If you could meet one of these animals, which one would you choose?

More to do

Give a stuffed animal to a child. This child names an animal! Then he passes the stuffed animal to another child. This child thinks of a different animal. Continue until everyone has held the stuffed animal and named one! Play the game, "Going To The Zoo!" Have each child, in turn, say, "I went to the zoo and I saw a _____." Each child adds to the animal names that were said before. Play it again! Use a different sentence, such as, "I went to the pet store and I bought a _____."

House Pets

What to do

1. Sit near the posterboard house. Place a selection of felt pens on the rug. Explain that tame animals live inside our house. They are called House Pets!

2. Name different kinds of house pets. Possible ideas are dogs, cats, birds, fish, hamsters, mice, snakes, lizards, guinea pigs, rats, frogs, turtles, even tarantulas!

3. Now draw House Pets! Each child chooses a felt pen and draws a house pet inside the posterboard house. Print the child's name by her pet.

4. Talk about each animal that is drawn. If a dog is drawn, ask what kind it is. Do you have a dog? What does a dog eat? Where can a dog sleep? If a dog gets dirty, can you give it a bath?

5. Continue until each child had drawn a House Pet. Look at all the House Pets! If you could have one of these House Pets, which one would you bring home?

More to do

Have the children draw a large house on a sheet a construction paper. Younger children may need help. Tear out house pet pictures from magazines and glue them inside the houses. Learn about pet care. Place a stuffed animal on the rug. If it is a dog, talk about how to care for a pet dog. Act out possible ways! For example, feeding: Pretend to scoop dog food into a bowl. Call your dog: Slap your knees and make kissing noises! Bathing: Turn on the water. Hold on to your nose and spray! Squirt on dog shampoo and rub it into your dog's hair. Rinse it out. Exercise: Tell the dog to sit! Place a collar around the dog's neck. Attach a leash and walk your dog around the classroom! Showing love: Take turns holding the stuffed dog and stroking it. Give it a hug. Your pet needs to know that you love him.

Age level

3+

Objective

To learn about tame animals

Materials

White posterboard
felt pens
tape

Preparation

Draw a large house on the posterboard. Tape it on a wall.

Baby Gorilla

Age level

3+

Objective

To learn that animals have babies and care for them

Materials

Brown construction paper
tape
black felt pen

Preparation

Roll a small sheet of brown construction paper into a tube. Tape it together. Draw two large eyes on one end of the tube. This is a baby gorilla! Make one for each child.

What to do

1. Animals have babies just like we do! Many animals are loving parents. They take good care of their babies. Place the baby gorillas on the rug. Each child chooses a baby gorilla.

2. Have the children pretend they are mother or father gorillas! Act out different things that a mother or father gorilla and a baby do together. Find a safe place for your baby gorilla! Then pretend to gather branches to build a nest. Now lay down by your baby. Rest together!

3. Demonstrate how a mother or father gorilla carries a baby. Kneel on the rug. Hold your baby gorilla in one hand close to your chest. Now walk on your two knees and one hand! Stay close together. Gorillas travel in groups!

4. Now the baby gorillas are bigger. Lay on the rug. Place your baby gorilla near you. Let your baby gorilla move away from you to play. Give the baby a gentle push! Your baby gorilla is moving too far away! Pull him back!

5. Baby gorillas like to ride on their parents' backs. Rest on all fours. Try to balance your baby on your back! Give the baby a piggyback ride!

6. Baby gorillas love to swing! Pick up your baby gorilla and swing the baby back and forth and around and around. Throw the baby in the air and catch the baby!

7. Take your baby gorillas home. Show everyone at home the things that a mother or father gorilla does with a baby.

More to do

Play mother or father and baby with different kinds of monkeys. Use orange paper to make a baby orangutan. Use black paper for a chimpanzee. Use white paper for a snow monkey from Japan!

Quiet Camouflage

What to do

1. What does the word camouflage mean? It means that you blend in with your surroundings. You wear the same colors. It is hard to see you! Explain that the children will be hiding in tall green grass to observe animals. Does anyone have the color green on? What other colors are you wearing?

2. Show the area with the green crepe paper strips. Tape a small strip of crepe paper on each child. Now you will blend in with the tall grass!

3. You need to move quietly to watch animals. If they hear you, they will move away! Practice walking quietly in a circle. Place your feet softly on the rug. Do not talk. Move toward the wild grass!

4. Quietly sit behind the wild grass. Give each child an animal viewer. You are ready to observe animals! Look through your animal viewer. Look for the wild animals in the classroom.

5. The teacher can direct some of the observations. Who can see the giraffe? Who can see a very large animal? Where is the parrot? Whisper when you talk!

6. Take your animal viewers home. See if you can find animals around your house!

More to do

Take a walk outside with your animal viewers. Sit in a quiet spot. Try to find animals through your viewers. Lay on your back. Look at the sky with your animal viewers! Lay on your stomach. Do you see any animals in the grass? When you see an animal, quietly tell the person near you!

Age level

4+

Objective

To understand the word "camouflage" and to learn how to observe animals

Materials

Green crepe paper
scissors
tape
yarn
magazines
construction paper
animal stickers

Preparation

Cut long strips of crepe paper. These are blades of grass. Cut at least ten. Hang the strips of paper from the ceiling or tape them on a string of yarn and tape the yarn between two chairs. Cut out wild animal pictures from magazines. (Calendar pictures are also great!) Tape these pictures around the room. Roll construction paper into tubes. Place an animal sticker on each one. These are animal viewers! Make one for each child.

Happy Habitats

Age level

4+

Objective

To learn that animals live in special places called habitats

Materials

Butcher paper
scissors
crayons
tape
wooden blocks

Preparation

Cut three large sheets of butcher paper. Draw a different habitat on each sheet. Draw tall wild grass on one sheet (grassland habitat). Draw mountains on the second sheet (mountain habitat). Draw a jungle with tall trees on the third sheet (jungle habitat). Tape these sheets on a wall a few yards apart.

What to do

1. Have the children help build a large square on the rug with wooden blocks. This is a house! Sit inside the house. Say the word, "habitat!" The children repeat it.

2. Explain that a habitat is a special place where animals live. Different animals live in different habitats. Their special habitat provides them with food and shelter. Where do we live (in a house, in an apartment, on a farm)? Your home is where you feel the most comfortable.

3. Visit the three habitats in the classroom. Visit the habitat with the wild grass. This is a grassland habitat! Special animals live here. Name some animals that live in the grasslands. Have the children repeat the animal names. (They will enjoy this!) Grassland animals are the elephant, the rhinoceros and the kangaroo!

4. Visit the mountain habitat. Many animals live in the mountains! Have the children repeat some mountain animals. These are the bear, the wolf, the deer and the bald eagle.

5. Visit the jungle habitat. Certain animals live in the jungle. Jungle animals are the tiger, the parrot and the orangutan!

More to do

Choose a child to name an animal. Now say "The Habitat" chant! Insert the name of this animal in the second line. Slap your knees while you are saying the chant!

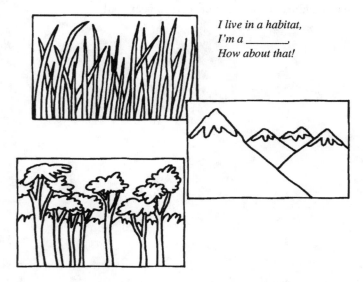

I live in a habitat,
I'm a _____,
How about that!

The Wild Grass

What to do

1. Who has grass near their house? What color is the grass? It is tame grass! Tame grass is cut before it grows too long. Have the children pretend to be tame grass. Sit on your knees. Sway slowly from a gentle breeze. Tame grass is short. There are no wild animals living in tame grass!

2. Some wild animals live in wild grass! Wild grass is tall. It has never been .cut! Stand tall. You are wild grass! Sway a little more in the breeze.

3. Now sit at the table. Explain that wild grass can be green, gold, red and brown! Draw a picture of wild grass using wild grass colors! Make your wild grass tall!

4. Encourage the children to draw animals hiding in their wild grass. Draw a pair of eyes in your wild grass. This is a wild animal hiding in the wild grass! Draw a patch of gray on your wild grass. This is an elephant! Draw black spots. This is a cheetah in the wild grass! Draw orange and black stripes for a tiger!

More to do

Say "The Wild Grass" chant! Slap your knees as you say the chant. Clap when you say the words, "Behind you!"

An elephant, a rhino and a kangaroo,
Walking in the wild grass,
Behind you!
Don't go running for they might catch you,
An elephant, a rhino and a kangaroo!

Age level

4+

Objective

To understand the grassland habitat

Materials

White paper
crayons

Preparation

Place white paper and a variety of crayons on the table.

The Great Big Elephant

Age level

3+

Objective

To learn about the elephant

Materials

Yarn
scissors
recorded music

Preparation

Cut a 3' string of yarn for each child.

What to do

1. Elephants are the largest land animals on the Earth! They live together in herds. They follow the oldest elephant! Pretend the class is a herd of elephants! Choose the oldest elephant. This elephant leads the herd around the classroom. Walk slowly on your hands and knees. Remember how big you are! Move carefully near the furniture and the other elephants!

2. Elephants greet each other by touching trunks. Continue to move around on your hands and knees. When you see a friend elephant, lift up your trunk (your arm) and touch trunks!

3. Elephants make different sounds. They scream, trumpet, grunt, rumble and purr. Try making sounds for each one!

4. Go on an elephant walk! Tie a string of yarn around each child's waist. Leave a foot of string hanging in the back. Play music. Form a line and hold onto the string of the elephant in front of you. The strings are the elephant's tails! Play music. Sway back and forth as you walk around the room. First the teacher leads the elephants, then the children take turns leading the elephant walk.

More to do

Elephants can pick up very small objects with their large trunks. Place napkins around the room. Place a peanut on each napkin. Have the children move on their hands and knees. Find a peanut! Use your nose to find one. Elephants smell with their trunks! When you find a peanut, pick it up with your trunk and place it in your mouth!

The Heavy Hippo

What to do

1. The hippo is a very heavy animal! It has tiny eyes, tiny ears, a large body and a very large mouth! Have the children spread their arms as wide as they can. This is a hippo with its mouth open!

2. Hippos spend most of the day in water. The water from a river protects their skin from the hot sun. Hippos can remain under water for five minutes. Go on a five minute hippo swim! Begin by walking on your hands and knees towards the river. Walk slowly. The hippo is very heavy! Take a deep breath. Slide down on your stomach. You are now under the water!

3. Move slowly around the room. You are walking on the river bottom! Look at all the fish in the river. They are not afraid of you. They know you will not eat them!

4. Lay down on the river bottom. Take a short rest. Five minutes has passed! It is time to surface. As you reach the top of the river, you see a mud hole! Roll around in the mud. The mud cools you off also!

5. Now you are hungry! Look for some crunchy grass to eat. Pretend to chomp on grass. Eat plenty! A hippo needs to eat 88 pounds of grass a day!

6. Night is coming. Rest on the grass. You will do the same thing tomorrow!

More to do

Say "The Hippo" chant! Say it slowly. Slap your knees in a slow rhythm.

> *Hippo-pot-a-mus,*
> *Don't get in a fuss,*
> *You can have your swim,*
> *Just....jump....in! (Clap your hands)*
>
> *Hippo-pot-a-mus,*
> *Don't get in a fuss,*
> *Find a muddy hole,*
> *Roll and roll and roll! (Rotate your fists around and around)*
>
> *Hippo-pot-a-mus,*
> *Don't get in a fuss,*
> *Eat your greens tonight,*
> *Take a giant bite! (Open your arms wide and then clap)*

Age level

4+

Objective

To learn the habits of the hippopotamus

Materials

Colored construction paper
scissors
magazines
tape

Preparation

Cut out fish shapes from different colored construction paper. Cut out fish pictures from magazines. Tape the fish shapes and pictures around the room.

Bounding Kangaroos

Age level

3+

Objective

To learn about the kangaroo

Materials

None

Preparation

None

What to do

1. When kangaroos are together, they are called a mob. Be a mob of kangaroos! When a kangaroo sits, it leans back on its tail to help it balance. Try it! Sit on your knees. Place one hand behind you on the rug. Lean on it! You are leaning on your tail!

2. When a kangaroo moves slowly, it crawls on all fours. Try the kangaroo crawl! Position yourself on your hands and knees. Move your front legs forward and together, like a little hop. Now move your hind legs forward and together. Kangaroo crawl around the room!

3. When a kangaroo wants to go faster, it bounds! It bounds on its hind legs only. It is a great hop! Do the kangaroo hop! Stand and hop once, as far as you can!

4. Sing "The Kangaroo" song to the tune of, "Do You Know the Muffin Man." As the children sing it, they hop around the room. When you finish the song, the kangaroos shake hands with each other. Sing it again! This time, crawl around the room!

   How do you do, my kangaroo,
   How do you do, my kangaroo,
   How do you do, my kangaroo,
   How do you do today!

More to do

Explain that when kangaroos are born, they are as small as a lima bean. After they are born, they crawl into their mother's pouch. When they get bigger, they jump out of the pouch! Pretend to be baby kangaroos. Give each child a string of yarn about 5' long. They each make a circle with the yarn on the rug. This is your mother's pouch! You were just born. Climb into your mother's pouch. You are called a joey! Now you have grown bigger. Jump out of your pouch and look around. When something frightens you or you get tired, jump back in your pouch!

Mountain Homes

What to do

1. Sit at the table. Have each child draw a mountain shape on a piece of paper (the younger children may need help doing this step). Explain that many animals live on a mountain. Some live near the top of the mountain. The children draw a line across the mountain approximately two thirds of the way up. This is a timber line. Above the timber line, you can find snow! Below the timber line, the trees grow. Have the children draw a forest of trees below the timber line.

2. Put snow on the mountains! Spread glue on the top of the mountain and stick cotton balls on the glue.

3. When you have finished putting the snow on, look closely at the mountain. Do you see any animals? They are well hidden in the forest. That is part of their camouflage! Explain that everyone can become mountain climbers. We will soon find and learn about some animals that live on the mountain.

More to do

Mountain animals often walk on narrow ledges! Cut a sheet of butcher paper 6' long and 2' wide. Place it on the rug. This is a narrow mountain ledge! Take off your shoes and walk across the ledge. Walk carefully! You don't want to fall down the mountain! Now cut a foot off the width. Walk this mountain ledge! Cut off six inches. Who dares to walk this narrow ledge?

Age level

4+

Objective

To learn about the mountain habitat

Materials

Glue
paper cups
crayons
white paper
cotton balls

Preparation

Pour glue into the paper cups. Make a glue cup for each child. Place the paper and crayons on the table.

Baby Bears

Age level

4+

Objective

To learn what mother bears teach baby bears

Materials

Brown or green crepe paper
scissors
tape
gray construction paper
bug stickers
different colored construction paper
crayons

Preparation

Cut crepe paper into 3' strips. Tape them low on the wall a few feet apart. These are trees! Cut gray construction paper into rock shapes. Place a bug sticker on each one. Put the rocks around the classroom. Draw a fish on a sheet of construction paper. Cut it out. Make a tree, a rock and a fish for each child. The children can help cut out the fish!

What to do

1. The children are baby black bears. The teacher is the mother bear! You live on a mountain and walk on your hands and knees. Walk on your hands and knees!

2. When baby bears are scared, they will quickly climb a tree. The bears hear a growl. It is a mountain lion! The children find a paper tree to sit by. Pretend to climb the tree. Stay in your tree until mother bear tells you it is safe. Mother bear stands tall on her hind legs to show the baby bears it is safe. (The teacher can stand tall!)

3. Mother bear shows her baby bears how to turn over a rock. Use your paw to flip over a rock! If there is an insect under the rock, eat it! Have the children find a rock. Flip over your rock with a paw. Did you find an insect? If you did, pretend to eat it!

4. Place the paper fish on the rug a few feet apart. They are swimming in a stream! Mother bear demonstrates how to catch a fish! Wade out into the stream. Look down into the water. When you see a fish, try to grab it with your paw! When you catch a fish, pretend to eat it. Try to catch another one!

5. Baby bears trot after their mother wherever she goes. The children follow the teacher around the room! When the mother bear lays down for a rest, the baby bears go off and play. When the mother bear wants to call them back, she huffs. The teacher huffs and the baby bears return to the mother bear.

More to do

Say "The Baby Bear" chant! After the teacher says a line, the children repeat it.

> *Baby, baby, oh baby bear,*
> *Where's your mother, oh mother bear?*
> *Have you got a sticker stuck in your hair?*
> *Baby, baby, oh baby bear!*
>
> *Baby, baby, oh baby bear,*
> *Where's your mother, oh mother bear?*
> *There's honey on your nose and don't you care,*
> *Baby, baby, oh baby bear!*
>
> *Baby, baby, oh baby bear,*
> *Where's your mother, oh mother bear?*
> *She's looking for you, oh baby bear,*
> *Baby, baby, oh baby bear!*

Nice Wolf

What to do

1. The class is a pack of wolves! A wolf pack shows affection. They are very caring. They gently paw each other. Have the children make a fist like a paw. Gently stroke each other! Wolves like to cuddle, so cuddle close together.

2. Wolves like to sit erect. Sit on your knees with your back straight. They can smell things that are far away. Everyone sniff! They hear well with their pointed ears. Place a straight finger by each ear. Turn your head back and forth and tell about a sound you hear.

3. Wolves communicate by their body position and by sound. They talk by howling to each other. Howl! Now stand on your hands and knees. Put your head high. This means, "I am the boss!" Now crouch low. Put your head down. This means, "I know!"

4. Wolves stay close to their families. Choose a father wolf. This child goes off to hunt for food. Now choose two mother wolves. One goes off and hunts for food too. The other mother stays and cares for the baby wolves. The remaining children are baby wolves. They play together on the rug! (The two wolves hunting for food search for the rabbit pictures on the wall! They bring the rabbits back to the pack!)

5. Wolves sleep out in the open, even when it snows. It's snowing! Curl up in a tight ball. Pull your legs and head close to your body. Close your eyes and remain very still. Now you will feel warm.

6. The children can take turns being the two wolves who hunt for food. For each hunt tape the rabbit pictures in a different place.

More to do

Make up a wolf story! The teacher starts the story. "Once there was a wolf and he lived in the forest. He liked to take morning walks. One day he walked down a path and past a stream. As he sat down to rest, he looked up and saw a _____." The child to the left of the teacher fills in the blank. Possible answers are trees, rocks, flowers, skunks, deer, a bear. Continue the story, pausing occasionally to give other children a turn to fill in another blank.

Age level

3+

Objective

To learn about and understand the wolf

Materials

Paper
felt pen
scissors
tape

Preparation

Draw two small rabbits. Cut them out. Tape them around the room.

The Wobbly Fawn

Age level

3+

Objective

To learn about fawns and camouflage techniques

Materials

Yellow construction paper
scissors
paper

Preparation

Cut large leaf shapes from yellow construction paper. Make one for each child.

What to do

1. Pretend to be fawns. Move around the room on all fours. Make your legs wobble! You have just been born. It is hard to walk.

2. When deer hear a rustling sound, they know something is near! The teacher is the mother deer. He or she rustles a piece of paper. The fawns find a hiding place in the room. Lie as quietly as you can! When the danger has passed, the mother deer walks around and taps each fawn on the shoulder. Return to the rug. Don't forget to wobble!

3. When the mother deer looks for food, she hides her fawns where they will be camouflaged. Have the fawns lay down. Curl up in a tight position. Lay very still! You are in a bunch of light colored leaves. They look like the color of your skin! The teacher places a yellow leaf on each child. The teacher says, "While I am gone, you will be safe. An enemy will not see you!" The teacher walks around the classroom and then returns to the fawns and removes their camouflage. It is safe to play!

4. A deer stands very still when it smells danger. Have the children stand on their arms and legs. Do not move! When the teacher sees a fawn moving, the fawn sits down. See who remains still the longest!

More to do

Make a fawn to take home. Give each child a lump of clay. Roll a tube shape for the body. Roll a smaller one for the neck. Pinch the neck on the body. Now pinch out a nose and tail! Add pointed ears. Stick four toothpicks in the body for thin wobbly legs. Color a paper plate yellow. The yellow is a nest of light colored leaves. Place the fawn on its camouflage!

Eagle Eyes

What to do

1. Bald eagles are big beautiful birds! Their wing span is eight feet! Give each child two strips of brown paper. Hold one in each hand. These are your brown wing feathers. Now stretch your arms wide. Flap your long wings! Fly gracefully around the room.

2. Bald eagles build nests high on a mountain at the top of a tall tree. Have the children find a place in the classroom for their nest and sit on it.

3. Pretend you are a bald eagle egg! Curl up in a ball. Explain that when you hatch, the first thing you will see is the blue sky. The teacher walks around the classroom and taps a child on the back. Your egg has cracked! Push out of your egg and look up. Can you see the sky? Help each child come out of her egg.

4. Bald eagles can see for miles around! They have very sharp eyesight! They can see a snake on the ground when they are flying high. Place the crepe paper snakes on the rug. Each child flies around the room once, swoops down and grabs a snake! The snake is delicious food for the bald eagle!

More to do

Draw a large eagle shape on a sheet of white construction paper. Draw one for each child. Cut thin triangles from brown and white construction paper. These are feathers. Glue feathers on your bald eagle! Glue white feathers on its head and tail. Glue brown feathers on its body. Color its eyes and beak yellow. Take your beautiful bald eagle home and hang it up high. Let it remind you to be strong and free!

Age level

4+

Objective

To learn about the strong and beautiful bald eagle and to learn to follow directions

Materials

Brown construction paper
scissors
crepe paper

Preparation

Cut strips of brown construction paper 2" wide by 2' long. These are wing feathers. Cut crepe paper into 1' long strips. These are snakes!

Love Me, I'm Endangered!

Age level

4+

Objective

To help children understand the word "endangered" and to encourage a caring attitude towards animals

Materials

Pink construction paper
scissors
felt pen

Preparation

Cut large heart shapes from pink construction paper. Make one for each child. Print the name of an endangered animal on each heart. Suggested names are Amazon parrot, tiger, orangutan, giant panda, mountain gorilla, rhinoceros, sea turtle, yellow-eyed penguin, monk seal, crocodile, pygmy hippopotamus, snow leopard, manatee, white whale, blue whale!

What to do

1. Place the paper hearts word side down on the rug. Ask the children, "What is an endangered animal?" (It is an animal that is close to extinction. It needs love and protection in order to survive!)

2. Explain that the name of an endangered animal is printed on each heart. Choose a child to turn over a heart. Read the name of the endangered animal. Have the children repeat the name. Print the name of the child on the heart! Continue until each child has turned over at least one heart.

3. Now remove the hearts. Pretend to place a large invisible box on the rug. Explain that there are endangered animal babies in the box. Carefully lift one out of the box. Identify it! If you find a baby gorilla, give it to the child who chose the gorilla heart! Hold it gently! Continue finding baby endangered animals in the box and giving them to the children.

4. They hold the baby animals gently and rock them in their arms. Give it a kiss. These animals need our love and protection.

5. Each child takes home their heart and their invisible endangered baby!

More to do

See who can remember the name of their special endangered animal! Draw a large Earth on a posterboard. Draw as many hearts on the earth as there are children in the class. The children tell the teacher the name of their endangered animal. Then they draw a happy face in one of the hearts! Title the picture, "Love Me, I'm Endangered!"

The Jungle House

What to do

1. Make a jungle! Explain that a jungle is going to grow on the paper! A jungle is like a very large house with many floors. On the first floor, or bottom of the jungle, is a layer of leaves and small plants. The children take turns painting large leaves at the bottom of the paper.

2. The second layer of the jungle is full of small trees! Take turns painting small trees above the layer of leaves and plants.

3. The third layer of the jungle is full of medium-sized trees. Now paint medium-sized trees above the small trees.

4. Large trees grow in the fourth layer of the jungle. The tops of these trees spread out like an umbrella! Paint them wide at the top.

5. Above the large trees, you can see the giant trees! Paint giant trees sticking out of the large treetops.

6. Jungles are full of many beautiful animals and colors! The tiger and parrot and orangutan are some of the beautiful animals. They are also endangered! Stand back and admire the jungle.

More to do

Say "The Jungle" chant! Slap your knees quietly in rhythm.

> *A tiger and a parrot and orangutan,*
> *Got together and softly sang,*
> *Love us in the jungle, a bee bop bang;*
> *A tiger and a parrot and orangutan!*

Age level

5+

Objective

To learn about the jungle habitat

Materials

Butcher paper
scissors
tape
green paint
bowl
paintbrushes

Preparation

Cut a large sheet of butcher paper. Tape it on a wall. Pour green paint in a bowl.

The Creeping Tiger

Age level

3+

Objective

To learn about the tiger, a large cat

Materials

Black construction paper
white chalk
two sponges

Preparation

Have each child draw white lines on a small sheet of black construction paper. This is a zebra!

What to do

1. The tiger is a large cat! How does a cat sound that lives in a house? "Meow!" How does a tiger sound? "RRRRRRoar!"

2. Tigers have thick pads on the bottom of their paws. They help the tiger move quietly! Sit in a circle. Take turns holding sponges in your hands. They are pads on your paws! Walk on your hands and knees around the outside of the circle. As the children move quietly around, say, "Tiger, tiger, round and round, creeping quiet on the ground!"

3. When tigers see an animal they want to eat, they creep low and quiet. They pounce on the animal at the last minute! Place the zebras around the room. Each child finds a zebra he wants to catch. Back away from the zebra. You have to catch it by surprise! Slowly creep towards it. Stay low! When you are close to the zebra, pounce on it!

4. The creeping tiger is tired! Lay on your backs. Yawn. Stretch! You are ready for a nap.

More to do

When the sunlight hits the leaves and grass in a jungle, it makes a light and dark design. The stripes on a tiger blend in! Tape a large sheet of butcher paper on a wall. Draw long black and orange stripes down on the paper. Fill the paper with tiger stripes! Now tape strips of green crepe paper on the butcher paper. Can you see the tiger behind the tall jungle grass?

Pretty Parrots

What to do

1. Place the tree branches on the rug. Stand on your tree branch! You are a wild parrot in the jungle. The tree you are sitting in is your territory. It is your special space! Now have the children fly off their branch. Fly around the room together. Parrots fly close together and will often touch wing tips! As you are flying, touch another parrot's wing tips (touch someone's fingers).

2. Parrots communicate through their body positions. Act them out!
   Get Away— Stand up. Hold up one foot and growl!
   I'm very upset— Shift your weight from one foot to another.
   I'm afraid —Place your arms (wings) against your body. Stand tall and thin. Stretch your neck upward!
   Watch out— Danger: Place your arms against your body. Lean forward and stretch and thin as you can. Now squawk loud to warn other parrots.
   I'm sleepy—Draw up one leg. Drop your chin. Flutter your eyes!

3. Place the paper flowers on the rug. Parrots are attracted to color! They eat bright jungle flowers. Choose a flower and pretend to eat your colorful flower!

More to do

Play Parrot Talk! Parrots can learn how to talk! Choose a child to be the bird trainer. The remaining children are the parrots. The bird trainer says a few words. The parrots repeat the words! Take turns being the bird trainer. Try making funny sounds!

Age level

3+

Objective

To learn about the large and beautiful parrots of the jungle and to learn how they communicate

Materials

Butcher paper
scissors
crayons
colored construction paper

Preparation

Cut butcher paper into strips 2' long and 6" wide. These are tree branches! Make one for each child. The children color their tree branches. Print their name on their branch. Cut circles from different colored construction paper. These are flowers.

Orange Orangutan

Age level

4+

Objective

To learn about the orangutan and to learn the habits of apes

Materials

Green yarn
scissors
tape

Preparation

Cut a string of yarn long enough to reach two opposite walls, or two pieces of heavy furniture. Cut additional strings of yarn 3' long. Tape the long string of yarn between two walls about 5' off the ground. Tape or tie the smaller strings of yarn across the yarn so they dangle down. Tape them about two feet apart. This is a jungle vine!

What to do

1. Orangutans are orange apes! Pretend the class is a family of orangutans. You are quiet apes and very affectionate. Sit close together. Sit quietly and smile at each other. You are happy apes. You love your jungle home!

2. An orangutan is always changing his facial expression. Look at each other! Move your face around to form different expressions.

3. Orangutans like to play around trees and swing from hanging vines. Stand at one end of the jungle vine. As you walk to the other end of the vine, hold on to each dangling vine. Move in a swaying motion. You are a swinging ape!

5. You are tired from such a busy day! Make a nest to sleep in. Pretend to climb a tree! Bend branches down to make a place to sit. Pull off leaves and place them on your branches. Turn around and around on your nest to pack the leaves together. Now sit down. Move around until you are comfortable. Now grunt! You are ready to sleep.

More to do

The orangutan likes company! Place sheets of paper and crayons on the table. Have the children draw a picture of one of the animals they learned about. Print the names of the animals on the papers. Tape them on the wall for all the children to see.

Jump In, Hold On and Let's Go—
Fun Rides with Transportation

Let's go! But how? Transportation offers miles of choices! After experiencing the activities in this chapter, the children will begin to think about different and creative ways to get from here to there. How did you get to school? by car? bicycle? Did anyone take a helicopter or a hot air balloon? Did you ride a camel? Why not?

Learning about transportation helps children identify many things that they see around them. How things work and why they are used are fascinating to a child's mind. How is a bicycle different from a school bus? If you wanted to get somewhere fast, would you take a plane or a boat? Are train tracks built on land or water? Many machines and animals that are used to travel are a mystery to children, which is another reason this topic is so appealing. Instead of walking to the playground, pretend to paddle a canoe, roller skate or ride a motorcycle. Transportation involves movement, going places, machines, noises and adventure!

In this chapter children will learn about land travel. Show them pictures of different cars. Design a car. Name your car! Talk about water travel. Take an imaginary submarine ride! Draw pictures of what you saw. Cover the pictures with wax paper for a watery view. Talk about air travel. Take a plane ride! Visit Hawaii! When you land, wear paper leis that you have made. Show pictures of the surrounding scenery. Get ready. Get set. Move! Transportation will take the children on exciting adventures.

Jump In, Hold On and Let's Go!
Fun Rides With Transportation

	Monday	Tuesday	Wednesday	Thursday	Friday
Week 1	**3+ Surprise Walk** *To introduce the word "transportation"*	**3+ Follow the Road** *To learn how to get to different places*	**3+ Pedal Pushers** *To learn about bicycles*	**4+ Bumpity Bump School Bus** *To learn about a school bus*	**4+ Here Comes a Train!** *To explore trains*
Week 2	**3+ Surfboard Boogie** *To learn about surfboards*	**4+ Boat Floats** *To discover that boats float*	**4+ Sailing Along** *To learn about sailboats*	**5+ My Home at Sea** *To learn that some people live on boats*	**4+ Submarine Ride** *To learn about submarines*
Week 3	**4+ Let's Go Ballooning!** *To become familiar with hot air balloons*	**3+ Glider Riders** *To find out about gliders*	**3+ Destination: Hawaii!** *To understand airplane travel*	**4+ Classroom Skydiving** *To learn about skydiving*	**4+ Rocket Ship Trip** *To understand the power of a rocket ship*
Week 4	**5+ Horsing Around** *To learn that animals are a form of transportation*	**3+ The Humpity Bumpity Camel** *To discover that camels are a form of transportation*	**3+ Make-Ups** *To use imagination*	**3+ Match-Ups** *To recognize similarities*	**3+ The Song Review** *To review the forms of transportation*

Surprise Walk

What to do

1. How could we get to school if there were no cars, no buses and no bicycles? Offer a clue. Look at your feet!

2. We can use our bodies to move from one place to another. This is the simplest form of transportation. Say that long word with the children!

3. Brainstorm ideas on different ways our bodies can move or transport us! Possible ideas are running, crawling, hopping, rolling and walking on our knees!

4. Try the different ways of moving!

More to do

Have the children take off their shoes and socks. Trace each child's left and right feet on separate sheets of paper. Each child colors in his or her own two feet. Hang the feet on a wall. Title the wall, "Feet Transportation!"

Age level

3+

Objective

To introduce the word "transportation"

Materials

None

Preparation

None

Follow the Road

Age level

3+

Objective

To learn that transportation takes you to a different location

Materials

Butcher paper
scissors
felt pen
small toy car

Preparation

Cut a 4' long sheet of butcher paper. Draw a 2" wide road down the length of the paper.

What to do

1. Place the paper road on the rug. Choose one child and draw a house at the left end of the road. This is the child's house.

2. We use transportation to take us from one place to another. Draw another house at the other end of the road. This is a friend's house. Who would like to visit a friend?

3. Each child draws another house, pushes the toy car from their house to their friend's house and back again!

4. When everyone has had a turn, ask, "What kind of transportation did you use to get to your friend's house?"

5. Leave the paper road out for the children to continue playing.

More to do

Cut out pictures of cars. Each child tapes his or her car along the road. If you run out of road space, tape the cars parked on the outside of the road. Then draw pictures along the road, such as trees, flowers, animals, people and other houses. Secure the paper road on a wall. Title it, "Car Transportation!"

Pedal Pushers

What to do

1. Place the picture on the rug, bicycle-side down. Tell the children that there is a type of transportation under this paper. Ask them to guess what it is! Offer clues. One or two people can ride on it. It has handlebars. You push it with your legs. It has a small seat. A bicycle! Show the picture after you have given all the clues. Who has ridden on one? Where have you gone on it?

2. Pretend to ride a bicycle! Sit on the rug. Grab the handlebars. Place your legs straight out on the rug. Move your knees up and down, one at a time. You are pushing bike pedals. Let's go! Start out slow. Gradually increase your speed. Ride up a hill! Lay on your back and pedal. Ride down a hill. Lean forward and stop pedaling. Coast down! To slow down push on the brakes. You do not need an engine to ride a bicycle. You supply the energy!

3. Sit at the table. Give each child a sheet of paper. Place crayons on the table. Ask the children to draw a picture of their house. When they are finished, tape the finished pictures around the classroom.

4. Now stand on the rug. Pretend to get on a bicycle! Pedal around the classroom and visit the homes of your friends! Honk as you pass each house!

More to do

Give each child a sheet of paper. Have them draw a road across their papers. Cut out pictures of bicycles from magazines. Glue the bicycles along the roads. Take turns riding a bicycle outside around the bike path. If you do not have a bike path, use chalk or sticks to make a road.

Age level

3+

Objective

To learn about bicycles

Materials

Magazines
scissors
construction paper
tape
white paper
crayons

Preparation

Cut out a picture of a bicycle. Tape it on a small sheet of construction paper.

Bumpity Bump School Bus

Age level

4+

Objective

To learn about a school bus

Materials

None

Preparation

None

What to do

1. Sing "The School Bus" song. Sing it to the tune of "Old Mcdonald Had a Farm."

   Riding a school bus all day long,
   Bumpity bump we go. (Bang two fists together)
   Riding the school bus all day long,
   Bumpity bump we go. (Bang two fists together)
   Stopping near and stopping far, (Clap to the left and then to the right)
   Wave to _____ in the car, (Name a child in the class)
   Riding a school bus all day long, (The child named above sings the
        rest of the song)
   Bumpity bump we go!

More to do

Draw a border around a sheet of white paper. This is a bus window! Talk about what you might see from a bus window. Ask the children to draw something they might see as they look through their window.

Here Comes a Train!

What to do

1. Give each child a felt material square and scissors. Make a train! Cut along the lines to separate the long strips. These are your train cars! Join the cars together with tape.

2. When a child's train is taped together, she decides which end is the engine and caboose. At the engine end, draw two headlights!

3. When the trains are finished, bring them to the train tracks. Notice that the tracks look like a road! What is missing? Draw the railroad ties across the tracks. Continue until you have completed the train tracks.

4. Choose a train conductor! This child places her train by the train station. Everyone says, "Here comes a train!" Then she pushes her train along the train track! When her train goes through the tunnel, everyone says, "Choo choo!" and pulls down on an imaginary cord!

5. As the trains make their journeys across the posterboard, talk about trains! Where is your train going? What is your train carrying? people? fruit? animals? If you were on the train, where would you like it to be going? If you built a train track through a mountain, what would you call it?

More to do

Give each child a large sheet of paper. Place crayons on the table. Draw train tracks! Add scenery around the track. Draw trees, mountains, houses, flowers, lakes and grass! Take the pictures home with the felt trains.

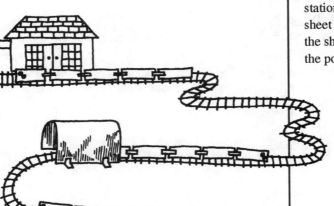

Age level

4+

Objective

To learn about trains, including that trains are the longest form of transportation

Materials

Small squares of felt for each child—use different colors
green posterboard
black felt pen
construction paper
tape
scissors

Preparation

Draw lines 2" apart down the felt squares. These are train cars. Draw a winding train track around the posterboard. Leave out the railroad ties; the children will add these. Draw a train station at one end of the tracks. Push a sheet of construction paper together at the short ends. Tape the short ends on the posterboard. This makes a tunnel!

Surfboard Boogie

Age level

3+

Objective

To learn about surfboards

Materials

Butcher paper
scissors
crayons

Preparation

Cut out 3' long surfboard shapes for each child.

What to do

1. Give each child a paper surfboard! Explain that surfboards come in many different colors and designs. Have the children place their surfboard on a flat surface. Place a pile of crayons by each child. Color in the surfboards! Create beautiful designs!

2. Print each child's name on the surfboards. When the surfboards are finished, stack them in a pile. Sit together on the rug. Talk about the surfboard. It is a form of transportation on the water. Does it have an engine? How does it move? How many people ride on one?

3. Pass out the surfboards. Demonstrate how to carry it! Place it under one arm, holding onto a long side. Now walk in place with the surfboards. You are headed for the beach!

4. Take off your shoes. Place your surfboard on the "sand" (rug). Carefully step on it, placing one foot in front of the other. Bend your knees slightly. Hold your arms out for balance. Sway back and forth with the wave. Now you are ready to put your surfboard in the water!

5. Pick up your surfboard. Yell, "Surf's up!" Run in place into the "water." Place your surfboard in the water. Lay on it and paddle with your arms. You are trying to catch a wave! Here it comes! Sit on your knees. Now stand in correct form. Ride that wave! Ride it all the way back to shore. Don't fall off! When you reach the shore, jump into the water. Grab your surfboard and catch another wave!

More to do

Play ocean music while you ride your surfboards. Play slow music for a calm ocean. Play fast paced music for a rough ocean! Instead of butcher paper, make surfboards out of cardboard or posterboard. Surf at home!

Boat Floats

What to do

1. Place the pan of water on the rug. Explain that the water is ocean water in a place called a harbor. It is a special place for boats! Place the sponge pieces on the rug. These are boats! Each child chooses a boat and places it in the harbor. The harbor is a safe place for boats. There are no waves or large sea animals in the harbor!

2. Place the wooden block in the pan. This is a dock. You walk on the dock to get to a boat! Place the twig people on the rug. Each child chooses a twig person, walks the person along the dock and places the person on one of the boats.

3. Look at the people on the boats. They will ride on their boats out of the harbor and into the ocean. Where can they go on their boats? Brainstorm ideas! Possible ideas are to an island, across the ocean, fishing!

4. Take one of the boats out of the water and place it on a dish. Is the boat moving? What does the boat need to move? Now place it back in the water. Boats are built to float. They provide transportation on water!

5. Send home a twig person and a piece of sponge with each child. Float your boat at home! Find a harbor to float it in. Find an object at home to make the dock!

More to do

Demonstrate how a boat can sink! Place a sponge in a pan of water. Explain that the boat is pushing down on the water. Place your hand in the air with your palm down. Move your hand down towards the rug. Now move your other hand, with palm up, to meet the hand moving down. When your hands meet, stop them! The bottom hand is the water pushing up on the boat. It keeps the boat from sinking! Now place a heavy rock on the sponge. What happens? The boat sinks! The boat is pushing down on the water with great force! The water cannot hold it up! Place your palms together. Push your top palm down and make your bottom hand sink to the rug. Take turns placing the rock on the boat and sinking it!

Age level

4+

Objective

To learn that boats float and move on water

Materials

Large shallow pan of water
sponges
scissors
one large block
2" twigs (twig people)
dish

Preparation

Fill the pan half full of water. This is the ocean! Cut the sponges in half.

Sailing Along

Age level

4+

Objective

To learn about sailboats—they run on wind and muscle power

Materials

White construction paper
felt pen
scissors
empty milk cartons
straws
tape
crayons
water table or large pan of water
masking tape

Preparation

Draw a large triangle on a sheet of white construction paper and cut it out to make a sail. Make one for each child. Cut milk cartons 3" from the bottom. These are the sailboats!

What to do

1. Make sailboats! Place the cut milk cartons on the table. Pass out straws. Tape the straw against the inside of the carton to make a mast on the sailboat!

2. Put these aside. Pass out the paper sails. Place crayons on the table. Explain that sails come in different colors and designs. Some sails have a rainbow on them. Some have circles or stripes. Some are all one color! Ask the children to color their sails!

3. When each sail is finished, tape it to the mast. Now the sailboat is ready to sail!

4. The children take turns placing their boats in the water table or a large pan of water. Before your boat can sail, you need to hoist up your sails. Pull down an imaginary line with your hands, alternating your hands as you pull. Your sail is going up! It takes muscle power to run a sailboat! Now place your sailboat in the water. Do you need an engine to start your sailboat? All you need is the wind! Pretend your hand is the wind. Gently push your sailboat in the pan.

5. Explain that people name their boats! Ask the children to think of a special name for their sailboat. Print their sailboat name on a piece of masking tape and stick it on their sailboat.

More to do

Place colored construction paper and felt pens on the table. Ask the children to draw and cut out members of their family. Place your family members in your boat. Give them a boat ride! Build a large boat bottom on the rug with wooden blocks. Or build the boat near a wall and lean a broom against the wall for a mast. Cut out a large sheet of butcher paper in the shape of a sail. Color it and then tape it on the broom. Now sit together in the sailboat. The teacher can lead everyone in the song, "Sail Your Boat!" Sing it to the tune of, "Row Row Row Your Boat."

> *Sail, sail, sail your boat,*
> *In the deep blue sea,*
> *Make a wish and catch a fish,*
> *A sailor I will be!*

My Home at Sea

What to do

1. Some people live on a boat instead of a house. Their boat is called a _____? Ask the children to guess what it's called! When the guesses are finished, slowly turn over the pictures on the wall. A houseboat!

2. Make houseboats! Place colored construction paper and the magazine pictures on the table. Give each child a glue cup, scissors and an empty shoe box.

3. Brainstorm what is found in a houseboat. Possible answers are a living room, a kitchen, a few bedrooms, a closet and a bathroom. Suggest ways to make the inside of your houseboat. Cut the construction paper into squares or large strips. Slightly fold a side and glue it onto the inside of the shoe box. You can make walls this way! Cut the paper to make tables and beds. Make a television! Make a refrigerator! Glue the house pictures in the various rooms. Be creative!

4. When the houseboats are finished, add the engine! Tape a small paper cup on the outside of a short end of the box. Tape it with the opened end up.

5. Now name the houseboats! The teacher can print the names on each child's houseboat.

More to do

Sing "My Houseboat" song to the tune of, "The Farmer in The Dell."

My houseboat on the sea,
My houseboat on the sea,
Who will come and live with me,
In my houseboat on the sea!

Daniel come and live,
Daniel come and live,
Daniel come and live with me,
In my houseboat on the sea!

Age level

5+

Objective

To learn that some people live on boats

Materials

Magazines
scissors
white paper
felt pens
tape
glue
small paper cups
different colored construction paper
shoe boxes

Preparation

Cut out magazine pictures of objects found inside a house, such as chairs, tables, pictures, lamps, ovens and beds. Draw a large picture of a house on a sheet of paper. Draw a large picture of a houseboat on another sheet of paper. Tape them on a wall picture side down. Tape the houseboat first! Pour glue into paper cups. Make a glue cup for each child.

Submarine Ride

Age level

4+

Objective

To become aware of transportation under the water

Materials

Paper tubes—ask parents for tubes from foil or plastic wrap
straws that bend at one end
scissors

Preparation

None

What to do

1. Explain that a submarine is a form of transportation that moves under the water. People ride on submarines! Does it sound fun? Let's find out!

2. Pass out a paper tube to each child. This is a submarine! Give each child a straw. Make a hole in the top of the tube (young children will need help making the hole) and push the straw into the hole. The bendable end should be sticking up. This is a periscope! You look through a periscope to see what is going on above the ocean.

3. Take turns taking a dive. If there is a Wendy in the class, say, "Captain Wendy, dive!" Then Wendy holds her submarine above her head (the surface of the ocean) and dives under, bringing her submarine down under the water (down to the rug). Say, "Captain Wendy, surface," and then she brings her submarine back up above her head to the surface of the ocean.

4. Say "The Submarine" chant.

   Down down down in the water, (Slowly move your hand down)
   Whoosh whoosh whoosh in the sea, (Rub your palms together)
   Dive dive dive to the bottom, (Touch the floor)
   A submarine ride for me! (Clap three times)

   Float float float by a whale, (Move your hands slowly in front of your body)
   Whoosh whoosh whoosh in the sea, (Rub your palms together)
   Sink sink sink to the bottom, (Touch the floor)
   A submarine ride for me! (Clap three times)

   Up up up to the surface, (Move your hand slowly up in the air)
   Whoosh whoosh whoosh in the sea, (Rub your palms together)
   Open the hatch, pull up the latch, (Place one palm upward and slap it with the oth...
   A submarine ride for me! (Clap three times)

More to do

Make submarine pictures! Cut white paper into large circles. These are portholes! Brainstorm ideas of what you might see under the ocean. Draw underwater pictures on the portholes. When the children finish, tape a circle of wax paper over each porthole picture. This will give them a watery look!

Let's Go Ballooning!

What to do

1. Sit together on the rug. Show the balloon. Ask the children if they think they can ride a balloon? They can ride a hot air balloon!

2. Explain that hot air rises! Move your hand upward. This is a layer of hot air! Now the air is cooling! Slowly move your hand downward.

3. Place the pieces of cloth on the rug. Each child chooses a piece of cloth. The cloth is flat on the ground and looks likes a balloon when there is no air in it. Give each child a small carton. This is the basket that you ride in. How do you blow hot air into the balloon so it rises?

4. Explain that there is a stove above the basket. It has a heater that makes hot air. A fan on the heater blows the hot air into the balloon. What happens to the balloon? The hot air fills the balloon and blows it up! Pretend to be the fan. Blow out five strong puffs of air!

5. Now attach your balloon (the piece of cloth) to your basket. Make a hole in each corner of the cloth and in each corner of the carton, if necessary. Have the children use four pieces of yarn to attach the cloth to the basket. The balloon is ready to take off!

6. Hold the hot air balloons up and slowly lift them into the air. The baskets will also rise! Pretend you are in the basket! Fly the hot air balloons around the room.

7. Call the children back to the rug. Hold your hot air balloon in the air. How does a hot air balloon land? Reduce the hot air that is blowing into the balloon. Pretend to turn down the fan. Now bring the balloons down a foot. Turn the fan down more. Bring the balloons down more! Gradually bring the balloons to the ground.

8. What a wonderful ride! What did you see so far above the ground? What looked tiny? What did you see close up?

More to do

Make paper hot air balloons to hang on the wall. Cut out large balloon shapes from butcher paper. Have the children color the balloons! Explain that hot air balloons come in many colors and designs! Cut squares from brown construction paper. These are baskets! Cut strings of yarn. Tape a string of yarn on each side of a basket. Now tape the other ends of the yarn to each side of the balloon. Tape the paper hot air balloons on a wall. Title the wall, "Let's Go Ballooning!"

Age level

4+

Objective

To become familiar with hot air balloons and to learn that warm air rises

Materials

Yarn
scissors
small squares of cloth approximately 6" x 6"
tape
blown-up balloon
small empty cartons such as strawberry cartons

Preparation

Cut yarn into 10" strings. Cut four for each child. Collect empty cartons. The children can bring them from home.

Glider Riders

Age level

3+

Objective

To learn the difference between a glider and an airplane

Materials

Four straws, popsicle sticks or pencils
tape
yarn
scissors

Preparation

Tape two straws together to form a cross. This is an airplane! Draw a black spot on the tail end to make an engine. Tape two more straws together to form another plane shape. This is a glider. It has no engine! Cut a 1' string of yarn. Attach the two planes together from the tail of the airplane to the front of the glider. Cut two 3' strings of yarn.

What to do

1. Place the two strings of yarn on the rug 6" apart, parallel to each other to form a runway.

2. Place the plane and the glider on the runway. The plane needs an engine to move it! The glider needs air! Move your hand around in the air. Move it quietly. A glider moves silently and gracefully.

3. Choose a glider rider! This child slowly moves the airplane down the runway. As the plane nears the end, she picks up the airplane and the glider. Now she moves both planes around in the air. The airplane needs to pull the glider high into the air.

4. After a minute, the teacher cuts the yarn that connects the two planes. The teacher flies the plane back to the runway. The glider rider flies the glider around the room.

5. When she brings the glider back down to the runway, tie the planes together again. Choose another Glider Rider!

More to do

Make gliders to take home! Color a sheet of white paper. After the papers are colored, demonstrate step by step how to fold the papers to form a glider. After they are folded, staple the bottom edge together. Place sticky stars on them for an added design!

Destination: Hawaii!

What to do

1. We are going to fly to Hawaii! What is the quickest way to get there? An airplane!

2. But you need a ticket to get on an airplane. Each child cuts out a ticket and finds the seat on the airplane that matches his or her ticket number.

3. When everyone is seated on the airplane, buckle up! It's time for take off! The teacher pretends he or she is the pilot. Talk into the loud speaker (your fist). Announce your name, your destination and possible weather conditions flying to Hawaii.

4. The teacher sits in front. Start the engine. Shake a jar of marbles! Make a "beep, beep" noise as a signal to fasten seat belts. As you leave the runway, tilt your heads back. You are ascending!

5. During the flight, the pilot can announce air conditions. Pretend to experience turbulence—jiggle in your seats! The plane is tilting to the left—lean to the left! The plane is descending—lean forward! As you lean forward, announce that you can see the island of Hawaii below.

6. As you land, make screeching noises. These are the airplane brakes! Once you leave the airplane, sit on the rug and show island pictures!

More to do

Bring a large cardboard box to the classroom. A good source for these boxes is your local market or appliance store. Cut out two wings of posterboard. Cut a slit on two sides of the box. Slide the wings through the slits and tape the ends down inside the box. Draw an instrument panel inside the box. Attach a paper plate for a steering wheel. Take turns flying the airplane!

Age level

3+

Objective

To understand airplane travel

Materials

Sheet of construction paper
scissors
felt pen
tape
jar of marbles
nuts
pictures of island scenery—a good source is from library books or calendars

Preparation

Cut a sheet of construction paper into 2" squares. Draw a small ticket shape on each square. Make one for each child. Place them on a table. Print a different number on each ticket! Arrange chairs side by side in two rows. This is the airplane! Place a single chair in front of the rows for the pilot seat. Tape numbers on each chair that match the ticket numbers.

Classroom Skydiving

Age level

4+

Objective

To learn about skydiving and what a skydiver needs to practice

Materials

Small stool or chair
large cardboard box
jar of marbles

Preparation

None

What to do

1. Explain that some people enjoy jumping out of airplanes with a parachute. They are skydiving!

2. The children will get a chance to "skydive." Each child will get a chance to jump out of the classroom "airplane." First we must practice the correct way to land. The teacher can demonstrate! The teacher stands on the stool or chair and jumps off. As the teacher jumps, he or she pulls an imaginary cord on his or her chest. This is the rip cord. It opens the parachute! Land on your feet with both knees bent. Then slowly fall to the rug, rolling over onto one side. Take turns standing on the chair. Hold each child's hand as they jump! Release their hand as they fall to the rug.

3. Now it's time to skydive! Place the cardboard box on the rug. This is the airplane! Place the stool or chair next to the box. This is the wing of the airplane. Choose a skydiver! The skydiver sits in the box. Shake the jar of marbles as the plane takes off. The pilot (another child or the teacher) is flying the plane. The skydiver is waiting to reach a certain height! When the teacher says, "Jump," the skydiver steps out of the box and onto the stool or chair. Jump! Don't forget to pull the rip cord! Continue with the other children.

More to do

Play recorded music. Dance with scarves! Pretend the scarfs are parachutes. Swirl them in the air. Open them up and dance. Throw them in the air and let them fall on you! Parachutes, like scarves, fall gracefully through the air.

Rocket Ship Trip

What to do

1. Make rocket ships! Place colored construction paper on the table. Place strips of tape on the edge of the table with most of the tape sticking out. This makes it easy for the children to pull the strip off.

2. Ask each child to choose a sheet of construction paper and put sticky stars on it. Roll the sheet to make a paper tube and tape the ends together. This is a rocket ship body!

3. Place the rectangular pieces of paper on the table. Each child chooses one and forms a cone shape. Tape the ends together. Now tape the cone over one end of the rocket ship body. Now the rocket ships are ready to blast off!

4. Bring all the rocket ships to the rug. Stand the rocket ships on Earth (the rug). Brainstorm ideas about rocket ships! They will get you to a destination faster than any other form of transportation. They are the most powerful form of transportation. Astronauts travel in rocket ships. They can travel into outer space!

5. Let's travel to the moon! Pass the jar of marbles around. Each child gives it a few strong shakes to start his or her engine. Now count down from ten to one. On the count of one, everyone says, "Blast off! "

6. Slowly move the rocket ships off Earth. Continue moving them in an upward direction. Stand up and level it off! Slowly move the rocket ships around the room. Move it silently. Space is very quiet!

8. When the teacher says, "I see the moon!" slowly head towards the paper moon on the wall. When your rocket ship has passed the moon, head back to Earth (the rug). Slowly land the rocket ships back on Earth.

More to do

Build a rocket ship! Collect three or four large cardboard boxes. Tape them on top of each other with heavy duct tape. Paint the boxes! Cut out circles from colored construction paper. Tape the circles on the boxes. These are control buttons! Place sticky stars on the boxes. Make a giant cone shape from posterboard or butcher paper. If the boxes are large enough, cut an opening on the bottom box large enough for a child. Take turns sitting inside the rocket ship!

Age level

4+

Objective

To understand the power of a rocket ship

Materials

Different colored construction paper
scissors
white paper
tape
sticky stars
jar of marbles

Preparation

Cut a 2" x 4" colored construction paper rectangle for each child. Cut out a large moon shape from the white paper. Tape it on a wall.

Horsing Around

Age level

5+

Objective

To learn that animals can be a form of transportation

Materials

Large cardboard box
scissors
broom
white posterboard
felt pen
tape
small chair
long rope

Preparation

Cut a small hole in one side of the box. Stick a broom handle down through the hole. Draw the large shape of a horses's head on white posterboard. Cut it out. Trace it on the remaining posterboard. Cut out a second horse head! Tape a head on each side of the broom that is sticking out of the box. You have made a broom horse! Place a small chair in the box for a saddle. Make a lasso from the rope!

What to do

1. Sit with the children near the broom horse! Explain that the broom horse is a tame horse. Notice the chair in the box. This is a saddle! You sit on the saddle to ride the horse. Pet the broom horse.

2. Explain that the horse was a wild animal. People tame horses! How do you tame a wild horse? Demonstrate! First you catch the horse! Stand a few feet from the broom horse. Swing the lasso! Try to swing the loop around the horse's neck or place it around the horse's neck! Now gently stroke the horse. Say, "Nice horse!" The horse will soon know that you want to be friends. Take turns catching the wild horse and taming it!

3. Now that the horse is tame, we can ride the horse! It is a form of transportation! Untie the loop on the lasso. Place the rope around the horse's neck. Tape the middle of the rope around the horse's neck below the head. Who wants to go horseback riding?

4. Choose a horseback rider! This child sits on the saddle and holds the reins. The remaining children slap their hands on their knees in an alternating pattern. This will sound like a horse galloping! Bounce up and down in the saddle! Move the reins up and down. You are traveling on a horse!

More to do

Explain that horses can travel at different speeds. A horse can walk! Slowly slap hands on the rug in an alternating pattern. A horse can trot. This is faster than a walk! Everyone slaps a little faster. A horse can canter. Canter with your hands! This is faster than a trot. Now gallop! Slap the rug as fast as you can. You will sound like a herd of horses!

The Humpity Bumpity Camel

What to do

1. People ride camels in the desert! Camels need little food and water when walking in a hot desert. They store fat in their humps. They use it for food! Have the children repeat the following verse one line at a time. Slap your hands on your knees as you say each line. Establish a slow rhythm. Repeat the verse again and say it faster! The camel is traveling at a faster speed! Repeat it a third time. The camel is running!

> *I need a little food. I need a little water.*
> *I humpity bump it, as I'm hotter and hotter!*

2. Say "The Camel" chant! Choose a child to fill in the blank with the name of an animal. Each child can have a turn to think of an animal name. Do related hand movements!

> *I do not think it wise to ride a _____, (Place hands out flat and on*
> *   top of each other, move them up and down)*
> *You'd tumble off and grow a little bump, (Clap on "bump")*
> *I think that you would look a little silly, (Laugh)*
> *So please take my advise and ride a hump! (Place hands in prayer position)*

More to do

Play "The Camel" game! Cut out six inch high camel shapes from yellow construction paper. Make two camels for each child. Print the word, "growl," on the back of half of the camels. Place the paper camels right side up on the rug. Choose a camel guide! The camel guide looks for a friendly camel. This child turns over a camel. If the word "growl" is showing, the camel is not friendly! Choose another camel. The child chooses until he finds a friendly camel to "buy" at the market. Take the camels home to remind you of the interesting camel!

Age level

3+

Objective

To learn about an unusual form of transportation—the camel

Materials

None

Preparation

None

Make-Ups

Age level

3+

Objective

To use imagination and to develop small motor skills

Materials

Construction paper
scissors
variety of small objects, such as paper cups, buttons, popsicle sticks, straws, rubber bands, plastic spoons, feathers, pipe cleaners, cotton balls, yarn
glue

Preparation

Cut different colored construction paper into small shapes such as squares and triangles.

What to do

1. Invent a form of transportation! Brainstorm the many forms of transportation that are already available. Who made the first one? Someone invented it!

2. Place a variety of objects on the table. Invent! Ask the children to glue together as many objects as they want in any way. Create a new form of transportation!

3. When the children finish their inventions, bring them to the rug. Each child shows her invention. Ask the inventor what the invention is called. Does it travel on land? Does it fly? Does it float? How many people does it carry? Do you push it or does it have an engine? Does it make a noise? Can you make the noise? Continue until everyone has shared their invention.

More to do

Have a transportation show! Place the inventions on a flat surface. Place a sign by each invention that describes its name and what kind of transportation it is. Tape magazine pictures of different forms of transportation near the display. Welcome other classrooms to visit your show!

Match-Ups

What to do

1. Sit on the rug. Place the picture halves on the rug with the transportation side showing.

2. Explain that everyone will be looking for picture halves that match. Look for matching colors and designs. Look for shapes that are similar. Mention the different kinds of transportation that are on the pictures.

3. Choose a child to find a match-up! This child chooses one of the picture halves. He searches for its matching half. Notice what it is! The teacher can help (if necessary) by offering verbal clues: look for something yellow, look for wheels, look for water, look for clouds!

4. When a correct match is made, he places both halves together on the rug. Then he chooses the next child to make a match-up. Continue until everyone has had a turn to match-up!

More to do

Place one half of each transportation picture in separate envelopes. Print on each envelope, "Transportation Match-ups!" Place the remaining halves on the rug. Give an envelope to each child. Take turns opening the envelopes and trying to find the matching half! When she does, she places both halves in her envelope. Take the envelopes home. Look for transportation pictures at home. Cut them out and cut them in half! Add them to your collection of match-up pictures.

Age level

3+

Objective

To recognize similarities and to increase matching skills

Materials

Magazines
scissors
felt pen
one envelope

Preparation

Cut out magazine pictures of different forms of transportation. Cut out a variety of cars, planes, boats, bicycles, surfboards, skateboards and even some animals! Cut out at least one picture for each child. Now cut each picture in half. Place the pieces in an envelope and mix them up. Print on the envelope, "Transportation Match-ups!"

The Song Review

Age level

3+

Objective

To review the forms of transportation

Materials

None

Preparation

None

What to do

1. Sing the following three songs to review different forms of transportation. In each song, one form of transportation is mentioned. You can sing each song many times, substituting different names of transportation each time. The children can help think of different transportation words to sing in the songs.

1. "The Ocean" song is said as a chant! Say it slowly. When you are doing the related movements, move smoothly and gracefully, like the peaceful movement of water.

> *Down from the mountain (Touch fingers together at eye level)*
> *And into the river, (Keep fingertips together, move hands down)*
> *Down from the river (Slowly roll hands around each other)*
> *And into the sea, (Move each hand outward)*
> *Flows the blue water (Move hands in a wavy motion)*
> *That carries the sailboat, (Place fist on open hand)*
> *Carries the sailboat, (Move above hands in a wavy motion)*
> *Out to sea! (Move hands slowly off to the right)*

2. Stand and sing "The Land" song to the tune of "London Bridge."

> *Build a house (Pound left fist into right hand)*
> *And plant a tree. (Pretend to dig a hole)*
> *Lay a road down (Move hand across floor)*
> *One-two-three. (Clap three times)*
> *Ride a school bus (Turn "steering wheel" around)*
> *Round the town, (Turn "steering wheel" around)*
> *Beep, beep, watch out for me! (Slap knee on each "beep," then point to self)*

3. Sing the first four lines of "The Air" song to the tune of, "It's Raining, It's Pouring." Sing the words "Up up up I go" and the word "In" at the same key that you start the song with. Then slowly lower the pitch four times as you sing, "my air-o-plane!"

> *I'm flying, I'm flying, (Keep palm down and fly hand around)*
> *Higher and higher, (Fly hand higher and higher)*
> *I'm having too much fun today, (Clap hands to rhythm)*
> *To ever want to land! (Fly hand down slowly and barely touch ground)*
> *Up up up I go, (Quickly bring hand back up again)*
> *In my air-o-plane! (Fly hand around)*

More to do

Place a large cardboard box in the classroom. This is a transportation box! It can take you anywhere—under the sea, around the land, high in the sky! Place a different object in the box relating to the type of transportation the child wants to use. For example, place a small horn inside if the box is a car. If the box becomes a plane, place a jar of marbles inside to make an engine noise.

Time Travel to Dinosaur Land

Let's take a giant leap into Dinosaur Land! Make tickets now! Make sure everyone makes a two-way ticket. But watch out, the children will not want to leave! These mysterious, fascinating giants are almost make-believe to a child, though they really existed. That is why dinosaurs will always sparkle eyes. Their larger-than-life image will roam classrooms forever!

Time Travel to Dinosaur Land

	Monday	Tuesday	Wednesday	Thursday	Friday
Week 1	**3+ Dinosaur Tickets** *To learn that dinosaurs lived many years ago*	**3+ Time Machine** *To discover that the Earth was different then*	**4+ Dinosaur Detectives** *To begin to understand dinosaurs*	**3+ Egg-Citing Discovery!** *To learn that dinosaurs laid eggs*	**4+ Ceolophysis, One of the First!** *To find out about Ceolophysis*
Week 2	**4+ Footprints to the Tyrannosaurus!** *To learn about Tyrannosaurus*	**4+ Apatasaurus, the Gentle Giant** *To explore the qualities of Apatasaurus*	**4+ Iguanodon, the Most Famous Dinosaur** *To learn about Iguanodon*	**3+ Anatasaurus, the Duck-Billed Dinosaur** *To learn that some dinosaurs could swim*	**4+ Ankylosaurus, the Armored Dinosaur** *To discover that some dinosaurs had armor*
Week 3	**4+ Stegosaurus, the Plated Dinosaur** *To learn about Stegosaurus*	**4+ Triceratops, the Three-Horned Dinosaur** *To learn about Triceratops*	**4+ The Dinosaur Riddle Chant** *To review dinosaur names*	**4+ No More Dinosaurs** *To understand "extinct"*	**3+ Freddy the Fossil** *To learn about fossils*
Week 4	**3+ A Bone Hunt** *To learn how dinosaur bones were discovered*	**3+ Rainbow Skin** *To encourage imagination*	**4+ Smooth or Bumpy** *To explore possible dinosaur skin textures*	**3+ Dinosaur Dancing** *To explore different ways to move*	**3+ Name-a-Saurus** *To review dinosaur names*

Dinosaur Tickets

What to do

1. Explain that everyone will be learning about dinosaurs. Ask the children how they think we get to Dinosaur Land? by plane? on a boat? We need to go back in time, many, many years! We need to ride in a time machine! The time machine does not need gas. It runs on imagination!

2. Before you can ride on the time machine, you need a ticket to Dinosaur Land. Each child needs to make a ticket before entering the time machine.

3. Make tickets! Give each child a paper ticket. Place crayons on the table. The children design and color their dinosaur ticket. Brainstorm ideas on what to draw on their ticket: a dinosaur jungle, volcano, rainbow, dinosaur egg. (Cover each ticket with contact paper to help preserve it.)

4. Each morning this month have the children give the teacher their ticket. (Keep the tickets in a special place in the classroom.)

More to do

What do you think Dinosaur Land looks like? Place a large sheet of butcher paper and crayons on the table. The children draw a large picture of Dinosaur Land on the paper. What do you think you will see there? Possibilities include mountains, trees, lakes, flowers, bugs, clouds, lightning, rain, grass, and dinosaurs! Display the mural on a wall. Title it, "Dinosaur Land!"

Age level

3+

Objective

To learn that dinosaurs existed many years ago

Materials

White construction paper
scissors
crayons
optional—contact paper

Preparation

Cut a 10" x 4" shape from white construction paper for each child. These are dinosaur tickets!

Time Machine

Age level

3+

Objective

To learn that the Earth was different when dinosaurs were alive

Materials

Yarn
scissors
tape
jar of marbles
large sheet

Preparation

Cut a piece of yarn and tape it on the rug in a circle, large enough to encircle the children. (Save the cut yarn for the next activity!)

What to do

1. Each child gives the teacher his or her dinosaur ticket. As they do, they can step into the yarn circle and sit down. This is the time machine!

2. Explain that a time machine travels back to a different time on the Earth. It is the same Earth, but many things will look different.

3. Now start the time machine! Cover the children with the large sheet. It is dark as you travel fast! Shake the jar of marbles. The engine is starting. Here you go!

4. The children can slowly rock back and forth. This is the motion of the time machine! Now slow your rocking down. The time machine is slowing down and will soon land!

5. We are in Dinosaur Land! Take off the sheet. Look around! Imagine the differences. Pretend to notice that many things are missing on the Earth. Each child can name an animal or object that is no longer on the Earth. Do you think you would like to live in a place like Dinosaur Land? Why? Why not? What would you miss the most? Are you ready to return to the Earth that you know?

6. Cover the children with the sheet! Shake the jar of marbles. You are traveling to the present time! Now pull off the sheet. You are back in civilization! Did anyone see a dinosaur? We will begin to look for dinosaurs on our next trip to Dinosaur Land!

More to do

Make time machines on paper! Give each child a sheet of paper and a string of yarn two feet long. Place glue on the table. Ask the children to place dabs of glue along their strings. Lay the strings in a large circle on the papers. Now pass out felt pens. Draw children inside the yarn. Draw yourself! Draw trees around the time machines. You have landed in Dinosaur Land!

Dinosaur Detectives

What to do

1. Make a large circle on the rug, with the yarn from the previous activity. Sit in the time machine. You have arrived in Dinosaur Land!

2. The children can step out of the time machine. Pick up the yarn and sit down again on the rug. It is time to look for a dinosaur!

3. Be Dinosaur Detectives! Place the dinosaur clues on the rug with the dinosaur stickers showing. Explain that a dinosaur clue is inside each folded paper.

4. Choose a child to be a Dinosaur Detective. This child chooses a dinosaur clue and hands it to the teacher. The teacher reads the clue! Continue until everyone has been a Dinosaur Detective!

5. Now look for a dinosaur! Remember the dinosaur clues. Walk around the room slowly and quietly. You do not want to scare a dinosaur! When you see a dinosaur, tell everyone! We all want to look at it.

6. When a child passes near the hidden dinosaur, shake a jar of marbles. That means someone is near the dinosaur. It is growling! Name the child who is near the dinosaur!

7. When someone finds the hidden dinosaur, take the dinosaur to the rug. See if the dinosaur clues apply to the dinosaur. Does it have legs that are under its body? Does it have a horn or a small head?

8. Give each child their dinosaur clue to take home. If you see a dinosaur near your home, let us know!

More to do

Make dinosaur panoramas to take home! The teacher can cut out magazine pictures of landscapes, such as trees, flowers, mountains, grass, lakes, the sky. Ask the children to help cut out pictures. They can save the pictures to use in their panorama. Each child can bring a shoe box and lid from home. Cut a small hole on the short side of each box. Cut another hole on the long side of each box. Place the shoe boxes, pictures and glue on the table. The children can glue the pictures in their shoe box. Glue them on the bottom and around the sides of the shoe box. Give each child a small picture or toy dinosaur to glue in their panorama! Now everyone can place the lid on their box. Look into the box to see Dinosaur Land! Shine a flashlight through the hole on the long side of a box. The panorama will light up!

Age level

4+

Objective

To develop a basic understanding of dinosaurs

Materials

Small sheets of white paper
felt pen
dinosaur stickers
picture of a dinosaur or a small plastic dinosaur
yarn (from the previous activity)
jar of marbles

Preparation

Print a dinosaur clue for each child on a sheet of paper. Fold the papers and place a dinosaur sticker on each one. Possible dinosaur clues: dinosaurs spent most of their time on land; dinosaur's walked with their legs under their bodies; look for large footprints; dinosaurs made loud noises; look for an animal that has a very long neck; look for an animal that has horns on its head; look for an animal that has a large heavy tail; look for an animal that has a small head and a large body; look for an animal that has very sharp teeth; and dinosaurs laid eggs. Hide a dinosaur picture or toy in the classroom. Hide it where it is not easily seen!

Egg-Citing Discovery!

Age level

3+

Objective

To learn that dinosaurs laid eggs

Materials

Dinosaur stickers
medium-sized rocks
brown sheet or cloth

Preparation

Place a dinosaur sticker on each rock. Place the rocks sticker-side down on the rug in a group. Place the sheet or cloth over the rocks. Make sure the rocks are covered. This is a nest of dinosaur eggs!

What to do

1. Sit around the nest of eggs. Explain that dinosaurs laid eggs! What other animals lay eggs? Give clues! Other animals include birds, fish, frogs, snakes, the platypus.

2. Point to the brown sheet. Explain that it is mud! Some dinosaurs made a nest in soft mud. Why would mud be a good place to lay eggs? (They can sink down if stepped on! The eggs are heavy and need a soft bed to prevent cracking. Mud hides the eggs from hungry dinosaurs. Mud could keep the eggs cool on very hot days!)

3. Do you think there are dinosaur eggs under the mud? Select a child to carefully remove the mud (the sheet or cloth). Look at the dinosaur eggs! Let's be quiet! We don't want to disturb the baby dinosaurs inside.

4. Now the child places the mud back over the dinosaur eggs. The eggs are ready to hatch! Count to ten. Count with dinosaur numbers! Dinosaur numbers are 1-a-saurus, 2-a-saurus, 3-a-saurus, etc. Slap your knees as you count each number. When you reach 10-a-saurus, clap! The eggs have hatched!

5. The teacher removes the mud. Each child chooses a dinosaur egg and turns it over. Look what kind of dinosaur hatched!

6. Place the dinosaur eggs in a safe and quiet place. A baby dinosaur needs peace and rest!

More to do

Paint the dinosaur eggs! Place them on the table with a selection of paints. Ask the children what color they think dinosaur eggs were. Paint the eggs! Leave the dinosaur sticker unpainted. You don't want the dinosaur to hide inside the egg!

Coelophysis, One of the First!

What to do

1. Read *The Coelophysis* story!

   Many years ago, the Earth was covered with thick forests. There were black volcanoes. Sometimes they would erupt and a tremendous rumble would fill the air. Small animals would shake. Spiders, turtles, frogs and dragonflies would hide. But one creature was different. It ran on two legs! It was the Coelophysis, one of the first dinosaurs!

2. With the children, follow the yellow footprints to the paper jungle. Choose a child to reveal the dinosaur picture of the Coelophysis! Explain that many small animals lived on the Earth with the Coelophysis. Some of the animals were spiders, turtles, frogs and dragonflies.

3. Sit at the table. Give each child a sheet of paper. Place felt pens on the table. Ask the children to draw a small insect or animal on their papers. The children can cut out their pictures and place them on the rug.

4. Sit around the small animals. Pretend you are a Coelophysis! When a Coelophysis walked, it leaned its body forward. It bobbed its head up and down. Its smaller upper arms were held close to its chest. Walk around like a Coelophysis! Try not to step on the animal life. The Coelophysis would rather eat them!

5. When a Coelophysis got tired, it sat down on its long tail. Ask the children to sit on the rug and lean back on one hand. Is that comfortable? Would you rather rest laying down?

6. A Coelophysis was eight feet long and three feet high! Tie an eight foot piece of yarn around the middle of a yardstick. This is a Coelophysis! Give each child a chance to walk around the room with the Coelophysis!

More to do

Do the Coelophysis Dance! Tie a long string of yarn around each child's waist. Play music with a lively beat! The Coelophysis was a fast moving dinosaur! Dance to the music, swinging the long Coelophysis tails!

Age level

4+

Objective

To learn that some dinosaurs were very small! The Coelophysis (See-loh-fy-ses) was one of the first dinosaurs.

Materials

Yellow construction paper
felt pens
scissors
green crepe paper
tape
picture of a Coelophysis
yarn
yardstick

Preparation

Draw a large footprint on yellow construction paper for each child. Cut them out. Print the name "Coelophysis" on each footprint. Cut six strips of green crepe paper 10" long. Tape them on a wall close together. (Keep this "jungle" on the wall for the other dinosaur activities.) Tape a picture of a Coelophysis behind the crepe paper. Place the footprints on the rug, leading to the dinosaur picture. Cut an 8' length of yarn.

Footprints to the Tyrannosaurus!

Age level

4+

Objective

To learn that the Tyrannosaurus was the most ferocious meat-eating dinosaur

Materials

Red construction paper
felt pens
scissors
picture of a Tyrannosaurus—try calendars or copy library book pictures or coloring book pictures
tape
felt pen

Preparation

Draw a large dinosaur footprint on red construction paper for each child. Cut them out. Print the word "Tyrannosaurus" on each footprint. Tape a picture of a Tyrannosaurus behind the crepe paper jungle from the previous activity. Place the footprints on the rug, leading up to the dinosaur picture. Save the footprints in each activity. The children can take home a set of dinosaur footprints when the activities are finished.

What to do

1. Sit and read *The Tyrannosaurus* story! Read it with an air of mystery!

   Dinosaurs hear a grumbling rumbling noise. They quickly turn their heads! A soft breeze is blowing. A smell of danger is in the air. Leaves crunch! A tall tree moves. Between two branches they see the large and frightening head of a Tyrannosaurus. Run! Tyrannosaurus is the largest of the meat eaters. He is the king of the dinosaurs!

2. Have the children follow the footprints to the paper jungle. Sit down. Choose a child to push the jungle apart and reveal the dinosaur. It is the Tyrannosaurus Rex!

3. A Tyrannosaurus stood on two legs. His front legs were small and close to his body. Ask the children to stand and pretend to be a Tyrannosaurus! Bend your arms at your elbows and place them in front of you. Prowl slowly around the room. Growl when you feel hungry!

4. You are tired from prowling. Rest on your stomach! To stand up again, the Tyrannosaurus gripped the ground with his small arms. His powerful large legs pushed him upward. Try it!

5. The Tyrannosaurus had very sharp teeth that were six inches long. Ask the children to place their fingertips together with knuckles bent. Move your hands apart and together like a jaw munching! Say "The Munch" chant while moving your hands.

   > *Munch...munch...munch,*
   > *Tyrannosaurus sees,*
   > *A yummy looking dinosaur*
   > *To eat eat eat!*
   > *Munch...munch...munch,*
   > *Tyrannosaurus eats.*
   > *Run yummy dinosaur, (Pound on rug)*
   > *Move your feet!*
   >
   > *Munch...munch...munch,*
   > *Tyrannosaurus eats,*
   > *Then big, big, yawn, (Spread arms wide, wider)*
   > *And sleep, sleep, sleep. (Lean head on hands)*

6. The Tyrannosaurus had sharp teeth and a head five feet long. Measure and mark five feet! Have a child stand at each mark. Whose head is larger, yours or Tyrannosaurus?

7. Ask the children why they think the Tyrannosaurus was called the king of the dinosaurs.

More to do

Do the Tyrannosaurus Dance! Play marching music or music with a strong beat. Stomp around the room! The teacher can stop the music at any time. When the music stops, the children stop and shake someone's hand nearby. Everyone says, pleased to eat you!

Apatosaurus, the Gentle Giant

Age level

4+

Objective

To learn that the Brontosaurus is now called the Apatosaurus

Materials

Gray construction paper
felt pens
scissors
tape
picture of an Apatosaurus
leaves

Preparation

Draw a large footprint on gray construction paper for each child. Cut them out. Print the name "Apatosaurus" on each footprint. Tape a picture of the Apatosaurus behind the crepe paper jungle. Place the footprints on the rug, leading to the dinosaur picture. Make small 3" footprints for each child. Print the letter "A" on half of them. Print the letter "S" on the remaining half. Tape half of the leaves on a wall at a height of four feet. Tape the remaining leaves on the wall at a height of two feet.

What to do

1. Follow the gray footprints to the paper jungle. Sit down. Choose a child to reveal the dinosaur picture. It's an Apatosaurus!

2. Read *The Apatosaurus* story!

   The loud roar of the Tyrannosaurus echoes through the jungle. The sound of thunder pounds faster and faster. See a massive body heaving itself towards a peaceful lake. It is a gigantic Apatosaurus running to safety! With a tremendous splash, the Apatosaurus disappears into the water. Now there is silence. The water in the lake ripples quietly. The Apatosaurus is safe; the Tyrannosaurus cannot swim.

3. The Apatosaurus had a very large body and a very small head! Ask the children to stand together in a tight group. They are the body of an Apatosaurus. The teacher can stand at the other end of the classroom. The neck of the Apatosaurus could stretch to the teacher!

4. Explain that the Apatosaurus could eat the leaves on the tops of very tall trees. A short dinosaur, like the Stegosaurus, ate leaves near the ground. Place the small footprints on the rug letter-side down. Each child turns over a footprint. If the letter "A" is revealed, you are an Apatosaurus! The children who chose the letter "A" can take a leaf off the tree that is growing near the top. If an "S" is revealed, you are a Stegosaurus. These children can take a leaf that is near the ground.

More to do

Place the leaves from the wall on the table. Place crayons on the table. Give each child a sheet of paper. The children can place a leaf under their paper and color over it with a crayon. Make many leaf tracings! When the leaf tracings are finished, put a dinosaur sticker on the paper. Print on each paper, "Plant Eaters!" Offer only stickers of dinosaurs that eat plants! Do not include the Tyrannosaurus or the small lizard-like dinosaurs on two legs.

Iguanodon, the Most Famous Dinosaur

What to do

1. Follow the green footprints to the paper jungle. Sit down. Choose a child to reveal the dinosaur picture. It's an Iguanodon!

2. Read *The Iguanodon* story!

   The air is hot. The forest is restless. Steam appears to be rising from a large swamp. Small animals are darting here and there. The noise of the jungle seems almost too loud! All of a sudden, the noise stops. A large human-like hand appears on a branch. Is it a giant? Is it a monster lizard? An arm appears. A large body follows on two thick legs. It is an Iguanodon, the most famous of all the dinosaurs!

3. Iguanodon bones were first discovered under a pile of rocks. Ask the children to walk around the room looking for the pile of rocks. (Don't let them look where you hid the bones!)

4. When the pile of rocks is discovered, have the children stand by it. The child who discovered it can carefully take it apart. What is under the pile? Three teeth! To whom do they belong? Maybe a giant lizard!

5. Now hunt for the bones. When each child finds a bone, he or she can sit on the rug.

6. To find out who giant bones belong to, scientists arrange and rearrange them. Each child can place his or her bone on the rug. Make sure the bones are touching. They will form a skeleton shape. When scientists studied the shape, they named the shape "Dinosaur." It looked like a giant lizard; dinosaur means terrible lizard! When scientists found the bones from the Iguanodon, they looked like a lizard called the Iguana, so they called this particular shape Iguanodon.

More to do

Place sheets of white construction paper on the table. Give the children scissors. Ask them to cut out dinosaur bones from the white paper. Give the children a bag to place their bones in. Take the bones to the rug. Place the bones on the rug and arrange them. Make sure they are touching! You have formed a skeleton! Look at the dinosaur skeletons. What name would you give this dinosaur?

Age level

4+

Objective

To learn that the discovery of the Iguanodon led to the name "Dinosaur"

Materials

Green construction paper
felt pens
scissors
picture of an Iguanodon
tape
rocks

Preparation

Draw a large footprint on green construction paper for each child. Cut them out. Print the name "Iguanodon" on each footprint. Tape a picture of an Iguanodon behind the crepe paper jungle. Place the footprints on the rug, leading to the Iguanodon. Place a pile of rocks in the classroom, somewhere not easily seen! Draw three 2" long teeth on white construction paper. Cut them out and place them under the pile of rocks. Draw long bones on sheets of white construction paper. Make them the length of the paper. Make at least one for each child. Cut them out and hide them in a special place in the classroom.

Anatosaurus, the Duck-Billed Dinosaur

Age level

3+

Objective

To learn that some dinosaurs could swim

Materials

Blue construction paper
black felt pen
scissors
tape
picture of an Anatosaurus
large and small marbles
small shallow pan
yellow cotton balls

Preparation

Draw a large footprint on blue construction paper for each child. Cut them out. Print the name "Anatosaurus" on each one. Tape a picture of an Anatosaurus behind the crepe paper jungle. Place the footprints on the rug, leading to the paper jungle. Cut a 10' length of yarn. Cut blue construction paper into four pieces. Roll each piece into a paper tube. Tape the loose edges together. Make a paper tube for each child. Place enough large and small marbles in a shallow pan so they do not move around!

What to do

1. Follow the blue footprints to the paper jungle. Sit down. Choose a child to reveal the dinosaur picture. It's an Anatosaurus!

2. Read *The Anatosaurus Story*!

   There is a loud splash in the lake. The fish are frightened. As the water settles down, you can see a huge shadowy form moving below the surface. It moves quickly for such a huge shape. It starts to rise! Large webbed feet are slowly moving towards you. Look up and see an enormous duck bill. Is it a giant duck? No! It's an Anatosaurus, the duck-billed dinosaur.

3. Explain that an Anatosaurus had webbed feet. They help you swim! Give each child four cotton balls. Place a cotton ball between each finger. You have a webbed foot like the Anatosaurus!

4. We know that the skin of the Anatosaurus was bumpy because a skin print was found on a rock. Show the shallow pan of large and small marbles. Pass it around so the children can move their hand over the top of the pan, feeling the large and small bumps. This is what the print looked like.

5. Some duck-billed dinosaurs had bumps on their heads! They were hollow bumps like a horn. Some people think they were used to make loud noises. A loud noise could say danger! What else could a loud noise mean? Brainstorm ideas! Now blow through the tubes. Make a loud noise!

More to do

Make a patch of Anatosaurus skin to take home. Cut sheets of construction paper into four pieces. Glue the pennies on the paper.

Ankylosaurus, the Armored Dinosaur

What to do

1. Follow the white footprints to the paper jungle. Sit down. Choose a child to reveal the dinosaur picture. It's an Ankylosaurus!

2. Read *The Ankylosaurus Story*!

Thump! Thump! Thump! What is that noise? Is it in front of you? Is it behind you? Thump! Thump! THUMP! Could it be the sound of heavy footprints? Walk closer to the sound. Crouch down and peek between two bushes. You see a thick bumpy tail thumping against a larger dinosaur. The smaller dinosaur is trying to protect itself! It is moving low in the plants like a heavy tank. It is an Ankylosaurus, the armored dinosaur!

3. The Ankylosaurus was fifteen feet long! Choose a child to hold one end of the yarn. The teacher can hold the skein and walk fifteen steps. Look how long the yarn is! That is the length of an Ankylosaurus!

4. When attacked, the Ankylosaurus would tuck its legs tight underneath itself. It would lay close to the ground, protecting its soft throat and belly. Let's try that! Lay on your stomachs. Bend your arms at the elbows and tuck them under you. Keep your head and stomach on the rug. The teacher can pretend he or she is a Tyrannosaurus! The teacher can touch the children lightly on their backs. The Tyrannosaurus is seeing if you are alive. Don't move! The Tyrannosaurus might go away!

5. The Ankylosaurus was covered with a thick bumpy armor. It was hard for another dinosaur to bite through it! The teacher can place a sock on his or her arm. Push small blocks into the sock, all the way down the sock. Then let the children try it.

More to do

Cut a sheet of butcher paper the length of the table. Place a variety of paints on the table in shallow containers. Give each child a sponge. Ask them to dip their sponges in the paint and make sponge prints on the paper. When the paper is covered with prints, it will look like the bumpy back of an Ankylosaurus! Tape it on a wall, and call it, "The Bumpy Back of an Ankylosaurus!"

Age level

3+

Objective

To learn that some dinosaurs were short and that their skin offered protection

Materials

White construction paper
felt pens
scissors
tape
picture of an Ankylosaurus
yarn
knee-high sock
small blocks

Preparation

Draw a large footprint on white construction paper for each child. Cut them out. Print the name "Ankylosaurus" on each one. Tape a picture of an Ankylosaurus behind the crepe paper jungle. Place the footprints on the rug, leading to the paper jungle.

Stegosaurus, the Plated Dinosaur

Age level

4+

Objective

To learn about the Stegosaurus

Materials

Pink construction paper
felt pens
scissors
tape
picture of a Stegosaurus
butcher paper
crayons

Preparation

Draw a large footprint on pink construction paper for each child. Cut them out. Print the name "Stegosaurus" in each one. Tape a picture of a Stegosaurus behind the crepe paper jungle. Place the footprints on the rug, leading to the paper jungle. Using butcher paper, cut out plate shapes that lined the back of a Stegosaurus. Cut one for each child. Shape them like ovals with a squared off bottom. Cut four long spike shapes. Cut a large body shape. Cut out four leg shapes. Cut out a small thin head.

What to do

1. Follow the pink footprints to the paper jungle. Sit down. Choose a child to reveal the dinosaur picture. It's a Stegosaurus!

2. Read *The Stegosaurus* story!

Quiet! Can you hear a crunch, crunch, crunch sound? Follow the sound into the jungle. You see large palms and strange looking plants. You hear the sound again. Crunch, crunch, CRUNCH! It's getting louder! Peek between two low bushes. You see a sharp branch on the ground. Wait a minute. It's moving! It's not a branch. It's the spiked tail of a Stegosaurus! And the noise? The Stegosaurus is munching on a crispy crunchy plant!

3. The back legs of the Stegosaurus were twice as long as the front ones! Ask the children to get on their hands and knees. Now lift your knees off the rug with your feet on the ground. Walk like a Stegosaurus!

4. Place the large paper body on the rug. Place the remaining paper pieces on the rug near the body. The children are going to assemble a Stegosaurus puzzle! Choose a child to pick a puzzle piece. If the child picks a spike, he can place the spike a few feet away from the body. The head can be placed at the front of the body. The plates can be placed along the back! When you have finished the Stegosaurus, look at its shape! Its shape consists of spikes, plates, a small head and a large heavy body.

More to do

Sit down and say "The Stegosaurus" cheer with the related body movements!

I'm walking through the jungle on my feet, (alternately slap rug with hands)
The heat is hard to beat, (Clap on "beat")
I'll look for a Stego (Make fist with right hand)
And you look for a Saurus (Make fist with left hand)
Then we can run into a ....
Stegosaurus! (Touch both fist together)

How can we tell a Stego, (Make fist with right hand)
How can we tell a Saurus, (Make fist with left hand)
How can we tell a Stegosaurus (Touch fists together)
From another dinosaurus? (Spread arms out wide)

You've got to see a plate, (Clap hands)
You've got to see a spike, (Clap hands)
You've got to see that everything (Pound fists one on top of each other)
Is put on right! (Pound fists one on top of each other)

You can hear a crunch, (Move right fingers and thumb up and down)
You can hear a munch, (Move left fingers and thumb up and down)
That's a Stegosaurus (Clap on "Stego")
Who is ouuuuut toooooo lunch! (Move right and left fingers and thumbs up and down)
Yaaaaaaaa, Stegosaurus! (Slap knees, then clap)

Triceratops, the Three-Horned Dinosaur

What to do

1. Follow the orange footprints to the paper jungle. Sit down. Choose a child to reveal the dinosaur picture. It's a Triceratops!

2. Read *The Triceratops* story!

   Near a large swamp, in the middle of the jungle, you hear a loud thump. The ground seems to shake. The leaves on the trees vibrate! What is happening? Is it an earthquake? Slowly you approach the sound. You see something close by. You duck behind a large tree! Two huge shapes are running towards each other. Two large heads are bent. The heads are going to hit! THUMP! Two mighty dinosaurs are fighting. They are Triceratops, the three-horned dinosaurs!

3. Point to the pictures on the wall. Notice that each picture is something large. The Triceratops was a little larger than one of the pictures! Choose a child to guess which one! Print this child's name on a strip of masking tape. This child sticks their name strip on the wall under the picture of their choice.

4. After all the children have guessed, point to the elephant. The Triceratops was a little larger then an elephant!

More to do

Do "The Triceratops" dance! Triceratops were big, so they moved slowly. Dance slowly to the music.

Age level

4+

Objective

To learn about the Triceratops

Materials

Orange construction paper
felt pens
scissors
tape
picture of a Triceratops
magazines
masking tape

Preparation

Draw a large footprint on orange construction paper for each child. Cut them out. Print the name "Triceratops" on each one. Tape a picture of a Triceratops behind the crepe paper jungle. Place the footprints on the rug, leading to the paper jungle. Cut out at least five magazine pictures of large objects. One of the pictures needs to be an elephant! Other pictures might be a truck, a whale, a building, a bus, a horse. Tape the pictures on a wall.

The Dinosaur Riddle Chant

Age level

4+

Objective

To review the dinosaur names

Materials

None

Preparation

None

What to do

1. Say "The Dinosaur Riddle" chant! Say it slowly. Slap your hands on your knees to establish a rhythm. The children can repeat each line after the teacher says it. See who can guess the name of the dinosaur before you say it!

> *Guess who was living in the dinosaur forest,*
> *Each little riddle is a dinosaurus!*
> *Who was the first and perhaps the nicest?*
> *The teeny tiny dinosaur (See-loh-fy-ses!)*
>
> *Who was the king of the dinosaur forest?*
> *The terrible and toothy Tyrannosaurus!*
> *Who ate the tallest trees in the forest?*
> *The gentle and gigantic Apatosaurus!*
>
> *Who looked like a lizard that is on the run?*
> *The interesting, incredible Iguanodon!*
> *Who looked like a duck swimming in the forest?*
> *The webbed and waddling Anatosaurus!*
>
> *Who looked like a turtle hiding in the forest?*
> *The lumpy and bumpy Ankylosaurus!*
> *Who munched and crunched on the fauna and flora?*
> *The plated and protected Stegosaurus!*
>
> *Who battled in the bushes where they often fought?*
> *The fighting and ferocious Triceratops!*
> *Now these are the riddles of the dinosaur forest,*
> *Tell me the name of a dinosaurus!*

2. When you finish the chant, ask the children who can remember the name of a dinosaur. You will get many responses!

More to do

Give each child a sheet of paper. Print the name of a dinosaur on each paper. Each child can draw a picture of that special dinosaur. Remind each child of the particular body shape of each dinosaur. Encourage the children to draw! The dinosaurs do not have to look like ones you have seen in a picture! When the pictures are finished, tape them on a wall in the same order that they appear in the chant. If you have two of the same dinosaurs, tape them under each other. Say the chant and point to the dinosaurs in each riddle.

No More Dinosaurs!

What to do

1. Ask the children if they saw a dinosaur on the way to school? Has anyone seen a dinosaur in their backyard? Why not? Let's find out!

2. Place the paper dinosaurs on the Earth picture. It's Dinosaur Land on the Earth! At one time they ruled the Earth! But what happened to them? They are extinct!

3. Demonstrate what the word extinct means. Choose a child to take a dinosaur off the Earth. Continue choosing children to remove dinosaurs. As each dinosaur is removed, comment on a possible reason why dinosaurs died. There are many possible reasons. The land became too cold. The land became too hot. Plants died, so many plant-eating dinosaurs starved. When plant-eaters died, the meat-eaters had nothing to eat. The dinosaurs became sick. Earthquakes increased. Fires spread. Some dinosaurs were trapped in sticky tar. Many dinosaurs were eaten by other dinosaurs. Small animals ate the dinosaur eggs.

4. When the last dinosaur is removed, look at the Earth. There are no more dinosaurs on the Earth. Not even one! They are extinct!

5. Place one dinosaur back on the Earth. Look! A dinosaur has been found! Are they extinct? No! Remove the dinosaur. Are they extinct now? Yes!

More to do

Act out the dinosaurs becoming extinct. Have everyone find a different place to stand in the classroom. You are dinosaurs! One by one, tap each dinosaur on the shoulder. Each dinosaur falls to the ground. You are no longer alive on the Earth! When all the children have fallen to the ground, the teacher looks around the room. He or she says, "I don't see any dinosaurs on the Earth. They are extinct!"

Age level

4+

Objective

To understand the word "extinct"

Materials

Colored construction paper
felt pens
scissors
white posterboard
crayons

Preparation

Cut out dinosaur shapes from different colored construction paper. Make one for each child. Draw a large Earth on the posterboard. Color it.

Freddy the Fossil

Age level

3+

Objective

To learn about fossils

Materials

White posterboard
blue and brown crayons
gray construction paper
felt pens
scissors
brown construction paper
wooden blocks

Preparation

Color the lower half of the poster-board blue. This is a lake. Color an inch of mud at the bottom of the lake. Draw a 3" long plant-eating dinosaur on gray construction paper. Cut it out. Draw body bones on one side of the dinosaur. Cut a piece of brown paper large enough to cover the dinosaur. Draw a 3" x 3" rock on gray construction paper. Draw two large eyes on the rock. Draw a bone shape on the other side. This is Freddy the Fossil!

What to do

1. Place the posterboard on the rug. Place the paper dinosaur on the rug, bone-side down. Stand six wooden blocks on the rug, near the poster-board. Place them a few inches apart. This is the dinosaur jungle! Hold up the rock with the eyes showing. Explain that this is a special rock. It is a fossil. Its name is Freddy! A fossil is a plant or animal that has hardened into stone! Freddy is going to tell you how that can happen.

2. Use the rock as you would a puppet! Have Freddy the Fossil tell *The Fossil* story!

Many years ago in Dinosaur Land, there lived a plant-eating dinosaur. He was a walking peacefully in the jungle. (Pick up the paper dinosaur and walk it through the blocks.) He was looking for crunchy green leaves to eat. All of a sudden, he heard a terrible noise. (Stop the dinosaur!) It was the roar of a Tyrannosaurus! (Roar!) The plant-eater ran for safety towards the large lake. (Slap hands on the rug! Run the dinosaur towards the lake.) He jumped in! (Place the dinosaur in the lake.) He swam to the middle of the lake. (Move the dinosaur to the middle!) The Tyrannosaurus could not swim. It went looking for someone else to eat! (Pound fists on palms.) Tyrannosaurus is stomping away!

The plant-eater was so tired from running that he couldn't swim. He sank to the bottom of the lake. (Place the dinosaur on the mud at the bottom of the lake.) Fish ate the dinosaur. Soon only the bones were left. (Turn the dinosaur over to the bone side.) The skeleton lay buried in the mud. (Place the paper mud over the skeleton.) Many years passed. The lake dried up. Now there was only dirt! (Color over the blue lake with a brown crayon. The children can help!) The mud became as hard as rock. The bones changed to stone. They became fossils!

3. Now Freddy the Fossil is going to ask a question. How do we know that dinosaurs lived on the Earth? (We find fossils in the dirt! They tell us that dinosaurs were once alive!) Show the bone on the back of Freddy. This rock is showing us that a dinosaur was here!

4. Does anyone have any questions they want to ask Freddy? Encourage the questions to be about Dinosaur Land!

More to do

Make fossil imprints to take home. Give everyone a mound of clay or dough. Place leaves on the table. Demonstrate how to make a leaf print in the clay. Press the clay flat. Lay the leaf on the clay and press down. Carefully lift the leaf up. You have a leaf fossil!

A Bone Hunt

What to do

1. Sit on the rug. Explain that you are going on a bone dig to look for dinosaur bones! You have to dig within a dig site. This is a place where you think the bones will be found.

2. Walk to the dig site. Give each child her plastic bag. Walk carefully in the dig site.

3. Hunt for dinosaur bones! Set a limit on the number of bones each child can find.

4. When a child finds a bone, she places it in the bag. Now clean the bones!

5. Give the child who is ready to clean her bones a small paintbrush. This child can sit on the ground and carefully brush the sand off her bone.

6. Place the dinosaur bones back in the bags when they are clean and bring them home at the end of the day.

More to do

Play Hide-a-Bone! Place yarn on the rug in a large square. This is a dig site! Cut out large bone shapes from white construction paper. Hide these dinosaur bones in the classroom. The children can hunt for a bone! When a child finds a bone, she can sit in the dig site.

Age level

3+

Objective

To learn how dinosaur bones are discovered

Materials

An uncooked chicken (or white posterboard)
a pot
yarn
scissors
masking tape
felt pen
plastic bags
paintbrushes

Preparation

Cook the chicken and save the bones. Or, cut white posterboard into small bone shapes, making a few for each child. Place yarn in the sandbox in a large square. This is the dig site. Hide the bones in the sand within the site. Have part of each bone showing. Print each child's name on a strip of masking tape. Place each strip on a plastic bag.

Rainbow Skin

Age level

3+

Objective

To learn that fossils tell us about the past but not what color a dinosaur was

Materials

White paper
felt pen
crayons

Preparation

Draw the large shape of a dinosaur on a sheet of paper for each child.

What to do

1. Sit at the table. Place a variety of crayons on the table. Ask the children if a fossil can tell us what color a dinosaur was. No! It only shows us that something, many years ago, was alive.

2. What color skin did a dinosaur have? Give each child a picture of a dinosaur. Brainstorm ideas! Do you think a dinosaur had spots. How about stripes? Do you think there was a rainbow dinosaur? Ask the children to color the dinosaur skins! Be creative!

3. Tape the colored dinosaur pictures on a wall. Look at the beautiful dinosaurs! Have each child point to his dinosaur picture. Talk about the color and design on each one. Title the wall, "What do you think dinosaurs looked like?"

More to do

Draw a small dinosaur on a piece of paper. Make it the same shape as the larger dinosaurs. Make a baby dinosaur for each child. the children can color the baby dinosaurs. Encourage the children to use similar colors and designs. Tape the baby dinosaurs on a wall next to the large dinosaurs. Can you see the dinosaurs that match? Perhaps they came from the same dinosaur family!

Smooth or Bumpy?

What to do

1. Place the objects and material on the table. Give everyone a glue cup. Ask the children, "If you could touch a dinosaur, what do you think it would feel like?" Brainstorm ideas!

2. Give each child a paper dinosaur. Ask the children to glue objects and materials on the dinosaur to give its skin texture.

3. When the dinosaurs have dried, tape them on a wall. Have each child point to her dinosaur. Talk about the objects on the dinosaurs. This one looks soft. This one looks lumpy!

4. Title the wall, "What do you think dinosaurs felt like?"

More to do

Make a giant Feeling Dinosaur! Tape a large sheet of butcher paper on the wall low enough for the children to touch. Draw a large dinosaur on the paper. The teacher tapes an object on the dinosaur. Ask the children to feel the object! Explain that it is our "Feeling Dinosaur"! Encourage the children to bring objects or material from home to tape on the dinosaur.

Age level

4+

Objective

To learn about possible dinosaur skin textures

Materials

Variety of objects or materials, such as crepe paper, construction paper, sponges, tin foil, cotton balls, paper bags, and marshmallows
scissors
glue
small paper cups
white paper
felt pens

Preparation

Cut up the above material into small squares, except the cotton balls and marshmallows. Pour glue into paper cups. Make a glue cup for each child. Draw a large dinosaur shape on a sheet of white paper for each child.

Dinosaur Dancing

Age level

3+

Objective

To explore different ways to move if you were a dinosaur

Materials

White posterboard
felt pens
scissors
balloons
paper cups
yarn
crepe paper
paper plates
party hats
pairs of socks
recorded music

Preparation

Draw large bones the length of the posterboard. Cut them out. Blow up balloons. Poke a hole on each side of the paper cups. String a piece of yarn through the holes. Make the yarn long enough to tie around a child's head. Cut crepe paper into 3' strips.

What to do

1. Explain how to Dinosaur dance! Display the above objects. Each object represents a different dinosaur. The crepe paper strips are the tails of a small dinosaur, the Coelophysis (See-loh-fy-ses!) The balloons are dinosaur eggs. The paper plates are the plates on the back of the Stegosaurus. The bones are dinosaur bones! The party hats are horns on the Triceratops. The paper cup masks are the duck bill of the Anatosaurus. The socks are the small arms of the Tyrannosaurus!

2. Ask the children to choose an object to dance with. The object they choose will determine the kind of dinosaur they are. For example, if a child chooses to wear the socks on his hands, he is a Tyrannosaurus!

3. Play music! The children dance with their dinosaur object. When the teacher stops the music, trade objects to become another dinosaur!

More to do

Do "The Last Dinosaur" dance! Sit in a circle. Choose a child to be the last dinosaur. This child chooses a dinosaur object. The last dinosaur stands in the middle of the circle. Play music! This child dances with the object. When the music stops, this child chooses another Last Dinosaur to dance.

Name-a-Saurus

What to do

1. Place crayons, stencils and cookie cutters on the table. Give each child a sheet of paper and a felt pen. Explain that the children can create their own new species of dinosaur!

2. Brainstorm ideas! You might have found the bones of a Flower-a-Saurus. Maybe you came across the bones of a Heart-a-Saurus. You could discover a Spot-a-Saurus in your backyard!

3. Use the stencils and cookie cutters to create designs on your dinosaur. Draw them with your felt pen. Color in your designs with the crayons.

4. As each child finishes her picture, she can tell the teacher what kind of dinosaur she drew. Print the name of the dinosaur on their paper. Each name will end in a_____a-Saurus!

5. Tape the picture on the wall and then sit on the rug. Now say the names of the known dinosaurs. The children can help remember the dinosaur names. When you have named the dinosaurs you have learned about, say the names of the newly discovered dinosaurs on the wall.

More to do

Sit and sing "The Name-a-Saurus" song! Sing it to the tune of, "Do You Know the Muffin Man." Sing the song again! The children can take turns thinking of a kind of dinosaur they discover.

> *I can dig dig dig underneath a log, (Dig with your hands)*
> *I can dig dig dig underneath a frog! (Make a fist jump on "frog")*
> *I can sneak upon one in a forest, (Tiptoe with fingertips)*
> *And capture me a _____a-Saurus! (Throw hands in air and then*
> *down on rug)*

Age level

3+

Objective

To review the dinosaur names

Materials

Crayons
stencils
cookie cutters
white paper
felt pens

Preparation

None

What's An Ocean?

Jump in! The ocean is an exciting and amazing place to explore. This is a world that is made for children. It is fantasy! It is full of bright colors, constant movement, beautiful fish and strange-looking creatures. Children are fascinated by a world under the water. Are there forests under the ocean? Yes! There are kelp forests. Are there gardens under the ocean? Yes! There are coral gardens. Do rabbits live under the ocean? No, but sea hares do! Who are the mysterious visitors in black suits (wet suits)? We are!

The ocean introduces children to new experiences, new information and feelings of respect for a special environment. Children will learn how to take care of, protect and help many of the sea animals found on a seashore and in the ocean. The activities in this chapter will stimulate many ideas and discussions. Enjoy the fun and adventure of each experience!

Shake Hands With an Octopus–
An Exciting Trip to the Ocean

	Monday	Tuesday	Wednesday	Thursday	Friday
Week 1	**3+ Ocean Adventure** *To introduce the concept of "ocean"*	**3+ Beach Fun** *To learn about beaches*	**3+ All About Sand** *To discover the properties of sand*	**4+ Beach Combing** *To learn about shells*	**3+ Seashore Surprise** *To review seashore knowledge*
Week 2	**4+ Why Tides** *To understand tides*	**4+ The Tidepool Story** *To learn about tidepools*	**3+ Something Fishy** *To learn about fish*	**3+ Four Fish Facts** *To discover more about fish*	**4+ The Sea Review** *To review the names of sea animals*
Week 3	**4+ Underwater Forest** *To learn about kelp forests*	**5+ Seahorse Tales** *To understand the amazing seahorse*	**4+ The Magic Octopus** *To appreciate how smart the octopus is*	**3+ Make Friends With a Moray Eel** *To discover that a Moray Eel is shy*	**3+ What's a Pinniped?** *To learn about seals*
Week 4	**4+ Beautiful Sharks** *To understand the misunderstood shark*	**3+ The Playful Dolphins** *To learn that dolphins are playful and friendly*	**4+ The Wonderful Whales** *To appreciate whales*	**3+ Sounds of the Sea** *To remember forms of sea life*	**4+ Fantastic Facts** *To review fascinating facts of sea life*

Ocean Adventure

What to do

1. Sit around the pan of water and pretend it is the Earth. Explain that the rocks are the land. Ask the children what the water is called (the ocean, the sea).

2. Look at the pan. Does the Earth have more land or more ocean? Each child can stir the water with a stick. Feel how much water is in the pan. Look how much ocean is on the Earth!

3. Ask these watery questions! Is the water in your bathtub an ocean? Is the water in your sink an ocean? Is the water in a rain puddle an ocean? What makes an ocean? Brainstorm many possible ideas—a large body of water, salt in the water, a place where saltwater fish live, a place where coral and kelp grow, water that touches a beach, water that surrounds the land on the Earth.

4. Display the pieces of sponge. These are small boats that can float in the ocean. Each child can choose a boat and place it on the water in the pan. Ask the children, "If you were on this boat, in the middle on the ocean, what do you think you would see?" Give each child a chance to float his or her boat and answer the question.

More to do

Make boats to take home! Form them out of dough, and pass out toothpicks to add a mast. Each child can cut his or her own flag from different colored construction paper and glue it on their mast. Place each boat on a paper plate. Everyone can think of a name for their boat. Print the boat's name on the paper plate. These boats can remind everyone of their ocean adventure that is about to start!

Age level

3+

Objective

To introduce the concept of "ocean"

Materials

Large shallow pan
water
three large rocks
sponge
scissors
stick

Preparation

Fill the pan with water. This is the ocean. Place three large rocks in the water a few inches apart. The rocks are land! Make sure a part of the rocks are above the water. Cut sponges pieces for each child. These are small boats!

Beach Fun

Age level

3+

Objective

To learn about beaches

Materials

Shallow pan
sand
water
salt

Preparation

Place an inch of sand in half of the pan.

What to do

1. Display the pan with sand. Ask the children if this a beach. No! It's missing something! Place a seashell on the sand. Is this a beach? No! Place a rock on the sand. Is this a beach? No! What is still missing?

2. Slowly pour water into the remaining half of the pan. Is this a beach? Almost! The children can sprinkle a pinch of salt in the water. Now it's saltwater! Let's call it an ocean. Is this a beach now? Yes! It is a body of saltwater by a sandy shore!

3. Explain that the beach is a very special place where people like to visit. Ask the children why they think it's a special place. There are many possible answers. It's warm! Laying in the sun makes you feel nice and relaxed. The ocean offers a beautiful view. The sound of the ocean is very soothing. There are many things to see. You can see shells, rocks, birds, sand crabs, kelp, tidepools and people! There are many things to do! You can run, play with a frisbee, swim, collect shells and build sand castles!

4. Place the pan on the table so the children can play with it. Or place sand, shells rocks and sticks in the water table for the children to play with.

More to do

Make beach pictures! Give each child a sheet of paper. Ask them to spread glue on the lower part of their paper. Place sand in paper cups and give one to each child. The children can shake the sand on the glue to make a beach! Shake the excess sand off. Using crayons, the children can color an ocean on the remaining part of their paper. Draw boats, whales and fish! Give each child an ocean sticker to place on his or her picture. Print the children's names on their papers. If a child's name is Rachael, print, "Rachael's Beach."

All About Sand

What to do

1. Sit on the rug around the pan of sand. Ask the children to touch the sand. Rub the sand between your fingers! How does it feel? soft? hard? warm? cold? Where does sand on the beach comes from? Brainstorm ideas! (The movement of the ocean grinds up rocks and coral into tiny pieces!)

2. Sand can change shape! It can pour. It can make an impression. Each child can add sand to the pan. Now lay a hand flat on the sand. Push down gently. Lift up your hand! Do you see a print of your hand?

3. Continue sitting on the rug and give each child a sheet of white paper. Place a spoonful of sand on each sheet. Lay on your stomachs. Look closely at the sand. What colors do you see? Are some of the pieces larger than others? Move the sand around with your fingers. Make a small design. People come to the beach to play in the sand!

4. Does the sand move at the beach? Yes! The wind can blow the sand from place to place. When sand is blown into large hills, a sand dune is formed! Pretend your hand is the wind. Ask the children to push the sand in the pan to form a hill. The shape of beaches is always changing!

More to do

What happens to sand when it gets wet? Pour some water in the pan of sand. Does it change color? Touch it! Does wet sand feel different than dry sand? Where do you see wet sand at the beach? What can you make in the sand? Sand castles! Wet the sand in the outdoor sandbox. Make sand castles with paper cups! Make other sand designs, such as turtles and whales. Dig a sea cave!

Age level

3+

Objective

To discover the properties of sand

Materials

Large shallow pan
sand
large spoon
white paper

Preparation

Fill the pan halfway with sand.

Beach Combing

Age level

4+

Objective

To learn about shells

Materials

White construction paper
felt pens
scissors
feathers, rocks, shells, sand dollars
small paper bags

Preparation

Draw a 3" fish bone shape on white construction paper for each child. Cut them out. Hide the shells, bones and feathers around the room. Trace one of each item on separate sheets of paper. Tape the tracings on a wall!

What to do

1. There are treasures to be found on the beach. They can be shells, rocks, fish bones, bird feathers! Looking for these treasures is called beach combing!

2. Let's go beach combing! Point to the pictures on the wall. The teacher says the name of the items to search for (name each variety of shell, sand dollar, rock, a fish bone, a feather).

3. Explain that shells are the homes of animals. The animals make the shells! They come in many colors and shapes. The shells in the classroom have no animal inside.

4. Give each child a paper bag. Explain that they can collect one treasure of each kind. To remember the different treasures, look at the pictures on the wall!

5. One more thing! Take off your shoes and socks. Most people walk barefoot when they are beach combing!

6. When each child has found the treasures, sit on the rug. Empty the treasures carefully on the rug. Shells break easily!

7. The teacher can point to each picture and ask, "Who found a moon shell? This is its shape. Look and see if you have one!" Continue with each pictured item.

8. If some children did not find all the treasures, look again! Everyone can help look for the missing treasures!

9. Take the treasures home! They will remind the children that the beach is a very special place. Ask the children how we can keep the beach special. Throw trash in a trash can! Don't remove more than you need from the beach. If you find a shell with an animal in it, leave it alone!

More to do

Fill a deep pan halfway with sand. Place small rocks and shells in the pan. Go beach combing in the pan! Place the pan on the table. Give a sieve to a child. This child can carefully sift through the sand. See what treasures you find each time you sift!

Seashore Surprise

What to do

1. Sit on the rug. Explain that there are surprise treasures in the paper bag. They are from the seashore!

2. The teacher secretly picks an object from the paper bag and places it in the oatmeal box. Now place the lid on the box and choose a treasure finder!

3. The treasure finder puts a hand through the lid opening and feels the object that is in the box. Guess what it is!

4. Now pull the object out of the box. Identify the object! This child can then choose the next treasure finder.

5. The teacher takes another object from the paper bag and places it in the oatmeal box. Continue with the other children.

More to do

Make starfish paintings! Cut out a 3" wide starfish shape from white posterboard for each child. Tape each starfish on a separate sheet of white construction paper. Give a starfish sheet to each child. Place a variety of paint on the table. Ask the children to paint a beautiful ocean picture on their paper. When the children are finished painting, remove the paper starfish from the pictures to reveal a starfish imprint!

Age level

3+

Objective

To review what was learned about the seashore through tactile stimulation

Materials

Empty oatmeal box
scissors
paper bag
various objects relating to the seashore, such as rocks, shells, feathers, bones, kelp, sand, a starfish

Preparation

Cut a hole the size of a child's fist in the lid of the oatmeal box. Place the beach items in a paper bag.

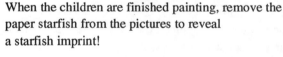

Why Tides?

Age level

4+

Objective

To understand the tides

Materials

Large shallow pan
sand
water
white paper
scissors
felt pen

Preparation

Fill one side of the pan with at least an inch of sand. Carefully pour water in the remaining side. Cut a large moon shape from white paper.

What to do

1. Sit around the pan of water. The ocean is always moving! Ask the children to sway back and forth. Even on a calm day, the ocean moves. Sway slightly!

2. The movement of the ocean is called the tide. The moon is like a giant magnet. It pulls on the oceans! When the moon is pulling on the water, it creeps up on the beach. It is high tide! When the moon stops pulling on the water, the ocean water is low on the beach. It is low tide! Each child can tilt the pan so the water creeps up on the "beach" and moves away from it.

3. If you walk near the water's edge, the water can creep up on you! It can surprise you and wet your feet! Each child can walk along the sand with their two fingertips. Walk near the edge of the water. The teacher can surprise you and tilt the pan to wet your "feet"!

4. Demonstrate the pull of the moon on the ocean water. Choose a child to be the moon. This child can sit in front of the other children. When the child holds the moon high, the others can lean forward. When the child holds the moon behind his or her back, the others can lean backward!

More to do

Sit and sing "The Tide" song! Sing it to the tune of, "The Worms Creep in, the Worms Creep Out." Sing it with an air of mystery!

> The tide creeps in, (Slowly walk fingers out)
> The tide creeps out, (Slowly walk fingers back)
> It wets your toes, (Wiggle toes)
> So you want to shout! (Shout!)
> Watch out, watch out, (Clap right, clap left)
> Watch out for me, (Point to self)
> I'm being chased (Rotate fists around each other)
> By the sneaky sea! (Tiptoe fingers)

The Tidepool Story

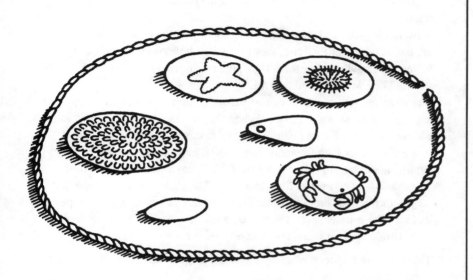

What to do

1. Place the yarn in a large circle at one end of the classroom. Sit at the other end of the classroom. Explain that a tidepool is a tiny pool along the shore. It is a very special place where certain ocean animals live. It can be completely covered with ocean water at high tide. At low tide, there is still some water in it and you can watch the animals in a tidepool!

2. Let's go find a tidepool! Take off shoes and socks. Pretend to walk along a beach at the water's edge. There is a tidepool! Let's sit around the tidepool. Sit quietly so we don't disturb or frighten this special busy world!

3. Display the box. Animals that live in the tidepool are in the box! We can help the sea animals return to their tidepool. Pass the box around the circle. Each child chooses a sea animal and shows the remaining children. As a child shows the sea animal, the teacher says an interesting fact about it. Then the child can place the sea animal in the tidepool. Continue until all the sea animals are in the tidepool!

Age level

4+

Objective

To learn about tidepools

Materials

Different colored construction paper
felt pens
scissors
box
yarn

Preparation

Draw a 2" circle on orange construction paper. Draw a crab shape in the circle. Cut the circle out. Draw a 3" circle on yellow construction paper. Draw a starfish shape in the circle. Cut the circle out. Draw a 3" circle on purple construction paper. Draw a circle with many long thin spines sticking out of it (a sea urchin). Cut the circle out. Draw a cone shape 1" in diameter on brown construction paper. Draw a hole at the top (a barnacle). Cut it out. Draw a 5" circle on green construction paper. Draw small flower petal shapes on it (a sea anemone). Cut it out. Draw a 2" long thin oval on dark blue construction paper (a mussel). Cut it out. Make one picture for each child. Place the cut out pictures in a box. Cut a long piece of yarn.

4. Information about the sea animals.

The hermit crab—When the hermit crab grows too large for his shell, he goes shopping for a new one! He will often try on several shells before he finds one that fits!

The starfish—The starfish can twist its body into many shapes. It moves very slowly, five inches a minute! If a starfish loses an arm, it grows a new one!

The sea urchin—The sea urchin eats kelp (seaweed). When in danger, it moves its sharp spines. Who likes to eat the prickly sea urchin? The sea otter!

A barnacle—Barnacles have a hole at the top of their shell. When they are out of water for too long, they close their hole so they won't dry out! Instead of crawling after food, they glue themselves to a rock, a ship or a whale. They wait for food to wash by!

The anemone—Anemones can be many different colors! In a group, they look like an underwater garden! When they are in a low water, they look like a saggy brown paper bag. When water covers them, they blossom into beautiful looking flowers! Their petals catch and poison their prey. A large anemone has a large appetite! It will eat a small shark or lobster!

The mussel—The mussel lives in a shell. The shell has two parts. What do you think holds them together? A muscle! The mussel has a spinner on its foot. The spinner spins a thread on a tidepool rock. This holds it on a rock. Inside the two shells are rainbow colors!

5. Tidepools are a special place by the sea. Tidepool animals live, eat and sleep together. Gently pick up the animals, but put them back where you found them. They are sharing their special home with you. Each child can pick up the tidepool animals. Pet them. Talk to them! Put one back and look for another one. Enjoy their watery world!

More to do

Say "The Tidepool" chant! Do the related body movements.

> *A mermaid came a knocking at the door, (Pound left fist on right hand)*
> *I'm just a little mermaid from the ocean floor! (Swim with arms)*
> *What do you want? said the crab on the shore, (wiggle fingers)*
> *I'll tidy up the tidepool for a dollar twenty-four! (Pretend to sweep)*

Something Fishy

What to do

1. Draw wavy ocean lines near the top of the paper. Now ask the children what kind of animal lives in water? Accept all sea animal answers! (The answer that you continue the activity with is fish!)

2. Explain that a fish is a sea animal. It always needs to be in the water. Draw a large fish shape on the butcher paper without a tail, eyes, fins, etc.

3. Ask the children what is missing. As the children respond, draw or color their answers. Possible answers are eyes, fins, gills, scales, bones on the inside.

4. As each body part is mentioned, talk about it! Large eyes help the fish see underwater. Fins help fish move. Tails push fish through the water. Fish breathe through gills. Fish have scales instead of skin or hair. Fish have a skeleton. Fish come in many beautiful colors.

5. When the fish picture is finished, place a variety of felt pens on the rug. Each child can choose a felt pen and draw a fish on the paper. Explain that many fish swimming together is a school of fish!

Age level

3+

Objective

To learn about fish

Materials

Butcher paper
scissors
tape
felt pens

Preparation

Cut a 3' x 2' sheet of butcher paper. Tape it on a wall.

More to do

Give each child a sheet of white construction paper. Place shades of blue and green crayons on the table. The children can color a beautiful ocean on their paper. While they are coloring their ocean, the teacher can draw and cut out 2" fish shapes from different colored construction paper for each child. Tape a string on the back of each fish. Make the string an inch shorter than the width of the papers. When the children finish their ocean, they can choose a colored fish. Tape the loose end of the string at the top of their paper. Now they can make their fish swim around in the ocean!

Four Fish Facts

Age level

3+

Objective

To learn more about fish

Materials

None

Preparation

None

What to do

1. How do people move? with flippers? with legs? Ask the children to demonstrate how they move around the classroom. Walk around the room! We are using our legs! Now ask, "If the classroom was filled with water and we were all fish, how would a fish move?" It would swim! How does a fish swim? Does it move in an upright position like you? Demonstrate the fish position! Lay on your stomach. Slightly bend your knees to make a tail. Stick your hands outward to make fins. Now rock back and forth. You are a fish swimming in water!

2. Fish move by bending their body and tail back and forth. This pushes them through the water. Pretend to be a fish swimming around the room. As you swim, move your body in a swaying motion.

3. When fish want to stop, they spread their fins out. Everyone swim around the room! When the teacher says, "Stop fish," spread out your arms and stop. When the teacher says, "Go fish," swim around the room.

4. When fish are frightened, they hide. They camouflage themselves! They hide in a place that matches their color. Swim around the room! When the teacher says, "Shark! Shark!," the children swim to a place that matches a color they are wearing. Remain very still! The teacher is the shark. He or she swims by each fish and does not see them. When the shark sits down on the rug, the danger has passed. It is safe to swim again!

More to do

Some fish are pets! Say the chant, "The Five Little Fishes." That is all mama will allow in the goldfish bowl! Or sing it to the tune of, "Five Little Ducks That I Once Knew."

Went to the pet store near my house, (Steer a car)
Mama said no to a little mouse, (Shake head from side to side)
Saw a goldfish in a bowl, (Point)
Mama said yes, and the man said, "Sold!" (Clap on "Sold" and say it loud)
One little goldfish in my bowl! (Hold up one finger)

Repeat this verse substituting "two..., three..., four..., five little goldfish in my bowl"

Went to the pet store near my house, (Steer a car)
Mama said no to a little mouse, (Shake head from side to side)
Saw a goldfish in a bowl, (Point)
Mama said NO! There's too many goldfish
in your bowl! (Wag finger sternly)

The Sea Review

What to do

1. Play "The Knock, Knock" Game! The teacher holds a block in each hand. He or she bangs them together three times while saying, "Knock, knock!"

2. Now the children say, "Who's there?" The teacher says, "A whale!"

3. The children say, "A whale who?" The teacher says, "A whale from the sea!" The children say, "Join the sea party!"

4. The teacher now gives the blocks to a child. This child bangs the blocks together and says, "Knock, knock!"

5. This child thinks of a different sea animal to name when the children say, "Who's there?" If the child names a shark, the verse will be, "A shark! A shark who? A shark from the sea! Join the sea party!"

6. Continue to pass the blocks until the other children have had a turn to join the sea party.

7. Now try and remember the different sea animals who joined the party! (You can play this game using the names of dinosaurs, land animals or the names of children in the room!)

More to do

Make a fish bowl review! Draw a large fish bowl on a sheet of white paper for each child. Ask the children to color in their fish bowl. Draw and cut out 2" paper fish from orange construction paper for each child. Print a sea question on the back of each fish. Tape the paper fish on a wall. Tape each child's fish bowl picture on the wall. Each child chooses a fish and answers their special sea question. Then they can tape their fish in their fish bowl. Suggested sea questions—Where does a fish need to live? What is a beach? What are you doing when you beach comb? What lives in a seashell? Name a kind of shell. What lives in a tidepool? How can we take care of a tidepool? What does sand feel like?

Age level

4+

Objective

To review the names of different sea animals

Materials

Two wooden blocks

Preparation

None

Underwater Forest

Age level

4+

Objective

To learn about kelp forests

Materials

Green crepe paper
tape
colored construction paper
scissors
felt pen
rocks
flashlight
rock for each child

Preparation

Tear off 3' strips of green crepe paper. Tape the strips from the ceiling. Tape many strips over the rug area. This is a kelp forest! Tear an extra 2' strip for each child (fronds). Draw 4" fish shapes on different colored construction paper for each child. Draw a square around each fish. Cut the squares out.

What to do

1. There is a forest under the water, a kelp forest! Place the crepe paper strips on the rug. Explain that kelp is a plant. It grows like giant trees under the water. Each child can choose a green strip of paper. It is a kelp plant!

2. Have the children place their kelp on the rug in front of them. What holds a kelp plant to the bottom of the ocean? It does not have any roots. Brainstorm ideas! (The bottom of the plant clings to rocks.) Give each child a rock to place at the bottom of his or her kelp plant.

2. Kelp does not have a rigid wooden trunk; it has a flexible stalk that bends with the flow of the water. Everyone stand! Be a stiff tree trunk. Don't move! Now be a giant kelp plant. With feet on the rug, sway back and forth. Move with the ocean!

3. Hundreds of different sea animals live in kelp. They eat the kelp. They hide in the kelp. They have babies in the kelp! Place the paper fish in the rug. Pass out scissors. Each child chooses a colored fish to cut out. Now tape the fish on the kelp plants!

4. Large leaves grow from the kelp plant. They are called fronds! Give each child a green frond to place on the kelp plant. The fronds grow toward sunlight, just like any plant! Where is the sun? Point to the sky! Which way do you think the fronds grow?

5. When people dive under the water, they can swim in the kelp forests. It is a strange and beautiful world! If you dive at night, you bring a flashlight. The kelp forest glows in the light! Darken the classroom. Sit quietly. You don't want to frighten the sea animals that live in the kelp forest. The teacher turns on the flashlight. Shine it in the kelp forest above you. Move the flashlight back and forth. Do you think it would be a mysterious experience? Do you think it would be pretty? Does it look scary? How about fun? Give everyone a turn to shine the flashlight in the kelp forest.

6. Place each child's paper kelp, rock, fish and frond in a small paper bag. Print on the bag, "My Kelp Kit." Take the kelp experiences home!

More to do

Draw many fish shapes on different colored construction paper. Cut around the fish shapes and place them on the table. The children cut out as many fish shapes as they want! The teacher can tape the colored fish on the kelp hanging in the classroom. Now darken the room! Shine the flashlight on the fish in the kelp. The classroom will seem to glow with underwater beauty! Sing the song, "Where the Green Kelp Grows!" Sing it to the tune of, "Do Your Ears Hang Low." Begin by singing it slowly. Gradually increase your speed!

In the sea, sea, sea, (Move hands in a wave)
I can go, go, go, (Clap on each "go")
To the very, very bottom, (Slap the floor three times)
Where the green kelp grows, (Move arms in a wavy motion)
All around, round me, (Turn around)
At the bottom of the sea, (Slap the floor three times)
Where the green kelp grows! (Move arms in a wavy motion)

Seahorse Tales

Age level

5+

Objective

To understand the amazing seahorse

Materials

Magazines
scissors
white paper
felt pens
tape
pipe cleaners
green crepe paper
white paper
picture of a seahorse (look in library
books!)

Preparation

Cut out magazine pictures of an ocean, kelp, a horse's head, a monkey's tail, a kangaroo's pouch, the large eyes of a chameleon and a fish tank! Or draw pictures of these things and cut them out. Draw tiny 1/4" question marks on a sheet of white paper. These are newborn sea horses! Fold a sheet of white paper in half to make a book shape for each child. Tape one of the pictures inside each book. Close the books and tape them on a wall. Cut pipe cleaners in half. Cut one for each child. Tear green crepe paper into 1' strips for each child.

What to do

1. Sit near the paper books. Explain that inside each book is a special tale. A tale is a story! Each tale gives a clue about a special sea animal.

2. Choose a child to pick a tale. This child shows the picture inside the book. Identify it. It is a clue to the special sea animal!

3. Suggested clues: It lives in the ocean. It can live in kelp forests. It has a head like a small horse. It has a tail like a monkey. It has a pouch like a kangaroo. It has large eyes that move in different directions, like a chameleon. It can live in a fish tank in a house. Their babies look like tiny question marks. It is not a whale. It is not a shark. It is not an eel. It is not a jellyfish!

4. If the correct answer is guessed during the clues, continue until all the clues are given! Do not reveal the correct answer yet! You can say, "Maybe!" If the correct answer is not given, slowly sound out the word sea horse! Now show a picture of a sea horse!

5. Give each child a pipe cleaner. Bend the pipe cleaners into the shape of a sea horse. Bend it into a question mark!

6. A sea horse does not swim like most fish. It swims in an upright position! Make the sea horses swim. Move them up and down in the air!

7. A sea horse has a long snout. The end of it opens and closes. This makes a smacking sound under the water. Make a smacking sound!

8. Give each child a strip of crepe paper. This is a piece of kelp. A sea horse swims in kelp! It holds onto kelp by twisting its tail around a thin stalk. Twist the end of the sea horses around the kelp.

9. Take the sea horses home. Twist the tail around an object in at home!

More to do

Fold a small sheet of colored construction paper in half. Tape a sheet vertically on the back of each child. Tape it along the folded edge. These are the fins on the back of a seahorse! When a sea horse moves its back fin, it swims! Play slow music! The children can gracefully swim around the classroom to the music.

The Magic Octopus

What to do

1. An octopus is very smart! It can remember something that it has learned. Place three paper cups on the rug. Show a marble. Place the marble under one of the paper cups.

2. Pretend that the marble is an octopus egg. The paper cups are rocks! The octopus has laid the egg under a rock. It will not forget where it laid its egg!

3. Pretend everyone is an octopus. The teacher can mix up the paper cups. Which octopus can find the egg?

4. Choose an octopus to pick up the rock that is hiding the egg. Guess again! The octopus picks up all three rocks (paper cups) until the egg is found.

5. Say the chant, "Oliver the Octopus" with movements.

   Oliver the Octopus (Hold up eight fingers)
   Lived in a cave, (Hold up eight fingers)
   If you said hello to Oliver, (Wave)
   Oliver waved! (Wave)
   1-2-3-4-5-6-7-8! (Clap on each count)

   Oliver the Octopus (Hold up eight fingers)
   Swam by his cave, (Hold up eight fingers)
   If you said hello to Oliver, (Wave)
   Oliver waved! (Wave)
   1-2-3-4-5-6-7-8! (Clap on each count)

   Oliver the Octopus (Hold up eight fingers)
   Crawled to his cave, (Hold up eight fingers)
   If you said goodbye to Oliver, (Wave goodbye)
   Oliver would say, (Wave goodbye)
   Goodbye! I'm too tired to wave! (Hold both cheeks and move face
        back and forth)

More to do

Make an octopus for each child! Open up a tissue. Place a cotton ball in the middle of the sheet. Pinch the tissue together under the cotton ball. This forms a round head. Tie a string of yarn under the head to secure it. Cut slits around the tissue to form arms. Make two eyes with a felt pen.

Age level

4+

Objective

To learn how smart the octopus is

Materials

Three paper cups
a marble

Preparation

None

Make Friends With a Moray Eel

Age level

3+

Objective

To learn that the moray eel is a very shy sea animal

Materials

Shoe box and lid
knife
scissors
construction paper
felt pen
brown or green sock

Preparation

Cut out the short sides of a shoe box. Draw a 3" fish on a sheet of construction paper. Cut it out.

What to do

1. The moray eel is a sea animal that is shaped like a large snake. It swims by moving its long body back and forth in the water. Its mouth opens and closes often. It makes it look mean! But the moray eel is only breathing! Pretend your arm is a moray eel. Weave your arm back and forth like a moray swimming. Now open and close your fingers. The moray eel is breathing, not trying to bite you!

2. The moray eel hides in between large rocks. When a fish swims by, the moray eel darts out and eats it! Then it will disappear inside a cave. Take out the shoe box. This is a moray eel's cave! Each child can stick their arm through the shoe box and out the far side.

3. Demonstrate how to pet a moray eel. Who wants to try? The teacher can wear a brown or green sock on an arm. Explain that there are brown and green eels! Stick your arm through the box and out the other side. Hold the paper fish in your other hand. Slowly wave the fish back and forth in front of the cave. Coax the eel to come out! Say to the eel, "Come on out! I have a nice fish for you to eat." Slowly move the eel out of the cave. Now pet the eel! Approach the eel with your hand moving high over the eel's head. Bring your hand down and gently stroke the eel behind its head. Pass the fish to the next child. This child can coax the eel out of its cave and pet it. The last child to pet the eel can feed it the fish!

More to do

There are many kinds of eels that live in the ocean. One kind is a rainbow eel! Make a giant rainbow eel to hang in the classroom Place a long sheet of butcher paper on the table. Draw a long eel down the length of the paper. Make it a foot wide! Place different colored paints on the table. Give each child a paintbrush. Paint the eel! Now draw and paint a second eel on another sheet of butcher paper, identical in shape to the first eel. Cut them both out and staple three sides together. Ask the children to crunch up newspaper and stuff the eel. Staple the remaining side together and hang it from the ceiling!

What's a Pinniped?

What to do

1. A seal is a pinniped. A pinniped is a fin-footed creature! Do you have fins or legs? Are you a pinniped?

2. What would it be like to have fins instead of legs? Find out! Everyone can rest on their stomachs. Place your hands close to your body. Lift your feet in the air. This is how a seal would be resting on the rug!

3. Now move like a seal! Lay on your stomachs. A seal can't use its rear flippers on land. It pulls itself along with its front flippers. Try moving yourself forward with only your hands!

4. You can teach a seal tricks. Pretend to be seals! Sit on your knees. The teacher is the seal trainer. The teacher can throw the ball to each child in turn. Each seal can throw the ball back! Try different tricks! Roll the ball back and forth. Bounce the ball back and forth. Sit on the rug and bend your knees. Place the ball at the top of your knees and let go. The ball will roll down your legs like a slide!

More to do

Explain the difference between a seal and a sea lion. You can see the ears of a sea lion! Sea lions like to play. Pretend to be sea lions. Sea lions like to body surf on a wave. Everyone can lay on their stomachs. Place your arms out to your side. Rock back and forth on a wave! Sea lions like to chase bubbles. Blow bubbles in the classroom. Chase them!

Age level

3+

Objective

To learn about seals

Materials

White paper
felt pens
medium-sized ball

Preparation

None

Beautiful Sharks

Age level

4+

Objective

To understand the misunderstood shark

Materials

Pink, blue, yellow, gray and white construction paper
felt pens
scissors
scarf
two spoons

Preparation

Draw and cut out 4" sharks from each of the colored papers. Make one shark for each child. Place the sharks on the rug with a scarf over them. Draw and cut out a small fish shape from colored construction paper.

What to do

1. Sit around the hidden sharks. Explain that there are sharks under the scarf! Ask the children what they think the sharks look like? Brainstorm ideas!

2. Take the scarf away and look at the sharks. They look beautiful!

3. Each child can choose a shark! Sit quietly with the shark. They are often shy. They usually do not want to bite you!

4. Sharks are strong, smooth swimmers. They move through the water very gracefully! The children can make their shark swim around the classroom. Move with smooth motions. The shark is a beautiful creature to watch!

5. Now swim the sharks back to the rug. Most sharks sink when they stop swimming! Slowly move the sharks. Keep the head in a slightly turned-up position. This helps to keep the shark from sinking to the bottom of the ocean.

6. Some sharks can rest on the bottom of the ocean. Swim the sharks to the bottom of the ocean and let it rest. A resting shark is hard to wake up! Gently stroke the sharks. They are still sleeping!

7. Sharks can feel small movements in the water. They can feel a fish passing by! The teacher can slowly move the paper fish past the sleeping sharks. Now they are hungry! The movement of the fish wakes them up. The teacher can swim the fish around the classroom. The children can make their shark follow the path of the fish!

8. Sharks have good hearing. They can turn toward a sound even in the dark! Use the scarf to blindfold a child. Pretend to be a shark in the dark! The teacher can bang two spoons together. The child listen for the noise and moves her shark towards the noise! Make the noise change directions.

More to do

Draw a large shark on a long sheet of butcher paper. Explain that some sharks will eat anything! Shoes, coats, jewelry, signs, license plates and toys have been found in a shark's stomach. Place magazines and scissors on the table. The children can cut out pictures of different objects. Spread a layer of glue over the shark's body. The children can stick the objects on the shark's stomach. Title the mural, "Have You Ever Been This Hungry?"

The Playful Dolphins

What to do

1. The dolphin is not a fish. It is a mammal like us. It breathes air! Ask the children to take a deep breath. That is what dolphins do before they swim under the water.

2. Dolphins move by pushing their tail up and down in the water. Move your hand like a dolphin swimming. Place your fingers together. Dip your hand up and down in a repeated motion.

3. Dolphins like to play. They enjoy riding the wavy water that boats make! The children pretend to sit on a moving boat. Sit in a circle. Rock back and forth. Now choose two children to be dolphins. The dolphins swim around the outside of the circle once. They move their hands up and down as they swim! The children on the boat can wave to the playful dolphins.

4. Dolphins also play by rolling over in the water. Pretend to be rolling dolphins. Roll around on the rug!

5. Dolphins are smart animals. They have a special language. It sounds like clicks. Try to talk like a dolphin. Make clicking noises with your mouth! This noise can also bounce off objects and return to the dolphin. It tells the dolphin how big an object is! With this echo, the dolphin can tell the difference between a large and small fish! Place the paper fish on the rug. Each child can choose a large fish and then a smaller fish. Make clicking noises to help the dolphin decide!

More to do

Some dolphins are caught and placed in large tanks for people to study. They can be taught many tricks! They can jump together! Place one child on each end of a long string of yarn. Hold the yarn a few inches above the rug. Choose two children to be two jumping dolphins! These two dolphins stand side-by-side. Jump over the yarn. Now jump back. The two dolphins can now hold the yarn. Choose two more children to be the jumping dolphins

Age level

3+

Objective

To learn that dolphins are playful, friendly creatures

Materials

Colored construction paper
scissors
felt pen

Preparation

Draw and cut out fish shapes from different colored construction paper. Use many colors. Make some 6", some 5", some 4", some 3", some 2" and some 1"! Make two fish for each child.

The Wonderful Whales

Age level

4+

Objective

To appreciate whales and to learn new vocabulary words relating to whales

Materials

Picture of a blue whale
optional—slow music or ocean music

Preparation

None

What to do

1. The whale is one of the most magnificent creatures on the Earth. They are living giants! The blue whale is the largest animal on the Earth.

2. The whale is a mammal like us. It breathes air. Pretend to be whales diving under the water. Stand up. Take a giant gulp of air! Now bend your body slightly and dive under. Swim slowly around the room like a pod of whales. Remember that you are very large! Have no fear of getting cold. You have a thick layer of fat under your skin, called blubber! (If possible, play slow music or ocean music.)

3. It is time to surface and take another breath of air. Swim back to the rug and stand up. First you need to let your air out. Exhale! When a whale exhales, it sprays a stream of water in the air. Exhale again. Now make a loud swishing sound with your mouth and move both hands upward. You have let your breath out!

4. Sit on the rug. You have a nose that you breathe with. Point to it! A whale has a blow hole. It is a hole on the top of its head! Make a blow hole with your hands. Touch fingertips together to form a circle. When the blow hole is open, the whale takes deep breath. Now make both hands into a fist. Touch your fists together with fingers touching. When the blow hole is closed, the whale dives under the water! Say "The Blow Hole" chant!

> *Open, close, open, close, (Fingertips together, then fists together)*
> *The giant whale dives under, (Swoop hands down)*
> *Open, close, open, close, (Fingertips together, then fists together)*
> *With a splash of thunder! (Clap on "thunder")*

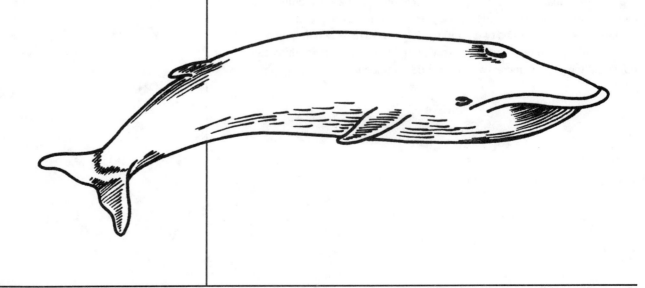

5. When a whale jumps straight out of the water and splashes back down, it is called breaching. You can hear the splash from a distance! Have everyone breach! Sit on the rug. Now jump straight up and come splashing down. Roll around on the rug! Breach again!

6. Sometimes a whale will lift its head straight up out of the water. Its body remains in the water. This is called spy-hopping!

7. Whales make many noises! They smack the surface of the water with their large tails. Place your arms up high and brings them down with a mighty slap on the rug. They also whine, squeak, hum and make a haunting sound. Try each sound! To make the haunting sound, cup your hands around your mouth. Make a long, slow oooooo sound, like a lonely ghost!

More to do

Sing "The Old Whale" song! Sing it to the tune of, "Where Oh Where Has My Little Dog Gone." Explain that some whales have become endangered. People should not hunt the whales! They should be allowed to live in peace and grow old. Sing this song slowly and with feeling. Sing it with love for the magnificent whales.

Where oh where has the old whale gone,
Where oh where can he be,
He's big and blue and beautiful too,
He's the blue whale of the sea!

Where oh where has the old whale gone,
Where of where can he be,
He's big and gray and beautiful too,
He's the gray whale of the sea!

Where oh where has the old whale gone,
Where oh where can he be,
He's black and white and beautiful too,
He's the killer whale of the sea!

Where oh where has the old whale gone,
Where oh where can he be,
He's white and bright and beautiful too,
He's the beluga whale of the sea!

You can continue this song using different whale names! As you sing this song, slowly move your hand up and down like a whale swimming in the water. Start the whale far off to the left. As you sing, it can slowly swim in front of you and disappear off to your right!

Sounds of the Sea

Age level

3+

Objective

To remember the many forms of sea life through the sounds they make

Materials

None

Preparation

None

What to do

1. Sit on the rug. You are at the seashore! Sit very quietly. You will be able to hear the different sounds of the sea.

2. Introduce each sound. The children can try the sound after the teacher identifies the sound and demonstrates it. Possible sea sounds:
   The surf—Make quiet swishing sounds with your mouth.
   A stormy sea—Clap your hands for waves crashing on the beach.
   Sea gulls—Make a high pitched short A sound, A..A..A!
   Sea lions—Make grunting sounds.
   Whales—Make haunting sounds.
   Dolphins—Make clicking sounds.
   Seahorse—Make smacking sounds.
   Whale's tail—Slap the rug!

3. Now begin a sea sound experience. The teacher says a name, such as sea gulls. The children make the sea gull sound! Then the teacher says, "Whale's tail." The children slap the rug. Continue in any order until all the sea sounds have been heard.

4. See who can remember the sea sounds. Each child can name a sound to make.

More to do

Extend the seashore experience. Try to think of other sea creatures you have talked about. Make a list of the added sounds and movements and do them!

Fantastic Facts

What to do

1. Print a sea question on the back of each fish. The following are a few suggestions.

   What is a whale doing when it is breaching?
   Can a whale breathe under the water?
   Can you make a whale sound?
   What sound does a dolphin make?
   How many arms does an octopus have?
   What color can a shark be?
   Is kelp a plant or an animal?
   Where is kelp found?
   Show with your finger how a seahorse swims.
   What sea animal has suckers?
   What has large eyes, fins and gills?
   Name an animal in a tidepool.

2. Place the fish on the rug and sit around them. Each child chooses a fish. The teacher reads the sea question on the back of the fish.

3. The child who chose the fish tries to answer the question. If he or she is not sure of the answer, everyone can help!

More to do

Make a picture of a sea lion on a piece of posterboard and place it on a chair. Put the paper fish on the rug behind the picture. Make a fishing pole from a pencil or stick and a string of yarn. Put a wad of tape at the end of the line. The children sit in front of the picture. Choose a child to go fishing! The child "hooks" a fish. The teacher reads the sea question on the back of the fish.

Age level

4+

Objective

To review fascinating facts of sea life

Materials

Colored construction paper
felt pens
scissors

Preparation

Draw 3" fish shapes on different colored construction paper for each child. Cut them out. Make one for each child. Print a sea question on the back of each fish. Tape the fish on the bucket! Cut a small slit under the W shape. This is the sea lion's mouth! Tape the opened end of a paper bag behind the slit.

Outside Fun and Games

The world outside has an air of magic; it conjures up visions of open spaces, exploration, and unrestrained movement, such as running, leaping and climbing high. Outside is a wonderful stage for games. Grass is a soft and attractive platform. It's an appealing and exciting place for group direction and fun. Besides all the fun, outside games offer choices and opportunities to grow, move and learn!

The games are divided into four different areas. There are chase games the first week. These games are great for decision making and perception skills. Who am I going to tag? Where do I run to in order to be "safe?" The second week has ground games. Being on the ground is a safe feeling. The ground is solid and stable! These games teach many concepts, such as hand-eye coordination and counting skills. A good sense of spatial awareness is developed! The third week has relay games. Recall abilities and controlled motor movement are increased. In the fourth week, there are story games. These games encourage listening skills and imagination! Children can play these games as long as the weather permits. Use the games whenever you can. They might go out of season, but they will never go out of style!

Gallops and Giggles and Outside Games

	Monday	Tuesday	Wednesday	Thursday	Friday
Week 1	**3+ Octopus** *To learn to make quick decisions*	**3+ Snow Rabbits** *To learn patience*	**3+ Dinosaur Party** *To develop concentration skills*	**3+ Frog in the Grass** *To increase perception skills*	**4+ The Birdies and the Worms** *To develop decision making skills*
Week 2	**3+ Turtle Ball** *To increase throwing and aiming skills*	**4+ Clean the Kitchen Sink** *To develop memory skills*	**3+ Tumbling Bears** *To develop spatial awareness*	**4+ Goosey Grass Says** *To encourage listening skills*	**4+ Caterpillar Ride** *To learn what our bodies can do*
Week 3	**4+ Beat the Clock** *To increase memory skills*	**3+ Follow the Snake** *To encourage perceptions skills*	**4+ Sponge Drop** *To learn the difference between left and right*	**4+ Ladybug, Ladybug** *To learn to make quick decisions*	**4+ Pair Up With a Dragonfly** *To increase control of large motor movements*
Week 4	**3+ Leave the Nest** *To increase perception skills*	**4+ Deep in the Jungle** *To encourage listening skills*	**4+ A Walk in the Grass** *To follow directions*	**3+ The Pink Pig Story** *To learn patience*	**3+ Run and Flop** *To encourage perception skills*

Octopus

What to do

1. Designate a place on the playground as a sea cave.

2. Ask the children to stand in a circle. They are fish!

3. Choose a child to be the octopus. Give this child the octopus arms to hold.

4. The octopus stands in the middle of the circle. The fish walk in a circle, around the octopus, and say,

   Oliver the octopus
   Can't catch me,
   A little tiny fishy
   In the deep blue sea!

5. At the end of the chant, the children stop and stand with their backs facing the octopus.

6. The octopus places the octopus arms on the ground behind a fish (a child). The octopus returns to the middle of the circle and sits down.

7. The teacher rings the bell and says, "Time for dinner!" All the fish turn around and look down. The fish who is near the octopus arms grabs it and runs around the circle once clockwise! The octopus jumps up and chases the fish. The octopus can only leave the circle through the empty space where the fish was standing and can only run clockwise. The fish tries to return to his or her same position in the circle without being tagged.

8. If a fish is tagged, it is eaten! It has to sit in the sea cave which belongs to the octopus. If a fish is not tagged, the octopus remains the octopus!

More to do

Here is another version! The game is played the same until after the chant. Then everyone stops and faces the octopus. The octopus passes out the octopus arms to eight different people. The octopus returns to the middle of the circle and sits down. When the teacher rings the bell and says, "Time for dinner," the fish, holding the arms, run to the safety of the sea cave. The octopus tries to tag a fish who is running! If a fish is tagged, it becomes the octopus.

Age level

3+

Objective

To learn to make quick decisions

Materials

Yarn
scissors
bell

Preparation

Cut eight 2' lengths of yarn. Tie them together at the top. These are octopus arms!

Color Rabbits

Age level

3+

Objective

To learn patience and to listen for auditory cues

Materials

None

Preparation

None

What to do

1. Choose a fox! The remaining children are the color rabbits.

2. Choose a place nearby to call the rabbit nest. Possible nests might be a tree, a bush or playground equipment.

3. Explain that rabbits can sit very still. A hungry fox will not see them if they remain still!

4. The color rabbits can sit quietly together on the grass. Remind them to sit or lay as still as they can. The teacher whispers a different color in each rabbit's ear.

5. The hungry fox walks slowly around the color rabbits. When the fox sees two color rabbits who look good to eat, the fox can tap them gently on the back. Then the fox sits on the grass, a few feet away from the color rabbits.

6. The fox names different colors. If one of the tagged rabbits hears the name of its color, this rabbit jumps up and runs to the safety of the rabbit nest.

7. If the fox tags a color rabbit, before it reaches its nest, it becomes the hungry fox!

8. If a color rabbit is not tagged, the fox can remain the fox or trade places with a willing color rabbit.

More to do

Play variations of this game! Instead of using colors, use different animal names. Try numbers, shapes, insects and things found in a house! If you give two children the same word, both children can run to safety.

Dinosaur Party

What to do

1. The dinosaurs are having a party. Everyone is invited except the Tyrannosaurus Rex! Choose a child to be the Tyrannosaurus.

2. Choose a spot on the playground to be the hiding place of the Tyrannosaurus. The Tyrannosaurus hides in the hiding place!

3. The remaining children put on their party hats and start the party. They stomp and growl on the grass! The teacher pounds on the pan with the spoon. This is the sound of the dinosaurs dancing!

4. While the dinosaurs are dancing, the Tyrannosaurus, at any time, can sneak out of the hiding place. The Tyrannosaurus runs into the party and surprises the dinosaurs. The first dinosaur tagged becomes the Tyrannosaurus Rex.

More to do

Draw and cut out 3" bone shapes from white construction paper. Tape the bones inside half of the party hats. Place the party hats on the children. No one knows which party hats have the dinosaur bones! Choose the Tyrannosaurus Rex. The game remains the same until the Tyrannosaurus tags a dinosaur. If the dinosaur tagged has a bone in his or her hat, this child becomes the Tyrannosaurus. If there is no bone in the hat, the Tyrannosaurus can choose a child to be the next Tyrannosaurus!

Age level

3+

Objective

To develop concentration skills

Materials

party hats
pan
spoon

Preparation

None

Frog in the Grass

Age level

3+

Objective

To increase perception skills

Materials

Green rubber frogs—at least four, or cut out frog shapes from green posterboard

Preparation

None

What to do

1. Have the children stand in a line in a designated area. This area should be at the far side of a yard.

2. Ask the children to close their eyes! The teacher places the frogs on the grass in different spots, as far away from each other as possible. Now the teacher yells, "Frog In the Grass!"

3. The children run and try to spot a frog. When they do, they grab it so it won't hop away!

4. Play it again! As an option, choose a child to hide the frogs in the grass. The children will want to play this many times!

More to do

Go on a variety of grass hunts. Hide rubber snakes or make them from green posterboard. Hide green ladybugs or green grasshoppers!

The Birdies and the Worms

What to do

1. Divide the children into two groups. One group are the worms. Give each of these children a pipe cleaner. The pipe cleaner represents a worm. The other group are the birdies!

2. Choose a spot on the playground to be the worm hole.

3. The birdies count slowly to ten. The worms run off and find hiding places on the playground. The worms need to be on the ground in their hiding places! On the count of ten, the birdies fly off to find a worm.

4. If a worm sees a birdie coming close, the worm can make a dash for the worm hole. If the worm is tagged on its way to the worm hole, it gives the birdie the pipe cleaner (a worm). The tagged worm sits out of the game. A worm cannot be tagged when it is on the ground. As soon as the worm runs, it can be tagged!

5. The game is over when all the worms are safe in the worm hole or have been tagged.

6. Now switch roles. The birdies can become the worms!

More to do

As an option, choose only one birdie and everyone else is a worm! The birdie collects as many pipe cleaners as possible before the game is over.

Age level

4+

Objective

To develop decision making skills

Materials

Pipe cleaners

Preparation

None

Turtle Ball

Age level

3+

Objective

To increase throwing and aiming skills

Materials

Medium-sized rubber ball
cardboard box large enough to hold
the ball

Preparation

None

What to do

1. Sit in a circle on the grass. Place the box in the middle of the circle. The box is a turtle shell!

2. Give the ball to a child. The ball is the turtle without its shell! The turtle is passed slowly around the circle. As it is passed to the right the children say, "ONE!" As the turtle is passed to the next child, the children say, "TWO!" Continue passing the turtle and counting until you reach the number ten.

3. The child who receives the turtle on the count of ten, keeps the turtle. Now say "The Turtle" chant!

   Turtle, oh turtle (Slowly crawl fingers on the grass)
   Oh turtle, on the ground, (Slowly crawl fingers on the grass)
   Don't cry turtle tears, (Wag a finger back and forth)
   Look what's found! (Wag a finger back and forth)

4. At the end of the chant, the child holding the turtle tries to throw the turtle into its shell (the box). If the turtle finds its shell, the child can take the turtle out of its shell and give it to the next child. If the turtle does not find its shell, say, "Poor Turtle!" Let the younger children have three tries to help the turtle find its shell.

5. Continue with the other children.

More to do

As a different variation, play Bedtime Turtle! At the count of ten, close your eyes. It's night and very dark out! When the turtle finds its shell, it goes to bed! With eyes closed, the child crawls on the grass towards the box. When the child finds the box, she drops the turtle in its shell!

Clean the Kitchen Sink

What to do

1. Sit in a circle on the grass near the pan of water. The teacher sits in the middle of the circle with the spoon and kitchen pan.

2. Give the dry sponge to a child. Explain that everyone is going to help wash the kitchen floor, but who is going to clean the kitchen sink? Let's find out!

3. The teacher begins to pound on the kitchen pan with the spoon. Everyone can sing "The Kitchen" song to the tune of "The Mulberry Bush." As you sing the song, the whole sponge is passed around the circle. The teacher beats out the rhythm with the spoon!

   Everybody can wash the floor,
   Wash the floor, wash the floor,
   Everybody can wash the floor,
   So early in the morning.

4. On the word "morning," the singing stops. Ask the child holding the sponge, "What do you have to do?" The child replies, "Clean the kitchen sink!" This child takes the sponge from the pan of water and scrubs the sink (the box).

5. This child is now out of the circle. When the child has finished cleaning the sink, he or she sits by the sink. This child can continue to sing with the children in the circle.

6. Now pass the sponge and sing "The Kitchen" song. Continue until there is one child left in the circle. This child is the winner! If the winner chooses, he can clean the kitchen sink.

More to do

Instead of passing a sponge, pass a dish towel. The child who is left holding the dish towel earns a sponge! Give this child a sponge to place in his or her lap. When everyone has earned a sponge, they can clean the kitchen sink or something on the playground. Dip the sponge in the pan of water and clean!

Age level

4+

Objective

To develop memory skills

Materials

Two sponges
scissors
pan of water
large cardboard box
spoon
kitchen pan

Preparation

Place the pan of water on the grass. Put one sponge in the pan of water. Place the large cardboard box near the pan of water.

Tumbling Bears

Age level

3+

Objective

To develop spatial awareness

Materials

Brown construction paper or felt
scissors
yarn

Preparation

Cut a teddy bear shape from brown
paper for each child. Cut a string of
yarn long enough to encircle all the
children. Place the yarn in a large circle on the grass. Place the paper bears
on the grass around the outside of the
circle.

What to do

1. Explain that everyone is a tumbling circus bear! The circle is a circus tent.
   Walk around the outside of the circus tent while you sing "The Circus"
   song. Sing it to the tune of, "Pop Goes The Weasel."

   Round and round the circus tent,
   Tumbling bears we go,
   Rumble, tumble on the ground,
   Start the show!

2. At the end of the song, do a tumble count! Say, "One tumble, two tumble,
   three tumble, Go!" On the word Go, clap! Now grab a tumbling bear and
   tumble into the circus tent!

3. Now place the tumbling bears outside the circle and start over. This time,
   remove one of the tumbling bears. When it is time to grab a bear and tumble, one child will be left without a tumbling bear. You cannot tumble
   into the circus tent without one!

4. The child who is left without a tumbling bear sits away from the circus
   tent. This bear is back in her cage! Continue the game until all the children are sitting in the bear cage except one child. This child can play the
   game alone and tumble in!

More to do

Cut out tumbling bears from different colored construction paper. Make two
bears of the same color for each child. Hide one set of colored bears in the
grass. Place the remaining bears around the circus tent. After the tumble
count, each child looks for a bear in the grass. When she finds a bear, she
runs to the circus tent, finds the matching bear and tumbles in!

Goosey Grass Says

What to do

1. Ask the children to stand on the grass. They are goslings (baby geese). The teacher is the oldest goose named Goosey Grass.

2. Play the game similar to Simon Says. The teacher says, "Goosey Grass says, 'turn around!'" Everyone turns around. The teacher might say, "Goosey Grass says, 'sit on the grass.'" Everyone sits on the grass.

3. The teacher continues with Goosey Grass directions until a statement is made without saying, "Goosey Grass says." The goslings should not follow the direction. They did not hear the words "Goosey Grass!"

4. Continue with more directions, saying "Goosey Grass" at times, and omitting it at others. Examples might be pound on the grass, hop on the grass.

More to do

With older children, give more detailed directions, such as find a partner and clap hands together. Be a pony and prance on the grass. Run off and bring Goosey Grass something small! The children can take turns being Goosey Grass!

Age level

4+

Objective

To encourage listening skills

Materials

None

Preparation

None

Caterpillar Ride

Age level

4+

Objective

To learn what bodies can do

Materials

None

Preparation

None

What to do

1. Who wants to ride a caterpillar? Choose a caterpillar rider!

2. The remaining children will make up the caterpillar. These children form a straight line on their hands and knees. Their sides should be touching. Everyone needs to remain very still.

3. The caterpillar is now ready to ride! The caterpillar rider crawls on the back of the caterpillar. Keep crawling until you reach the middle of the caterpillar. Now lay on your stomach. It is time for your ride!

4. The children who make up the caterpillar slowly rock back and forth on their hands and knees. The teacher can rock back and forth to demonstrate the correct direction. Now the caterpillar rider turns over. Go for a ride on your back!

5. Then the caterpillar rider crawls off the caterpillar. Choose another caterpillar rider! Continue until all the children have had a caterpillar ride. (It will be hard to wait!)

More to do

Think of different ways to ride the caterpillar. Try kneeling. Try sleeping on the caterpillar. Close your eyes! Sit on the caterpillar with your legs stretched out.

Beat the Clock

Age level

4+

Objective

To increase memory skills

Materials

White posterboard
felt pens
white construction paper
scissors
paper bag
chair
tape dispenser
timer

Preparation

Draw a large circle on white poster-board. Draw large numbers inside the circle to represent the numbers on a clock. Cut 3" squares from white construction paper for each child. Print a clock number on each square. Place these numbers in a paper bag. Lean the posterboard against a chair on a grassy area. Place the tape dispenser on the ground. Place the paper bag at least fifteen yards from the clock.

What to do

1. Form a straight line facing the clock. The line should be near the paper bag. Explain the rules! The teacher times the game on his or her watch. The teacher will then choose a child to run to the paper bag. This child will pick a number from the paper bag and identify it. Then the child will run to the clock. When the child reaches the clock, he will pull tape from the dispenser and tape their number over the printed number on the clock. (During this time, everyone can cheer!)

2. After he has taped his number on the clock, he runs back to his space in line and sits down. The next child in line continues the game. Continue until every child has placed a number on the clock and is sitting down.

3. When everyone is sitting down, the teacher can yell, "You beat the clock!" The teacher tells the children how long it took.

4. Repeat the game, trying to improve the time.

More to do

Draw and cut out a mouse shape for each child. Place the mice in a paper bag. Say the rhyme, "Hickory Dickory Dock." Now the first child in line can grab a mouse from the bag and tape it on the clock. This child runs back and sits down in his space. Play this game with a posterboard ladybug. Choose spots from a bag and tape them on the ladybug! Draw a large fish on a poster-board. Each child pours water from a pitcher into a paper cup. Carefully run to the fish and throw your water on it!

Follow the Snake

Age level

3+

Objective

To encourage perception skills

Materials

Green construction paper
scissors
yarn

Preparation

Cut out a winding snake shape from green construction paper. Cut a long piece of yarn, at least 20'. Lay the yarn in a winding pathway on the grass. This is a grass snake!

What to do

1. Stand in a group on the left side of the grass snake. Choose a child to hold the paper snake.

2. Move your arms like sneaky, slithery snakes as you say the following verse:

   Sneaky snake.
   Sneaky snake.
   Who will you slither to?

   Now say the word "Go," and clap at the same time! The child holding the paper snake runs along the left side of the grass snake, following its winding shape. As the child reaches the end of the snake, the child turns around and follows the other side of the snake, all the way around and back to the group of children.

3. When the child returns to the group, she gives the paper snake to another child. The runner then sits down. Repeat the snake verse! The next child follows the snake path up and back. Continue with the rest of the children.

More to do

Give each child long pieces of yarn. The children place their yarn in a winding pathway on the grass. You have made a grass snake! Run along your grass snake. Run along someone else's grass snake! Pick your grass snake up and form a different shape on the grass.

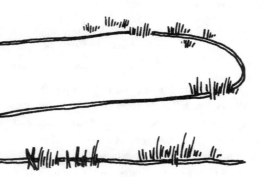

Sponge Drop

What to do

1. Place the bucket of water on the grass. The children stand in a straight line on the left side of the bucket. Mention that everyone is on the left side of the bucket!

2. Give each child a sponge. Hold the sponges in the air like you are about to wash a window. Explain that you are window washers and the teacher is the boss! Now sing "The Window Washer" song, to the tune of, "Here We Go Round The Mulberry Bush." As you sing, "scrub" with the sponge!

   > *Washing a window all day long,*
   > *All day long, all day long,*
   > *Washing a window all day long,*
   > *When is it time to quit?*

3. The teacher now says, "I'm the boss and it's time to quit!" The children clap and cheer! The teacher says, "On your mark, get set, quit!" After the word "quit," say the name of the child farthest from the bucket. This window washer runs down the front of the line and drops his sponge in the bucket of water. He now stands to the right of the bucket.

4. Repeat with the name of the window washer farthest from the bucket. (The next child at the end of the line.) This child runs and drops her sponge in the bucket of water. Then she stands next to the other window washer. Continue in this manner until everyone has quit and is standing in line on the right side of the bucket.

5. Tell the children that all the window washers on the right side of the bucket can go home. The children can run off and find a place on the playground to call home.

More to do

Begin the game on the right side of the bucket and finish on the left side of the bucket! Try this game with your eyes closed! The children in line hold out their arms. The child who is going to the bucket walks and feels his way by following the line of arms!

Age level

4+

Objective

To learn the difference between left and right

Materials

Bucket
water
sponges

Preparation

Fill the bucket half full of water.

Ladybug, Ladybug

Age level

4+

Objective

To learn to make quick decisions

Materials

Red posterboard
felt pens
scissors

Preparation

Draw a 6" circle on red posterboard. Draw black spots on the circle. Cut it out. This is a ladybug!

What to do

1. Divide the children into two groups. Each group stands in a straight line, facing each other. The lines should be at least ten yards apart.

2. Give one child the ladybug. Explain that the ladybug needs to fly home. The blackbird has told her that her children are in danger! The children can help the ladybug fly home.

3. All slowly count to ten. On the count of ten, yell, "Fly home!" The child holding the ladybug runs to the opposite line and gives the ladybug to any child.

4. The child now holding the ladybug runs to the opposite line and gives another child the ladybug. The child who gave up the ladybug sits down in the empty spot. Everyone can encourage the flying ladybug by saying, "Fly Home!" Say it often!

5. Continue the ladybug flight until all the children are sitting down. The ladybug has arrived home!

More to do

Cut out small red circles from red posterboard. Draw black spots on them. These are the ladybug's children! Hide the ladybug's children in the playground before the game. When the game is finished, the children can hunt for them!

Pair Up With a Dragonfly

What to do

1. Place sheets of colored construction paper on the grass in a straight row. Place them a few feet apart. Explain that they are wildflowers. The children will become fast darting dragonflies!

2. Choose a pair of children to dart first. Give the dragonfly pair the paper tube. Each child holds one end of the paper tube with one hand, one child uses the left hand and the other child uses the right hand. The children are standing on opposite sides of the tube. The tube is the body of the dragonfly. The children are the wings!

4. Explain that dragonflies dart from flower to flower. They move fast. You can hear their wings buzzing! The dragonfly pair will dart back and forth between the flowers. Demonstrate how to dart between the flowers. The teacher first walks around the right side and then around the left side of the flower (colored construction paper). When the teacher reaches the last chair, everyone can yell, "Fly back!" The teacher flies back to the waiting dragonflies.

5. Now the dragonfly pair is ready to fly. The remaining children make a buzzing noise! The dragonfly pair take off and dart between the flowers.

6. When the dragonfly pair has flown back, the teacher gives the paper tube to another pair of children. Now they are ready to fly. Continue with the rest of the pairs.

More to do

Give each child a paper tube. (You can make them from rolled up construction paper.) Everyone has a dragonfly body! Place the flowers around the playground in different spots. They can be far away from each other. Now place your dragonfly bodies on the grass. Rub your palms together quickly. Warm up your wings! When the teacher says, "One dragonfly, two dragonfly, three dragonfly, go," pick up your body and fly away! Fly around each of the flowers. When you are tired, fly back to the teacher.

Age level

4+

Objective

To increase control of large motor movements

Materials

Colored construction paper
long paper tube (from wrapping paper or tin foil)
black felt pen
tape
long paper tube (from wrapping paper or tin foil)
chairs

Preparation

None

Leave the Nest

Age level

3+

Objective

To increase perception skills

Materials

Yarn
scissors
paper cup

Preparation

Cut a piece of yarn long enough to encircle the children. Place the string of yarn on the grass in a large circle.

What to do

1. The children sit inside the circle. The teacher is the mother bird.

2. Ask the children to roll into a ball. They are bird eggs! When each child hears his egg crack, he can hatch out of his egg and stretch. The teacher walks inside the nest and claps his or her hands over each egg. This is the sound of an egg cracking! When you hear it, you can stretch.

3. Now you are hungry baby birds. Everyone can peep! Peep loudly. You are very hungry!

4. The teacher picks a baby bird who looks ready to leave the nest. If the child's name is Daniel, the teacher says, "Baby bird Daniel, you can leave the nest!" This child flies to the teacher. The teacher gives Daniel a paper cup. Daniel is to find food to bring back to the nest. He flies away in search of food! Possible food items are a small rock, a twig, grass, dirt, sand, a leaf, a bug!

5. The child places the food in the cup and returns to the nest and places the food in the center of the nest.

6. The other baby birds peep! The teacher calls another child to leave the nest. The game continues until everyone has left the nest and brought back food for the baby birds.

More to do

Give each child special instructions concerning the food item to find. Special instructions might be find something brown, find something skinny, find something round, find something green, find something that smells good, and find something that is flat!

Deep in the Jungle

What to do

1. Stand together on the grass. Everyone says "The Jungle" chant with suggested movements.

   > *Deep in the jungle (Sway like grass in the wind)*
   > *Where the wild grass grows, (Sway like grass in the wind)*
   > *I heard a noise! Shhhh! (Stop, put finger to lips)*
   > *I turned around, (Turn around)*
   > *I hid upon the ground! (Hide eyes)*
   > *Now take a peek, (Peek through fingers)*
   > *What do you see? (Sit on knees)*
   > *I see a _____ (Point to a child to name an animal)*
   > *Coming to capture me!*

2. The teacher tells how to escape. Possible ideas might be run away, jump away, crawl away, swim away, tiptoe away, grab a friend and find a hiding place, freeze (stand still)!

3. The children follow the suggestion! The teacher then calls the children back and everyone repeats the chant. A different child names an animal and a different suggestion is used to escape. Continue until everyone has named an animal.

More to do

Before the game, choose a child to be the wild animal. This child hides somewhere on the playground. At the end of the chant, when the children are escaping, the wild animal jumps out of hiding, gives a loud roar and chases the children! The first child tagged becomes the next wild animal.

Age level

4+

Objective

To encourage listening skills

Materials

None

Preparation

None

A Walk in the Grass

Age level

4+

Objective

To learn how to follow directions and how to use imagination

Materials

None

Preparation

None

What to do

1. Let's take a walk in the grass. Everyone stretch! Take a deep breath. Shake your legs, one at a time. Now we are ready. The teacher says, "Follow me! I wonder what we will see on our walk!"

2. Walk briskly around the playground. Explain that we need to loosen up our muscles!

3. Pretend to approach a thick jungle. It is too thick to walk through. We need to crawl!

4. There's a large lake in the distance. Run to it! Stop at the edge and jump in. Pretend to swim in the lake.

5. When you get out of the lake you see a giant mud puddle. Let's jump in! Roll around in the mud. Rub it on your face and arms. Have a mud fight!

6. Now we need some rain to wash off the mud. Sit in a circle. Listen for rain! Begin to slap your knees, first one knee and then the other knee. Do it faster! Hear the rain coming! Now dance in the rain. Doesn't the rain feel good?

7. Next we arrive at a mountain to climb. Climb a climbing structure on the playground or slide down a slide!

8. When you come down from the mountain you see a merry-go-round. Go for a ride! Everyone hold hands to form a circle. Start walking slowly around. Now walk faster. Lean back and go fast!

9. Your walk in the grass is almost over. Walk slowly. Look around. What do you see? What do you hear? Lay on the grass. Let your bodies sink into the Earth. What a wonderful walk!

More to do

Go on a surprise walk! During the walk, see an unexpected bear! Run from the bear! Find a hiding place. Send someone out to see if the bear has gone away. Then resume your walk! The next time you go for a walk in the grass, see a dinosaur! Before you take a walk, the children can offer suggestions on things to see and do on your walk.

The Pink Pig Story

What to do

1. Sit in a circle. The teacher tells *The Pink Pig* story!

   Once upon a time there was a hungry farmer. He was sooooo hungry, you could hear his stomach growl! (The children growl.) Then he had an idea. (Clap!) The hungry farmer went out to look for a pig. He walked through the woods. (The children slap their knees.) Then he heard a pig noise. (Everyone oink!) He ran to where the noise was. (The children slap their knees faster.) He froze! He saw a pink pig walking in the woods. He looked at his watch and said, "Time to eat!" (The children repeat, "Time to eat!")

2. Now choose a child to be the pig. Give this child the pink pig. This child walks around the outside of the circle. The rest of the children sway back and forth and say "The Pig" chant.

   > *Tick, tock goes the clock,*
   > *Time to cook a ham,*
   > *But oh my gosh, the pig said,*
   > *Catch me if you can!*

3. The children in the circle continue to sway and slowly repeat the words, Tick, tock, tick, tock. Continue to say these words until the child who is the pig stops and drops the pink pig in someone's lap.

4. If the pig was dropped in Robert's lap, say, "Robert! Catch the pig!" Robert jumps up and chases the pig around the circle. The pig attempts to return to Robert's space and sit down before he or she is tagged. (Both children run in a clockwise direction.)

5. If the pig is not tagged, the child chasing the pig becomes the next pig. If the pig is tagged, the pig sits in the pig pen (the middle of the circle). The child who tagged the pig, becomes the pig.

6. Now repeat the chant. The next child who is tagged, replaces the child in the pig pen. The original child in the pig pen sits in the circle again. Continue with the rest of the children.

More to do

Make a pink pig for each child. The children close their eyes! Hide the pink pigs in the grass. Tell *The Pink Pig* story. Then say "The Pig" chant without choosing a pig. At the end of the chant, the children run off and try to catch (find) a hidden pig!

Age level

3+

Objective

To learn patience and counting skills

Materials

Pink construction paper or pink felt
felt pens
scissors

Preparation

Draw a 6" pig on pink construction paper or pink felt. Cut it out.

Run and Flop

Age level

3+

Objective

To encourage perception skills

Materials

White posterboard
felt pens
scissors
red and green construction paper
tape

Preparation

Cut one 12" circle from white poster-board. Cut a 12" red construction paper circle and tape it to one side. Cut a 12" green construction paper circle and tape it to the other side.

What to do

1. The teacher is the mother bunny. The children are the baby bunnies! The mother bunny is going to show the baby bunnies how to watch out for the wolf.

2. Explain that there are two things a bunny needs to know—how to run and how to flop! Tell the story called *The Run and Flop Bunnies.*

Once there was a tiny bunny who lived in a burrow with his brothers and sisters. One night, when the bunnies were snugly tucked in bed, the mother bunny told them about the wolf. If you smell a wolf, you must remember two things. You must run fast! Only when you have lost the wolf can you flop and rest. Now repeat after me, "run and flop!" (The children repeat these words "run and flop!") The mother told her bunnies not to worry. If she smelled a wolf, she would quietly hold up a green sign. If you see the green sign, she said, you better run fast! When the wolf has gone, I will hold up a red sign. This means you can flop! Now go to sleep! (The children can lie on the grass and pretend to sleep.) In the morning, the mother bunny told her babies to go and play. But remember, she warned them, be watching me! If I smell a wolf, I will hold up my signs.

3. After the children disperse, the teacher holds up the red circle. Do not give any verbal cues! As the children notice the red circle, they run off!

4. Now hold up the green side of the circle. As soon as the children notice the green circle, they flop on the ground.

5. Give the children a chance to be the mother bunny and hold up the red and green sign!

More to do

Make more signs using different colors. Use them when the bunnies are playing! When you hold up a yellow sign, the children scream! When you hold up a brown sign, they find a hiding place. When you hold up a black sign, they lay very still and hide their eyes. This is a good test of a bunny's memory!

Index

The GIANT Encyclopedia of Theme Activities For Children 2 to 5

Over 600 Favorite Activities
Created by Teachers for Teachers

A nationwide contest with thousands of entries produced this large book. There are 48 themes filled with more than 600 teacher-developed activities that work. From the alphabet and art to winter and zoo there are themes for every season and every day of the year.

All activities are clearly described and ready to use with a minimum of preparation. This is an ideal resource for a busy teacher. The book has a special strengthened binding which allows it to lie flat on a table. 512 pages.

ISBN 0-87659-166-7
19216

Gryphon House
Paperback

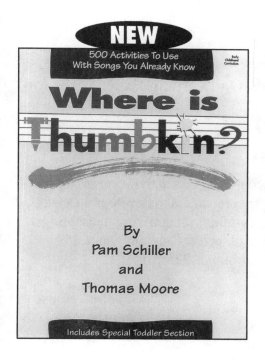

Where is Thumbkin?

500 Activities to Use with Songs You Already Know

Pam Schiller, Thomas Moore

These are the songs teachers and children are already singing together every day. The book is organized month-by-month, and has sections for toddlers, threes, fours, five and six year olds. These simple learning activities can be used in circle time, for transitions, or for special music time. A list of related children's literature and recordings accompanies each set of activities. 256 pages.

ISBN 0-87659-164-0
13156

Gryphon House
Paperback

The Learning Circle

A Preschool Teacher's Guide to Circle Time

Patty Claycomb

Here's the perfect collection of circle time activities - for every day, month and season. These activities give children a chance to talk about themselves and their friends while enjoying hands-on learning discoveries.

You'll find circle time activities for music and movement, games, the senses, communication, crafts, the human body, nutrition, the ocean, land forms, plants, dinosaurs and inventions. 205 pages.

ISBN 0-87659-115-2   **Gryphon House**
10007   **Paperback**

Do Touch

Instant, Easy, Hands-On Learning Experiences for Young Children

LaBritta Gilbert

This popular collection of hands-on activities uses simple materials, can be quickly prepared and develops specific skills - pairing, fitting, forming, categorizing, measuring, sorting and more. Clear objectives and directions are enhanced by expert illustrations. 225 pages.

ISBN 0-87659-118-7   **Gryphon House**
10010   **Paperback**